In association MasterCard

CONTENTS

MW01705668

Cover Picture: Coopershill House, Riverstown, Co Sligo, Ireland (see page 207).

INTRODUCTION BY THE EDITOR

Johansens guides, now in their 15th year, have developed from one single hotel guide into what this year is a set of five – Recommended Hotels, Recommended Inns with Restaurants, Recommended Country Houses and Small Hotels, Recommended Business Meetings Venues and now, for the first time, Johansens Recommended Hotels in Europe. The market place has grown and we have grown with it. Our principles, nevertheless, have remained constant. The annual inspection of candidates for inclusion in our guides reinforced by the thousands of reports from Johansens guide-users sustains our criterion of excellence.

We are publishers and as such we form the link between two groups of clients: hoteliers who, if accepted for membership, pay an annual fee and their guests, who are in many cases purchasers of our guides. We value both these relationships hoping that our contribution to excellence in hospitality, now not only in Britain but in all Europe, will be of great benefit to the diverse clientele which we so proudly serve.

Rodney Exton, Editor.

In association with MasterCard

KEY TO SYMBOLS

13 rms Total number of rooms	13 rms Nombre de chambres	13 rms Anzahl der Zimmer
MasterCard accepted	MasterCard accepté	MasterCard akzeptiert
Visa accepted	Visa accepté	Visa akzeptiert
American Express accepted	American Express accepté	American Express akzeptiert
Diners Club accepted	Diners Club accepté	Diners Club akzeptiert
Quiet location	Un lieu tranquille	Ruhige Lage
Access for wheelchairs to at least one bedroom and public rooms	Accès handicapé	Zugang für Behinderte
Chef-patron	Chef-patron	Chef-patron
M 20 Meeting/conference facilities with maximum number of delegates	M 20 Salle de conférences – capacité maximale	M 20 Konferenzraum-Höchstkapazität
8 Children welcome, with minimum age where applicable	8 Enfants bienvenus	8 Kinder willkommen
Dogs accommodated in rooms or kennels	Chiens autorisés	Hunde erlaubt
At least one room has a four-poster bed	Lit à colonnes	Himmelbett
Cable/satellite TV in all bedrooms	TV câblée/satellite dans les chambres	Satellit-und Kabelfernsehen in allen Zimmern
Direct-dial telephone in all bedrooms	Téléphone dans les chambres	Telefon in allen Zimmern
No-smoking rooms (at least one no-smoking bedroom)	Chambres non-fumeurs	Zimmer für Nichtraucher
Lift available for guests' use	Ascensrur	Fahrstuhl
Indoor swimming pool	Piscine couverte	Hallenbad
Outdoor swimming pool	Piscine de plein air	Freibad
Tennis court at hotel	Tennis à l'hôtel	Hoteleigener Tennisplatz
Croquet lawn at hotel	Croquet à l'hôtel	Krocketrasen
Fishing can be arranged	Pêche	Angeln
Golf course on site or nearby, which has an arrangement with hotel allowing guests to play	Golf	Golfplatz
Shooting can be arranged	Chasse	Jagd
Riding can be arranged	Chevaux de selle	Reitpferd
Hotel has a helicopter landing pad	Hélipad	Hubschrauberlandplatz
Licensed for wedding ceremonies	Cérémonies de noces	Konzession für Eheschliessungen

In association with MasterCard

Published by
Johansens, 175-179 St John Street, London EC1V 4RP
Tel: 0171-490 3090 Fax: 0171-490 2538
Find Johansens on the Internet at: http://www.johansen.com

Editor:	Rodney Exton
Publishing Director:	Andrew Warren
P.A. to Publishing Director:	Angela Franks
Associate Publisher:	Peter Hancock
Secretary to Associate Publisher:	Carol Sweeney
Regional Inspectors:	Christopher Bond Geraldine Bromley Julie Dunkley Susan Harangozo Joan Henderson Marie Iversen Pauline Mason Mary O'Neill Brian Sandell
Production Manager:	Daniel Barnett
Production Controller:	Kevin Bradbrook
Designer:	Matthew Davis
Copywriters:	Sally Sutton, Jill Wyatt
Sales and Marketing Manager:	Mike Schwarz
Marketing Executive:	Juliet Brookes
Marketing Assistant:	Rebecca Ford
Managing Director:	Martin Morgan

A HOBSONS DIRECTORY

MEMBER ASTA American Society of Travel Agents *Integrity in Travel*

DPA DIRECTORY PUBLISHERS ASSOCIATION

BRITISH HOSPITALITY ASSOCIATION

Hobsons Publishing plc,

a subsidiary of the Daily Mail and General Trust plc

ISBN 1 86017 131 1

Printed in England by St Ives plc

Colour origination by Meridian House plc

Distributed in the UK and Europe by Biblios PDS Ltd, Partridge Green, West Sussex, RH13 8LD. In North America by general sales agent: SunWelcome, INC., Clearwater, Florida (direct sales) and The Cimino Publishing Group, INC. New York (bookstores). In Australia and New Zealand by Bookwise International, Findon, South Australia.

HOW TO USE THIS GUIDE

If you want to identify a Country House or a Small Hotel whose name you already know, look for it in the national indexes on pages 239–234.

If you want to find a Country House or a Small Hotel in a particular area you can

- Turn to the Maps on pages 223–229
- Search the Indexes by County on pages 230–234
- Look for the Town where you wish to stay in the main body of the Guide. This is divided into Countries. Place names in each Country are in alphabetical order.

The Indexes list the Country Houses and Small Hotels by Counties, they also show those with facilities such as conference centres, swimming, etc.

The Maps cover five different regions. Each Country House and Small Hotel symbol (a green square) relates to a Country House or a Small Hotel in this guide in or near the location shown.

Mini Listings pages 217–221: The Inns (a red triangle) on the Maps are listed in order of place names and divided nationally so that, if you cannot find a Country House or a Small Hotel locally, you may be able to find an Inn nearby at which to stay.

The Prices, in most cases, refer to the cost of one night's accommodation, with breakfast, for two people. Prices are also shown for single occupancy. These rates are correct at the time of going to press but they should always be checked.

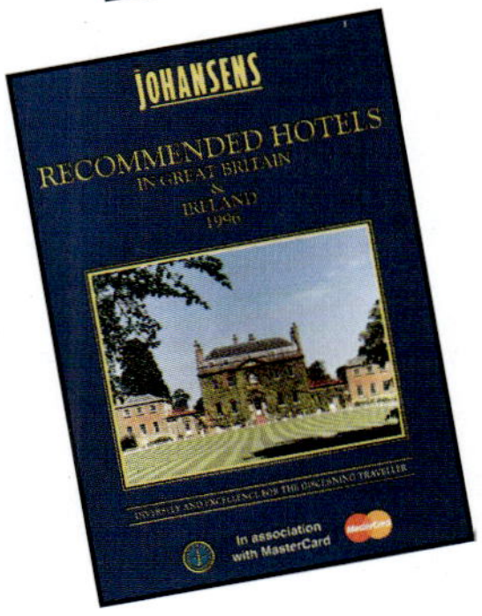

INTRODUCTION

By Brian and Lindy O'Hara of Coopershill House, Riverstown, Co Sligo, Winner of the 1995 Johansens Country House Award

It is with great pride and some trepidation that we find ourselves asked to write the introduction to this guide. As winners of the Johansens Country Houses "Award for Excellence" 1995, we feel that for this year we represent the owners of all the properties featured, and we wholeheartedly recommend that you make optimum use of the finest guide of its type available for Great Britain and Ireland.

It gives us particular pleasure to be the first Irish winners of a Johansens award. We hope that this may be propitious during these days of renewed peace initiatives in Northern Ireland and that increased tourism to both North and South may result. It continues to be our proud tradition that from no other nationality does a visitor receive a more genuine welcome than that given by the Irish people.

Coopershill is Brian's family home and has always been a favourite house of the extensive O'Hara family. It is a house of great warmth and character where guests seem immediately to feel at home; it is the charm of this old Georgian house that particularly appeals to our guests.

Thank you for reading this introduction to what we feel is "our" guide. We hope that you will spend many happy days and nights in Johansens recommended country houses and small hotels.

Céad Mile Fáilte - a hundred thousand welcomes!

AWARD 1995 J WINNER

JOHANSENS AWARDS FOR EXCELLENCE

The names of the winners of the 1996 Awards will be published in the 1997 editions of Johansens guides.

The winners of the 1995 Awards are listed below. They were presented with their certificates at the Johansens Annual Awards dinner, held at The Savoy on 31st October 1994, by Giles Shepard CBE.

WINNERS OF THE 1995 JOHANSENS AWARDS

Johansens Country Hotel Award for Excellence
Amberley Castle, Arundel, West Sussex

Johansens City Hotel Award for Excellence
The Chester Grosvenor, Chester, Cheshire

Johansens Country House Award for Excellence
Coopershill House, Riverstown, Co Sligo

Johansens Inn Award for Excellence
The Lamb, Burford, Oxford

Johansens Most Excellent Value for Money Award
Lower Bache, Leominster, Herefordshire

Johansens Most Excellent Service Award
Hotel Maes-Y-Neuadd, Harlech, Gwynedd

Candidates for awards derive from two main sources: from the thousands of Johansens guide users who send us guest survey reports commending hotels, inn and country houses in which they have stayed and from our team of twelve regional inspectors who regularly visit all properties in our guides. Guest survey report forms can be found on pages 487–496. They are a vital part of our continuous process of assessment and they are the decisive factor in choosing the value for money and the most excellent service awards.

The judges each year are invited from among the winners of previous years awards.

The Judges for the 1995 Awards were:-

David Shentall, Kinloch House, Winner of the 1994 Johansens Country Hotel Award
Malcolm Reed, The Swallow, Birmingham, Winner of the 1994 Johansens City Hotel Award
Hugo Jeune, The Rising Sun, Lynmouth, Winner of the 1991 Johansens Inn Award
Anne McClure, 4 South Parade, York, Winner of the 1994 Johansens Value for Money Award

Grasmere, Allan Bank and Helme Crag, Cumbria

Johansens Recommended Country Houses in England

Castles, cathedrals, museums, great country houses and the opportunity to stay in areas of historical importance, England has much to offer. Whatever your leisure interests, there's a network of more than 550 Tourist Information Centres throughout England offering friendly, free advice on places to visit, entertainment, local facilities and travel information.

British Travel Centre
12 Regent Street
Piccadilly Circus
London SW1Y 4PQ
(Personal callers only)

English Heritage
Keysign House
429 Oxford Street
London W1R 2HD
Tel: 0171-973 3396
Offers an unrivalled choice of properties to visit.

Historic Houses Association
2 Chester Street
London SW1X 7BB
Tel: 0171-259 5688
Ensures the survival of historic houses and gardens in private ownership in Great Britain.

The National Trust
36 Queen Anne's Gate
London SW1H 9AS
Tel: 0171-222 9251
Cares for more than 590,000 acres of countryside and over 400 historic buildings.

The Heart of England

Here you have the essence of England, the country's very heart. From the thatched villages of Shakespeare Country, to some of the world's finest potteries in Stoke on Trent.

The Heart of England Tourist Board
PO Box 15
Worcester
Worcestershire WR5 1BR
Tel: 01905 763436

Cumbria

England's most beautiful lakes and tallest mountains reach out from the Lake District National Park to a landscape of spectacular coasts, hills and dales.

Cumbria Tourist Board
Ashleigh
Holly Road
Windermere
Cumbria LA23 2AQ
Tel: 015394 44444

Northumbria

The north east region of England is steeped in folklore and history and is celebrated as one of the most important centres of early English Christianity.

Northumbria Tourist Board
Aykley Heads
Durham
Co Durham DH1 5UX
Tel: 0191-384 6905

The North West

This region offers the very best in history and heritage, stunning countryside and vibrant towns and cities including Chester, Lancaster, Liverpool and Manchester.

The North West Tourist Board
Swan House
Swan Meadow Road
Wigan Pier
Wigan WN3 5BB
Tel: 01942 821222

Yorkshire & Humberside

Scenic coastline with lively resorts, and spectacular seascapes. Unspoilt natural grandeur in dales and moors. Historic cities, picturesque villages, impressive castles and stately homes.

Yorkshire & Humberside Tourist Board
312 Tadcaster Road
York
North Yorkshire YO2 2HF
Tel: 01904 707961

East Midlands

This region includes the coastal resorts of Lincolnshire, waterways such as the Grand Union Canal, the Trent & Mersey Canal and the Rivers Trent, Soar and Witham. Most of the Peak District National Park lies in Derbyshire.

East Midlands Tourist Board
Exchequergate
Lincoln
Lincolnshire LN2 1PZ
01522 531521

East Anglia

A place of farms and pine forests, quiet villages and thatched cottages, medieval towns and charming cities, lively seaside resorts and quaint villages.

East Anglia Tourist Board
Toppesfield Hall
Hadleigh
Suffolk IP7 5DN
Tel: 01473 822922

West Country

England's favourite holiday destination with a mild climate all year round and over 600 miles of contrasting coastline. Discover another world of legend, mystery and romance.

West Country Tourist Board
60 St Davids Hill
Exeter
Devon EX4 4SY
Tel: 01392 76351

Southern England

This area has connections with great literary figures. In the 19th century, Oxford was a centre for the pre-Raphaelite painters and many of their works can still be viewed in the city.

Southern Tourist Board
40 Chamberlayne Road
Eastleigh
Hampshire SO50 5JH
Tel: 01703 620006

South East

The region has 257 miles of coastline stretching from Gravesend, Kent, to the Witterings, West Sussex. The Channel Tunnel links this corner of England to mainland Europe.

South East England Tourist Board
The Old Brew House
Warwick Park
Royal Tunbridge Wells
Kent TN2 5TU
Tel: 01892 540766

Laurel Villa

LAKE ROAD, AMBLESIDE, CUMBRIA LA22 0DB
TEL: 015394 33240

OWNER: Brian Seedhouse
CHEF: Jenny Gittins

9 rms | 9 ens | SMALL HOTEL

S: £50
D: £60–£80

Originally built as a gentleman's residence in the mid 1800s, on the outskirts of the village of Ambleside, Laurel Villa has been lovingly restored and refurbished by Brian and Jenny. The bedrooms here are spacious and use has been made of wallpapers and fabrics based upon the designs of William Morris complemented by furniture made of mellow pine. All the bedrooms overlook the fells and have en suite facilities to a very high standard. Two of the bedrooms feature a four-poster bed whereas others have coronet or half-tester beds.

Jenny's menus are based on traditional British fare accompanied by a selection of English wines. The full Cumbrian breakfast includes locally made Cumberland sausages.

There is a private car park to the rear of the house. Special rates are available throughout the year. Closed at Christmas.

Places of interest nearby: Situated in the heart of the Lake District, Ambleside is an ideal base for tours of the fells and surrounding villages. A host of water sports can be enjoyed on Lake Windermere, while tennis, golf and bowling facilities are available nearby. **Directions: Take the one-way system around Ambleside to Windermere. Laurel Villa is 100 yards past the last shop on the right-hand side.**

For hotel location, see maps on pages 223–229

Nanny Brow Hotel

CLAPPERSGATE, AMBLESIDE, CUMBRIA LA22 9NF
TEL: 015394 32036 FAX: 015394 32450

OWNERS: Michael and Carol Fletcher

S: from £60
D: from £70
Suites: from £75
(including dinner)

18 rms | 18 ens | SMALL HOTEL

Designed and built in 1902 by a London architect for his own use, this elegant country house sits peacefully under Loughrigg in five acres of gardens and woodland. It has access on to the fell and enjoys spectacular views of the River Brathay.

The hotel, noted for its award winning restaurant, has a warm and friendly atmosphere. There are log fires on chilly evenings and fresh flowers are replenished daily.

All suites and rooms are individually designed and furnished in traditional quality. Croquet, fishing, spa bath and solarium are within the grounds and guests also have free use of a local private leisure club. Dogs ares accepted and children have free accommodation if sharing their parents' room.

Personally managed by resident owners Michael and Carol Fletcher who are proud of their achievements and their caring and attentive staff, under the leadership of manager Rachel Gennard, the hotel is recommended by most major guides for fine wine and cuisine. For the second consecutive year an AA Red Rosette has been awarded. A full colour brochure can be sent on request.

Places of interest nearby: The hotel has fishing rights on the River Brathay, and the gardens lead directly onto Loughrigg Fell. Dogs are accepted by prior arrangement.

Directions: From Ambleside take A593 Coniston road for 1½ miles; the hotel is on the right-hand side.

Appleton Hall

APPLETON-LE-MOORS, NORTH YORKSHIRE YO6 6TF
TEL: 01751 417227 FAX: 01751 417540

OWNERS: Norma and Graham Davies
CHEF: Rob Meynell

S: £50–£60
D: £100–£120
Suite: £120
(including dinner)

10 rms | 10 ens | SMALL HOTEL

Appleton Hall is in the centre of the pretty Yorkshire village of Appleton-le-Moors – which is on the southern side of the North Yorkshire Moors National Park. The hotel is surrounded by beautiful landscaped gardens where guests can sit and relax or wander at their leisure. The elegant refurbished rooms assure visitors they have come to a peaceful and comfortable country house where Graham and Norma Davies and their staff guarantee a high standard of service and hospitality.

The ten en suite bedrooms are all fully equipped to provide the modern necessities – two have their own lounges. One of the rooms has a four-poster bed.

There is a small well-stocked cocktail bar to pass the time before dinner. The delectable five-course table d'hôte menu changes daily and is accompanied by a comprehensive selection of wines.

Places of interest nearby: A walkers' and bird-watchers' paradise, or visit Harrogate and York, returning to inviting log fires on chilly afternoons. **Directions: Leave the A1 at the Thirsk turning, taking the A170, signposted Scarborough. Shortly after passing through Kirkbymoorside the road to the village is on the left.**

10 12

For hotel location, see maps on pages 223–229

BURPHAM COUNTRY HOTEL

OLD DOWN, BURPHAM, NR ARUNDEL, WEST SUSSEX BN18 9RJ
TEL: 01903 882160 FAX: 01903 884627

OWNERS: George and Marianne Walker

10 rms | 10 ens

S: from £31.50
D: from £63–£70

This charming Country Hotel, reputed to have been a hunting lodge for the Duke of Norfolk in times gone by, is situated in one of the most peaceful and unspoilt villages in West Sussex. Nestling in a fold of the South Downs, it offers superb views of the surrounding countryside.

The spacious bedrooms are comfortably furnished. A range of modern facilities include colour TV, hair dryer, tea and coffee making facilities, direct-dial telephones and radio/alarm clocks. Guests are requested not to smoke in their rooms.

Pre-dinner drinks can be enjoyed by the open fire in the comfortable Cocktail Lounge. An interesting and varied menu offers excellent cuisine which is attractively presented by Marianne Walker who is Swiss and renowned for her Rösti. A good wine list adds to the pleasure of the meal. Special breaks are available throughout the year.

Golf, riding, fishing and sailing are all readily available in the locality. Racing at Goodwood and Fontwell.

Places of interest nearby: Burpham has a beautiful and historic Norman church, while Arundel, with its Wildfowl Sanctuary and renowned Castle, is three miles away. The coast lies within six miles. **Directions: Burpham is signposted off A27 east of the bridge over the railway at Arundel station. The Hotel lies within about 2½ miles.**

For hotel location, see maps on pages 223–229

THE BEECHES FARMHOUSE

WALDLEY, DOVERIDGE, NR ASHBOURNE, DERBYSHIRE DE6 5LR
TEL: 01889 590288 FAX: 01889 590288

OWNERS: Barbara and Paul Tunnicliffe
CHEF: Barbara Tunnicliffe

10 rms | 10 ens

S: £38.50
D: £46

The Beeches hotel and restaurant was opened in 1986 by Barbara and Paul Tunnicliffe. It is situated on the dairy farm which Paul's family has worked for 50 years. Located in the Derbyshire Dales, The Beeches is surrounded by lots of things to see and do, whatever your age or interests. Families are most welcome: children love staying on the working farm, for, where they can, they watch the cows being milked and feed the many pet animals. For executives there are spacious en suite rooms with direct-dial telephones and access to the fax.

At the heart of The Beeches' popularity is Barbara's splendid cooking. Like the dishes she demonstrates at the BBC Good Food Show, Barbara's menus feature bold country recipes. Specialities include local boneless beef rib with port, Guinness and pickled walnuts and casserole of spiced lamb with apricots and miniature herb dumplings. Vegetarian and fresh fish dishes are also offered. Everything is freshly prepared with seasonal ingredients.

Places of interest nearby: Sudbury Hall, Calke Abbey, Tutbury Castle, the Potteries museums and Alton Towers.

Directions: Heading east to west on the A50 Derby –Stoke road, turn right at Doveridge down Marston Lane, signposted to Waldley. At Waldley take first right turn, then first left to The Beeches

12 M

For hotel location, see maps on pages 223–229

Biggin Mill House

BIGGIN-BY-HULLAND, NR ASHBOURNE, DERBYSHIRE DE6 3FN
TEL: 01335 370414 FAX: 01335 370414

OWNERS: Penny and Mark Bazeley

2 rms | 1 ens

S: £60
D: £75

Set well off the beaten track, Biggin Mill House is a beautiful stone farmhouse which provides its guests with an ideal base from which to explore the beautiful Derbyshire Dales. A mile long track leads to the house, which is situated in 3 acres of wooded grounds with a stream.

Peace and quiet are guaranteed in this lovely retreat, with its welcoming and homely atmosphere. The guests' lounge has a beamed ceiling, log burner and cosy furnishings, while the dining room is predominantly oak furnished and decorated in gentle woodland colours. An extensive breakfast menu is available including oak-smoked kippers, porridge with maple syrup and cream and home-made croissants for example.

There are two comfortable and delightfully decorated bedrooms, with every modern comfort including one room with a spa bath. They offer uninterrupted views of the grounds and surrounding countryside. Penny prepares delicious dinners by prior arrangement.

The proprietors of Biggin Mill House provide a written guide and map to the wonderful walks from the grounds which cover the local countryside.

Places of interest nearby: The market town of Ashbourne, Carsington Water, Kedleston Hall and the Peak District. **Directions: A hideaway off the A517, four miles from Ashbourne, eight miles from Belper. Full details provided when making your reservation.**

For hotel location, see maps on pages 223–229

In association with MasterCard

Blagdon Manor Country Hotel

ASHWATER, DEVON EX21 5DF
TEL: 01409 211224 FAX: 01409 211634

OWNERS: Tim and Gill Casey

7 rms | 7 ens | SMALL HOTEL

S: from £45
D: from £90

Nestling in eight acres of beautiful rural Devon, Blagdon Manor is a lovely Grade II listed building offering guests total peace and comfort. Although records suggest that the Manor has existed in some form since Saxon times, the present building dates back to the 17th century.

Inside the manor, heavy oak beams, worn slate flagstones and handstitched soft furnishings recreate the feel of a past era. The bedrooms are individually and attractively furnished and include a television, hair dryer and hospitality tray.

Guests dine together in a dinner-party atmosphere and enjoy the very best of English cuisine, prepared from the finest ingredients. Superb homemade desserts and sweets complement the meals. The hotel is fully licensed.

Places of interest nearby: Blagdon Manor is ideally placed for taking a walk on Dartmoor, Bodmin Moor or the coastal path or a quiet wander around quaint fishing villages. There is also a wealth of historical houses and magnificent gardens. **Directions: From Launceston join A388 towards Holsworthy. Pass both Chapman's Well and first sign to Ashwater, turn right at second sign to Ashwater, then first right. Hotel driveway is on the right.**

CHAPEL HOUSE

FRIARS' GATE, ATHERSTONE, WARWICKSHIRE CV9 1EY
TEL: 01827 718949 FAX: 01827 717702

OWNERS: David and Patricia Roberts
MANAGER: David Arnold

10 rms | 10 ens | SMALL HOTEL

S: £42–£55
D: £55–£65

Chapel House was the dower house of the now demolished Atherstone Hall, home of the Bracebridge family since the early 18th century. The oldest part of the house dates from about 1720 and subsequent additions were made until 1879. Many original features have been retained and others carefully restored so that the house now furnished in traditional style retains the elegance of an earlier age. Chapel House is discreetly tucked away in the corner of Atherstone's market square within a well-tended, walled garden that still is a particularly attractive feature of the property.

Chapel House has acquired an enviable reputation for high quality, imaginative food and an excellent selection of wines. Chef Gary Thompson uses only the freshest ingredients and his particular specialities are fish and game. Special dietary needs can be catered for by prior arrangement. Closed on Christmas Day and Boxing Day. Chapel House is just 25 minutes from the centre of Birmingham and is convenient for the NEC.

Places of interest nearby: Bosworth Battlefield, Tamworth Castle, Arbury Hall, Lichfield and Coventry Cathedrals and the many industrial museums of the Midlands. Also close is the Belfry Golf Centre.

Directions: Two-and-a-half-miles from the A5 junction 10 on the M42. Located in the market square of Atherstone beside the church.

For hotel location, see maps on pages 223–229

PETTY FRANCE

DUNKIRK, BADMINTON, AVON
TEL: 01454 238361 FAX: 01454 238768

OWNER: Bill Fraser

20 rms | 20 ens | SMALL HOTEL

S: £65–£85
D: £85–£110

Built in warm Cotswold stone and set in beautiful countryside, this 18th century country house has been transformed into a delightful private hotel. The owner calls the elegant surroundings 'pleasure gardens', the only sport being croquet!

Bill likes to welcome new arrivals personally and his staff are equally hospitable.

Reflecting the Georgian era are the spacious, flower filled, public rooms. The restaurant has a sophisticated menu based on local produce. Vegetarians are not forgotten and the cheeses include Cheddar-Denhay from Dorset and Little Rydings goats' milk cheese. The fine wine list provides a choice of further pleasures.

The charming bedrooms are either in the main house or in the old stable block. The latter have more privacy and character, but are smaller. All have en-suite shower rooms or private bathrooms, as well as telephone and television.

There are three small air-conditioned conference rooms, accommodating up to 25 people each, equipped with modern display equipment.

Places of interest nearby: Well located for businessmen, close to Bristol, Bath, Gloucester and Cheltenham. Golf, riding, tennis, squash and fishing are available **Directions: From the M4, Junction 18, take the A46. Head North for five miles; Petty France is just off the main road on the left.**

25 M

For hotel location, see maps on pages 223–229

EAST LODGE COUNTRY HOUSE HOTEL

ROWSLEY, NR MATLOCK, DERBYSHIRE DE4 2EF
TEL: 01629 734474 FAX: 01629 733949

OWNERS: Sue and Peter Mills
CHEF: Richard Harrison

14 rms | 14 ens | SMALL HOTEL

MasterCard VISA AMERICAN EXPRESS

S: £55
D: from £78

East Lodge Country House Hotel was originally built as the East Lodge to Haddon Hall, the Derbyshire seat of the Duke of Rutland and sold as a private home in the 1920's. Converted to a hotel in the 1980's, East Lodge is now owned and run by Sue and Peter Mills and their attentive staff. It is ETB 4 Crowns Highly Commended.

The attractive lounge with log fire, charming restaurant and spacious hall offers high levels of comfort combined with a warm and relaxed atmosphere. The 14 en suite bedrooms are tastefully furnished, each havings its own distinctive character. The imaginative table d'hôte and à la carte dinners are served daily in the restaurant with lighter meals available in the lounge. A wide selection of wines are on offer at affordable prices.

Set in 10 acres of attractive gardens and surrounded by rolling Derbyshire countryside, East Lodge provides an ideal setting for relaxing breaks, conferences and corporate activity/team building events.

Places of interest nearby: Peak National Park, which boasts some of the country's most spectacular walks. The famous stately homes, Chatsworth House and Haddon Hall, are within two miles. Bakewell, Buxton, Matlock and Crich are a short drive away. **Directions: Set back from the A6 in Rowsley village, three miles from Bakewell. The hotel entrance is adjacent to the B6012 junction to Sheffield/Chatsworth.**

60 M

In association with MasterCard

THE PEACOCK HOTEL AT ROWSLEY

ROWSLEY, NR MATLOCK, DERBYSHIRE DE4 2EB
TEL: 01629 733518 FAX: 01629 732671

OWNERS: Jarvis Hotels Ltd
MANAGER: Pat Gillson
CHEF: Robert Moakes

14 rms | 14 ens

S: £85
D: £65
(including dinner)

Once the Dower House to Haddon Hall, this superb 17th century country house is now a marvellous hotel. With gardens leading down to the River Derwent it has a special lure for anglers!

When first a hotel in 1820 it attracted bathers who plunged into the nearby River Wye! Fishermen are spoilt here. There are 12 rods on the River Wye and two on the Derwent. Tickets are available for residents, and the Haddon Estate Head Keeper offers advice and tuition. Fish caught will be cooked by the hotel or put in the freezer. What's more the dedicated can enjoy the Angler's Picnic, brought to the riverside. Walkers in the Dales get a delicious picnic in a thermally insulated knapsack.

The hotel is beautifully furnished throughout, with antiques and flowers in abundance. The bedrooms are extremely comfortable and thoughtfully equipped.

The restaurant is for both residents and non-residents. They can enjoy an aperitif in the delightful bar or lounge before dining in the restaurant where no smoking is the rule. A variety of menus reflect prices for two, three or four courses, followed by eight different liqueur coffees. There are excellent traditional facilities for small meetings.

Places of interest nearby: Haddon Hall, Chatsworth House and Crich Tram Museum. **Directions: From M1/junction 28, head for the A6. Rowsley is midway between Matlock and Bakewell.**

20 M

For hotel location, see maps on pages 223–229

WAREN HOUSE HOTEL

WAREN MILL, BAMBURGH, NORTHUMBERLAND NE70 7EE
TEL: 01668 214581 FAX: 01668 214484

OWNERS: Peter and Anita Laverack
CHEF: Alan McMullan

7 rms | 7 ens | SMALL HOTEL

S: from £55
D: from £110
Suite from: £140
(including dinner)

"To visit the North East and not to stay here, would be foolish indeed". So says one entry in a visitors book that is filled with generous and justified praise for this delightful traditional country house which lives up to all its promises and expectations and beyond. The hotel is set in six acres of gardens and woodland on the edge of Budle Bay Bird Sanctuary overlooking Holy Island and two miles from the majestic Bamburgh Castle.

The owners, Anita and Peter Laverack, do not cater for weddings or similar events, so they are able to offer a rare commodity of peace and tranquility even during the busy summer months. Throughout the hotel the antique furnishings and the immaculate and well-chosen decor evoke a warm, friendly and charming ambience.

Seated in the candle-lit dining room, surrounded by family pictures and portraits, guests can select dished from the daily changing menu and wines from over 250 bins. Dogs by prior arrangement. Special short breaks available all year.

Places of interest nearby: The Farne Islands are just a boat trip away, while Bamburgh, Alnwick and Dunstanburgh Castles along with Holy Island are nearby. Waren House is open all year. **Directions: There are advance warning signs on the A1 both north and south. Take B1342 to Waren Mill. Hotel (floodlit at night) is on south-west corner of Budle Bay just two miles from Bamburgh.**

10 M | 14

For hotel location, see maps on pages 223–229

In association with MasterCard

Apsley House

141 NEWBRIDGE HILL ROAD, BATH BA1 3PT
TEL: 01225 336966 FAX: 01225 425462

OWNERS: Anne and Chris Baker

7 rms 7 ens

S: £45
D: £55–£85

One mile from the centre of Bath, this elegant Georgian house was reputedly built for the Duke of Wellington in 1830, and is set in a delightful garden.

The new hosts, Anne and Chris Baker, greet guests with a warm welcome into their home, with its magnificently proportioned reception rooms which have been refurbished in great style and comfort.

A quite delicious breakfast is the only meal served, although drinks are available. Anne and Chriss Baker will readily recommend local restaurants and inns which visitors will enjoy.

The bedrooms are quite romantic with lovely drapery and delightful en suite bathrooms. Televisons almost seem to intrude in this timeless décor. The minimum age for guests' children is ten years.

Places of interest nearby: There is so much to see and do in Bath, the centre of which is just 25 minutes stroll from Apsley House. The magnificent architecture includes the Assembly Rooms, mentioned so often in Jane Austen's and in Georgette Heyer's historical novels, the Royal Crescent and the Roman Baths. Fascinating museums, the thriving theatre and excellent shopping all add to one's enjoyment of this lovely city. The Cotswolds and Mendip Hills are within driving distance. **Directions: The hotel lies one mile west of the centre of Bath, on the A431 which branches off A4, the Upper Bristol Road.**

14 M 10

For hotel location, see maps on pages 223–229

BATH LODGE HOTEL

NORTON ST PHILIP, BATH, AVON BA3 6NH
TEL: 01225 723040

OWNERS: Michael and Shirley O'Dwyer

5 rms | 5 ens

S: from £65
D: £75–£85

The Bath Lodge Hotel, originally called Castle Lodge, was built between 1806 and 1813 as one of six lodges added to a former gentleman's residence known as Farleigh House. This splendid building, with its towers, battlements, portcullis and heraldic shields, is redolent of Arthurian romance and offers guests a delightful setting in which to escape the stresses and strains of modern life.

The rooms, which are superbly decorated and furnished, are beautifully located and have many castellated features within them. Three rooms overlook the magnificent natural gardens with its cascading stream and the adjacent deer forest.

The main entrance hall, lounge and conservatory all contain oak beamed ceilings, natural masonry and large log burning fireplaces. All the rooms are furnished in keeping with this unique building.

An excellent breakfast is served at the hotel and there are plenty of good restaurants to chose from in Bath itself.

The hotel has a no-smoking policy, although guests may smoke in the conservatory area if they wish.

Places of interest nearby: Stonehenge and Longleat. Bath Lodge is an ideal location for enjoying the vast number of tourist attractions associated with this World Heritage City. Wells and Bristol are also both within easy reach.

Directions: From Bath take the A36 Salisbury road. Bath Lodge is on your left after approximately seven miles.

Bloomfield House

146 BLOOMFIELD ROAD, BATH, AVON BA2 2AS
TEL: 01225 420105 FAX: 01225 481958

OWNERS: Bridget and Malcolm Cox

6 rms | 5 ens

S: £35–£55
D: £50–£110

This elegant country house, Grade II listed, was commissioned in 1800 by a notable Mr Henshaw, later to become Lord Mayor of Bath. It nestles in grounds that afford magnificent views over the city.

Bloomfield House is one of the most comfortable and relaxing country houses in the area and is furnished with handsome antiques, hand-woven silk curtains and French chandeliers.

The main bedrooms feature canopied or four-poster beds, including "The principal bedroom of the Mayor and Mayoress of Bath (1902/3)". Remote control colour TV, direct-dial telephone and tea/coffee making facilities are available in all bedrooms. There is ample parking.

There are also two separate spacious apartments each comprising two double/twin bedrooms, bathrooms, large lounge and kitchen which are available for families on a short, long or self-catering basis.

Riding, golf, swimming, sauna and leisure facilities are available by arrangement.

Places of interest nearby: The Cotswolds, Castle Combe, Stourhead, Stonehenge and Longleat. **Directions: From the centre of Bath take the A367 Wells road for 1/4 mile towards Exeter. Fork right after The Bear Pub; Bloomfield House is on the right before the third road junction.**

For hotel location, see maps on pages 223–229

EAGLE HOUSE

CHURCH STREET, BATHFORD, BATH, AVON BA1 7RS
TEL: 01225 859946 FAX: 01225 859946

OWNERS: John and Rosamund Napier

8 rms | 8 ens

S: £34–£42
D: £44–£68

Three miles from Bath lies the charming conservation village of Bathford. Behind a high stone wall, wrought-iron gates and elegant façade, this Georgian home, designed by John Wood, stands in 1½ acres of grounds, giving far-reaching views of the surrounding countryside.

The eight bedrooms, including some large family rooms, all have private facilities, colour television, hairdryers and tea and coffee-making facilities. Cots and extra beds can be provided upon request. There is a spacious drawing room, where meetings for up to 12 people can be held, and a second, smaller lounge. Although dinner is not served at Eagle House, the owners, John and Rosamund Napier are always glad to help with reservations for tables in one of Bath's many good restaurants.

Set in a walled garden adjacent to the main house is a cottage with two bedrooms, two bathrooms, sitting room and kitchen, which can be occupied for stays of two nights or more. It offers complete privacy with views across the valley and a new grass tennis court.

Places of interest nearby: The beautiful city of Bath, Castle Combe, the National Trust village of Lacock, the Cotswolds, Longleat House, Avebury and Stonehenge.

Directions: From the A4 take the A363 towards Bradford-on-Avon. Go 150 yards, then fork left up Bathford Hill. Take first right into Church Street; Eagle House is 200 yards on the right.

IRONDALE HOUSE

67 HIGH STREET, RODE, NR BATH, AVON BA3 6PB
TEL/FAX: 01373 830730

OWNERS: Jayne and Oliver Holder

2 rms

S: £50
D: £50

In an unspoilt area of countryside close to the Somerset border, this detached, late 18th century house has been extensively refurbished to the highest standards. Set in the quiet village of Rode, near the green, Irondale has a beautiful walled garden and enjoys wonderful views towards Bath which is just 10 miles away.

Both guest bedrooms in the house are pleasantly decorated, comfortably furnished and have their own bathrooms. The lounge, overlooking the gardens and hills, is an ideal place in which to relax and unwind – it is a room which has the atmosphere of a private sitting-room.

Owners Jayne and Oliver Holder often share a drink with their guests in the evening, but dinner is available by arrangement only. However, there are several good pubs and restaurants in the locality. Private parking is available.

Places of interest nearby: Bath, Rode Bird gardens, Longleat, Salisbury and Wells. **Directions: From the the A36 Bath–Salisbury road take the A361 towards Trowbridge. Turn left beside The Bell pub, right at T-junction and Irondale is the first large house on the left after the village green.**

en famille

For hotel location, see maps on pages 223–229

MONKSHILL

SHAFT ROAD, MONKTON COMBE, BATH, AVON BA2 7HL
TEL & FAX: 01225 833028

OWNERS: Michael and Catherine Westlake

3 rms | 2 ens

S: £30–£45
D: £50–£65

Five minutes from the city centre of Bath lies this secluded and very comfortable country residence, surrounded by its own peaceful gardens and enjoying views over one of the most spectacularly beautiful parts of the Avon Valley. You can be assured of a warm welcome at Monkshill, where the emphasis is on luxurious comfort and complete relaxation. The spacious drawing room with its fine antiques, Steinway Grand and open log fire, is for the exclusive use of the guests and the gardens offer a great variety of interest throughout the year.

The tranquillity of the Limpley Stoke Valley is one of Monkshill's most enchanting features. A narrow country lane or, if you prefer, an old Monks' footpath leads down into the quiet and unspoilt medieval village of Monkton Combe with its excellent pub and scenic brook. The famous Kennet and Avon canal close by leads into Bath.

The house itself is renowned for luxury accommodation, and the individually styled en-suite bedrooms, all with TV and tea/coffee facilities, are graciously appointed and command excellent views over the gardens, woodland and valley below.

Places of interest nearby: In this designated 'Area of Outstanding natural Beauty' are many historic villages, country inns and well sign-posted walks. **Directions: Take A3062 to the crossroads south of the city. Turn left into Bradford Road and right into Shaft Road.**

8 M

In association with MasterCard

NEWBRIDGE HOUSE HOTEL

35 KELSTON ROAD, BATH, AVON BA1 3QH
TEL: 01225 446676 FAX: 01225 447541

OWNERS: Newbridge House Hotel (Bath) Ltd
MANAGER: Gill Mead

10 rms | 10 ens

S: £60
D: £80

Newbridge House is an elegant Georgian manor with wonderful views across the Avon valley to the west of the historic Roman city of Bath. Throughout the hotel great care has been taken to furnish and decorate its lovely rooms in keeping with the architecture. In the kitchen the emphasis is on good basic ingredients rather than heavy sauces. The restaurant menu often features game as well as fresh fish from Cornwall. Chef may suggest a starter of tomato and goats cheese tart flavoured with basil followed by fillet of salmon topped with turbot mousse and a light coriander sauce accompanied by one of our fine wines.

Private meetings are especially well catered for in this quiet retreat only one and a half miles from the centre of Bath. The new management team have ensured that every facility is provided, supported by an extremely high standard of housekeeping.

Several of the bedrooms have a balcony with country views and some also have open fires.

Places of interest nearby: Bath, Stourhead, Longleat, Stonehenge. **Directions: From the centre of Bath take the A4 towards Bristol, then right at traffic lights onto A431 Kelston road. 1½ miles from the city centre.**

40 M

For hotel location, see maps on pages 223–229

Paradise House

HOLLOWAY, BATH, AVON BA2 4PX
TEL: 01225 317723 FAX: 01225 482005

OWNERS: David and Janet Cutting

10 rms | 10 ens

D: £48–£70

In the peaceful grounds of this early 18th century mansion house, guests could be forgiven for forgetting that they are only seven minutes' walk from the Roman Baths, Pump Room and Abbey in the centre of the beautiful Georgian city of Bath. The city is also notable as a fashionable shopping centre and home of the arts.

Situated in a quiet cul-de-sac, Paradise House has been carefully modernised and restored to a high standard to enhance its classical elegance. Ornate plaster ceilings and a fine marble fireplace can be seen in the public rooms, where antique and contemporary furniture are combined with pastel fabrics to create an attractive effect. The large walled garden, with its fish pond and rose covered pergola, is a delightful sun-trap from which guests can enjoy views of the city and surrounding hills. A boules court is a recent addition.

Proprietors David and Janet Cutting are on hand to assist guests with advice on what to see in Bath. Although neither lunch nor dinner is served at the hotel, the hosts have details of the 80 or so local restaurants (advance booking is advisable in high season).

Places of interest nearby: The Cotswolds, Bristol, Wells and Glastonbury. **Directions: Entering Bath on the A4 London Road. Later, turn left to the A36. Take first left after viaduct onto A367 Exeter Road. Go left at Day and Pierce and down hill into cul-de-sac.**

WIDBROOK GRANGE

TROWBRIDGE ROAD, BRADFORD-ON-AVON, WILTSHIRE BA15 1UH
TEL: 01225 864750/863173 FAX: 01225 862890

OWNERS: John and Pauline Price

19 rms | 17 ens | SMALL HOTEL

S: £52–£59
D: £75–£85

According to the ancient rent books, Widbrook Grange was built as a model farm in the 18th century amid eleven acres of idyllic grounds, traversed by a stream. No longer a farm, Widbrook still reflects its agricultural heritage. Together resident owners John and Pauline Price have converted the Grange with skill and care to combine contemporary comforts with a traditional ambience.

All of the bedrooms, whether a spacious four-poster room or one that is petite and cosy, are well appointed with facilities and antique furnishings. Some of the bedrooms are in the recently converted 200-year old stone barn which forms the courtyard. Dinner is available from Monday to Thursday, and there are also many excellent restaurants locally about which your hosts can advise you. An old bread oven adds to the rustic charm of the breakfast room, where a hearty start to the day is assured. The Manvers suite, with its oak table and carver chairs has been designed for board meetings, seminars and private functions.

Widbrook can now boast a superb indoor heated swimming-pool and gymnasium. There is an arrangement with nearby Kingsdown Golf Club. Riding and fishing can also be arranged.

Places of interest nearby: Longleat House and Safari Park, Bath, Avebury and Stonehenge. **Directions: From Bradford-on-Avon take the A363 Trowbridge Road, the Grange is on the right after the canal bridge.**

40 M

For hotel location, see maps on pages 223–229

THE LODGE

BEAMINSTER, DORSET DT8 3BL
TEL: 01308 863468

OWNER: Michael O'Rourke

3 rms | 2 ens

S: from £30
D: £60–£70

On the edge of the charming town of Beaminster lies The Lodge a fine, Grade II listed Georgian house built in 1794. It is set in four acres of lovely grounds, and is graced by several handsome cats.

Fine examples of original wood, plasterwork and fireplaces are to be found inside The Lodge. The comfortably, spacious bedrooms offer pleasant outlooks and are furnished with antiques. Good English home cooking is provided by the kitchen, with most of the ingredients coming straight from the garden.

Leisure activities for the energetic include walking, riding or tennis on one of the new all-weather courts – tennis coaching is available on site. Those who prefer more relaxing pastimes can choose between golf, fishing or swimming in the pool set in the walled garden. **Places of interest nearby:** The coast is just seven miles away and there are numerous historic houses and superb gardens in the vicinity, including Parnham House with its famous craft workshops. **Directions: Beaminster is on the A3066 between Crewkerne and Bridport. From Dorchester use the A356/B3164. The entrance to The Lodge is on the main road north of the town centre.**

ST PETER'S HOUSE

OLD MARKET, BECCLES, SUFFOLK NR34 9AP
TEL: 01502 713203

OWNERS: Charles and Jennie Broome

3 rms

S: £25
D: £40

St Peter's House Hotel stands on the site of a fishermen's chapel (dating back to pre-conquest times) and that is how the hotel gets its name. Some of the chapel's remains are incorporated into the present day structure, which is an early Georgian, Grade I listed building.

The ground floor has been completely restored to its 18th century style, known as 'Strawberry Hill Gothic', and there is even some original paint visible. The beautiful stained glass windows are protected from the elements by external glazing.

This elegant setting provides excellent accommodation, with small, bright and welcoming bedrooms and lovely public rooms. The menu provides freshly cooked, good quality food, complemented by an excellent wine list.

The front of St Peter's is on the old market square, while the back opens onto a lovely 'secret' garden that sweeps down to the river and offers views of the swans, ducks, ducklings and boats. Private moorings on the River Waveney provide easy access via the garden to the house.

Beccles is a tourist centre with superb leisure and sports facilities. The Norfolk Broads and surrounding area offer wonderful opportunities for fishing and bird watching.

Places of interest nearby: The coastal towns of Lowestoft and Great Yarmouth, and the city of Norwich, are only 20 minutes drive away. **Directions: Beccles is on the A143 between Bungay and Lowestoft.**

35

For hotel location, see maps on pages 223–229

Bovey House

BEER, SEATON, DEVON EX12 3AD
TEL: 01297 680241 FAX: 01297 680270

OWNERS: Francisco and Kay Fernandez-Llorente

9 rms | 8 ens

S: £55
D: £95–£110
(including dinner)

Henry VIII in 1543 gave this beautiful 16th century manor, as part of her dowry, to his sixth and final wife, Catherine Parr, who surprisingly survived him. The king had previously taken the house from Sherborne Abbey in 1539 during the dissolution of monasteries. With Thomas Hardy country to the east and Exmoor, home of the Doones, to the north, guests feel immersed in legend and history as they approach the hotel down the tree-lined avenue to the walled garden.

The reception area is Jacobean and the graceful drawing room has a magnificent Adam ceiling. The oldest part of the house is the 15th century Inglenooks Bar where locals and visitors alike enjoy informal meals in the 'eating house' both at lunchtime and evening, accompanied by superb wines rather than mead! The Dining Room is magnificent, with Tudor linen-fold panelling. There are creative à la carte and table d'hôte menus, yet served amidst a family ambience. The bedrooms are spacious, nearly all of them en suite and many with four-posters, the ceiling of one depicting Charles II hiding in the oaktree.
Places of interest nearby: Guests enjoy strolling in the three acre garden, walking along the fascinating coastline or exploring Exmoor, Dartmoor and Exeter with its magnificent cathedral. Sailing and riding can be arranged.
Directions: A3052, take turning to Beer Quarry Caves then turn right and right again.

20 M

For hotel location, see maps on pages 223–229

DANNAH FARM COUNTRY GUEST HOUSE

BOWMAN'S LANE, SHOTTLE, NR BELPER, DERBYSHIRE DE56 2DR
TEL: 01773 550273/630 FAX: 01773 550590

OWNERS: Joan and Martin Slack
CHEF: Joan Slack

8 rms | 7 ens

S: £32.50–£55
D: £50–£75

Set amid undulating countryside high above the Ecclesbourne Valley, Dannah Farm is part of the Chatsworth Estates on the edge of the Peak District. This is an exceptional farmhouse conversion so it is not surprising that in addition to being Highly Commended by the ETB (3 Crowns) and AA Premier Selected, the hotel won the 1993 National Awards for Excellence and Innovation and the 1994 Best of Tourism Award for the East Midlands. As the Georgian farmhouse is still part of a 128-acre working farm, guests and their children will discover plenty of activity within the grounds.

Four-poster, twin-bedded, double and single rooms are offered, all overlooking rolling pastures. There are two residents' lounges and large, safe gardens.

The restaurant has rapidly earned a fine reputation. Aromas of freshly baked bread, home-made soups and piquant sauces escaping from the kitchen whet the appetite for dinner, which is served with good wines in relaxed surroundings and is by arrangement. **Places of interest nearby:** The countryside is criss-crossed with footpaths with walks in all directions. Dannah Farm is optimally placed to enjoy the many attractions of the area – Chatsworth, Haddon Hall, Dovedale and water-sports at Carsington. **Directions: From Derby take the A6 Matlock road. At Duffield turn left onto the B5023 towards Wirksworth. At the traffic lights at Cowers Lane turn right onto the A517 towards Belper, then take the first left to Shottle. Bowman's Lane is 100 yards past the crossroads.**

For hotel location, see maps on pages 223–229

Bibury Court

BIBURY COURT, BIBURY, GLOUCESTERSHIRE GL7 5NT
TEL: 01285 740337 FAX: 01285 740660

OWNERS: Jane Collier, Andrew and Anne Johnston

20 rms | 17 ens | SMALL HOTEL

S: from £48
D: from £68–£76
Suite: £95

Past visitors to Bibury Court are reputed to have included Charles II and during the reign of George III, the Prince Regent. This gracious mansion dates from Tudor times, but the main part was built in 1633 by Sir Thomas Sackville, an illegitimate son of the 1st Earl of Dorset. After generations of illustrious owners, it became a hotel in 1968.

The great house is set on the outskirts of Bibury, which William Morris called "the most beautiful village in England". As a hotel, it is run on country house lines with the main objectives being the provision of good food and wine in informal and pleasurable surroundings. Log fires during the cooler months add to the comfort of guests.

There are some lovely panelled rooms in the house, many containing antique furniture. Many of the bedrooms have four posters, most have private bathrooms, and for those who like greater privacy there is the Sackville suite.

Trout fishing is available in the Coln, which forms the southern boundary of the hotel's six acres of grounds, and there are golf courses at Burford and Cirencester. Watersports and riding are available nearby. The hotel is closed at Christmas.

Places of interest nearby: Bibury Court is ideally placed for touring the Cotswolds, while Stratford, Oxford, Cheltenham and Bath are all within easy reach.

Directions: Bibury is on the B4425, seven miles from Burford and seven miles from Cirencester.

20 M

BIGGIN HALL

BIGGIN-BY-HARTINGTON, BUXTON, DERBYSHIRE SK17 0DH
TEL: 01298 84451 FAX: 01298 84681

OWNERS: Mr and Mrs J Moffett

15 rms | 15 ens

S: £30–£45
D: £45–£70

Centrally situated in the Peak National Park, Biggin Hall is a 17th century, Grade II listed property set in eight acres of grounds. Situated 1,000 feet above sea level, the air may particularly benefit insomnia and asthma sufferers. Visitors come here for the peace and quiet and to enjoy the landscape with its dry-stone walling, deep wooded valleys, heather-clad moorlands and historic market towns and villages. Walkers will appreciate the many uncrowded footpaths nearby.

The rooms of this house feature massive oak timbers and antiques, with one containing a superb four-poster bed. One of the sitting rooms has an open log fire where guests can enjoy a convivial atmosphere. A recently converted 18th century stone building, comprising four self-contained studio apartments and two-roomed suites, each with a private bathroom, is situated 30 yards from the main house. The traditional farmhouse cooking puts emphasis on free-range produce, wholefoods and natural flavours. Dogs are accommodated in the apartments only. **Places of interest nearby:** Chatsworth, Bolsover Castle, Kedleston Hall, Alton Towers, American Adventure Theme Park, Buxton, Ashbourne and Bakewell. **Directions: This country house is situated at the end of Biggin Village, which is off the A515, nine miles from Ashbourne and ten miles from Buxton.**

20 M | 12

Lower Brook House

BLOCKLEY, NR MORETON-IN-MARSH, GLOUCESTERSHIRE GL56 9DS
TEL/FAX: 01386 700286

OWNERS: Sybil and Ann Porter-Miles

3 rms | 3 ens

S: £28–£30
D: £45–£50

Lower Brook House has been skilfully created from a well-built detached property dating back to the 17th century and it epitomises the traditional Cotswold stone house of its period. It is quietly situated in the village of Blockley, famous in the 1700s for its silk trade. Standing within attractive gardens Lower Brook House offers a warm welcome to those in search of good hospitality and comfortable accommodation.

The hostesses take great care to ensure that guests' requirements are swiftly attended to. The three en suite bedrooms have antique furnishings and plenty of interesting bric-à-brac. One of the rooms has a four-poster bed and all have tea and coffee facilities, a colour TV and hairdryer.

Memorable breakfasts are provided along with unlimited amounts of fresh and cooked fruits, but evening meals are not provided. However, there are a number of places that serve good food in the local area.

Places of interest nearby: Blockley is a short drive from Cheltenham, Oxford and Stratford-upon-Avon. It is also a good point of departure for day trips around the picturesque local villages – perhaps to hunt for antiques.

Directions: As you enter the village from Moreton-in-Marsh, Lower Brook House can be found on your right.

For hotel location, see maps on pages 223–229

In association with MasterCard

HARROP FOLD

BOLTON-BY-BOWLAND, CLITHEROE, LANCASHIRE BB7 4PJ
TEL: 01200 447600

OWNERS: Peter and Victoria Wood

4 rms | 4 ens | SMALL HOTEL

MasterCard VISA S: £45 D: £60–£65

Harrop Fold Country House Hotel belongs to the 280-acre farm bought by Peter and Victoria Wood in 1960. It is set in the hamlet of Harrop, in a secluded valley, and is almost unknown except to local country folk. Harrop is thought to mean either 'valley of the hares' or 'high dell'.

The farmhouse, reputedly of Viking origins, is built of local stone with thick walls, mullioned windows and low, beamed ceilings. Innovations and renovations have turned it into a comfortable country house. 'A touch of luxury in the back of beyond' is just one of the many praises showered upon this establishment.

The delightful cosy bedrooms offer numerous comforts and many afford beautiful views of the fold. First-class service is complemented by the best in English country cooking. Meals are served in a peaceful environment amid antiques and family treasures.

Harrop Fold is a splendid retreat offering respite from the rigours of modern life. Guests can wander across farmland, saunter by fresh, sparkling streams or merely sit and relax on grassy slopes.

Places of interest nearby: The Ribble Valley, Leighton Hall, Skipton Castle, Trough of Bowland and the Yorkshire Dales. **Directions: Leave M6 junction 31 – A59 to Skipton. Three miles past Clitheroe take left to Sawley and Bolton-by-Bowland. Turn left to Holden to Copy Nook pub. At Holden follow signs to Harrop Fold.**

16

For hotel location, see maps on pages 223–229

Langtry Manor

DERBY ROAD, EAST CLIFF, BOURNEMOUTH, DORSET BH1 3QB
TEL: 01202 553887 FAX: 01202 290115

OWNER: Pamela Hamilton Howard
MANAGER: Tara Howard

18 rms | 18 ens | SMALL HOTEL

D: £89–£159

Originally called the 'Red House', this fine hotel was built by King Edward V11 (then Prince of Wales) as a home for his mistress, Lillie Langtry.

The bedrooms and suites are exquisite. The Edward VII Suite is furnished as it was when this magnificently spacious room was first built although today's occupants have the advantage of an en suite bathroom! The Lillie Langtry Suite has a pretty four-poster bed, heart shaped corner bath and Romeo and Juliet balcony. Ideal for anniversaries, birthdays and honeymoons.

While the Manor was being constructed, Edward and Lillie stayed in Langtry Lodge just a few yards away. Today it offers accommodation furnished to the same high standards as the main hotel and guests are invited to use the Manor's dining room, lounge and bar.

For breakfast sample the delights of kedgeree, home-made marmalade and freshly squeezed orange juice or enjoy a continental breakfast in your room. Sumptiuos dinners are served in the magnificent dining hall with minstrals gallery. Saturday night guests are invited to take part in a splendid six-course Edwardian Banquet.

Places of interest nearby: Hardy country, the New Forest, art galleries, theatres and gardens. **Directions: Take the A338 Wessex Way to the station on left. First exit at roundabout, over next roundabout, first left into Knyveton Rd, second right into Derby Rd.**

For hotel location, see maps on pages 223–229

Dial House Hotel

THE CHESTNUTS, HIGH STREET, BOURTON-ON-THE-WATER, GLOUCESTERSHIRE GL54 2AN
TEL: 01451 822244 FAX: 01451 810126

OWNERS: Lynn and Peter Boxall

10 rms | 9 ens

S: £53.50
D: £107–£125

In the heart of the Cotswolds lies Dial House Hotel, a small 17th Century country house which combines the charm and elegance of a bygone era with all the facilities of a modern hotel. Proprietors Lynn and Peter Boxall have 26 years experience in the hotel industry and extend a warm welcome to their guests.

The hotel is open throughout the year and roaring log fires burn throughout the winter months. In the summer, lunches are served in the delightful and secluded walled garden. Chef Stephen Jones creates delicious, freshly cooked food for the à la carte restaurant, which creates an aura of old England with its inglenook fireplace and oak beams. Dial House has received an AA Rosette Award for its cuisine and every care is taken by friendly staff to provide guests with an interesting choice of dishes and good quality wines.

An open fire in the comfortable lounge creates an ideal setting to finish of an evening with coffee and liqueurs. The décor of the bedrooms is light and cheery and some overlook the garden. All are en suite, centrally heated and equipped with tea and coffee making facilities.

Places of interest nearby: Stratford-Upon-Avon, Bath and Cirencester, Warwick Castle, Blenheim Palace, Cheltenham, Slimbridge Wildfowl Trust and Oxford.

Directions: Bourton-on-the-Water is four miles south west of Stow-on-the-Wold off the A429.

For hotel location, see maps on pages 223–229

Box House Hotel and Restaurant

BOX, WILTSHIRE SN14 9NR
TEL: 01225 744447 FAX: 01225 743971

OWNER: Charles Tull
CHEF: Darren Francis

9 rms | 9 ens | SMALL HOTEL

S: £65–£80
D: £75–£95
Suites: from £100

As soon as you pass through the gates to Box House, you will discover a handsome Georgian mansion, set in nine acres of beautiful landscaped gardens , and standing resplendent above the green valley through which the "Bybrook" quietly meanders to the River Avon on the outskirts of Bath.

Enjoy an apéritif in the relaxing atmosphere of the sitting room, or beside the log fire in winter before appreciating the excellent cuisine and dining in one of the elegant dining rooms, having chosen from the varied and seasonal menus. The wine list is interesting and reasonably priced.

Private meeting and dining suites are available for conferences and business meetings, with specialised equipment available.

The individually designed bedrooms are spacious, with superb views, and the bathrooms fitted to the highest standards. Guests can enjoy the wonderful outdoor swimming pool, and they can also dine alfresco.

The City of Bath is nearby with its Roman Baths and many other attractions which are within easy reach of Box House. **Places of interest nearby:** Guests can swim in the outdoor pool. Riding, shooting, fishing and air-ballooning can be arranged. Bath is nearby with its famous Cathedral and other historical buildings, and many West Country beauty spots are in easy reach. **Directions: Leaving the M4 at junction 17 take the A429 to Chippenham, then A4 signposted to Bath. Box House has its walled entrance on the right in the village.**

CROSS LANE HOUSE HOTEL

ASTLEY ABBOTS, BRIDGNORTH, SHROPSHIRE WV16 4SJ
TEL: 01746 764887 FAX: 01746 768667

OWNERS: Brian and Vanessa Binns

8 rms 8 ens

S: £37.50–£55
D: £60–£75

The discerning traveller will be charmed by the peace, quiet and comfort offered by this delightful house, now under the new ownership of Vanessa and Brian Binns. The origins of the house are 17th century, although there have been additions over the years. It is set in two acres of Shropshire's beautiful countryside, with unforgettable views to the south and west over the Severn Valley.

Special features of the house include the tiled entrance hall dating back to the time of William IV, an original inglenook fireplace, and exposed beams throughout. Despite these reminders of a bygone age, Cross Lane House offers every modern comfort and some thoughtful extras which are guaranteed to ensure a memorable stay.

An excellent and varied menu is provided in the dining room, cooked by Vanessa Binns who won the BBC Master Chef award in 1992. All the dishes used freshly cooked produce, which is attractively presented and complemented by a good wine list.

Places of interest nearby: Ironbridge the birthplace of the Industrial revolution, the Coalport China Museum, the Severn Valley Railway, Midland Motor Museum and the Aerospace Museum at nearby Cosford. **Directions: Cross Lane House is on the B4373 Bridgnorth–Broseley Road, one mile north of Bridgnorth.**

12 M

For hotel location, see maps on pages 223–229

Chelwood House

CHELWOOD, NR BRISTOL, AVON BS18 4NH
TEL: 01761 490730 FAX: 01761 490730

OWNERS: Jill and Rudi Birk

11 rms | 11 ens | SMALL HOTEL

S: £49–£59.50
D: £69–£94

Only minutes from Chew Valley Lake, Chelwood House enjoys an enviable location between Bristol, Bath and Wells – all cities of exceptional historic and cultural interest. A former dower house dating from 1681, the hotel's upper rooms enable visitors to take in far-reaching views over the meadows and rolling Mendip Hills. An impressive staircase leads to the guest rooms; three have four-poster beds of different national styles – French, Victorian and Chinese. Antique furniture, ornaments and paintings from the personal collection of owners Rudi and Jill Birk furnish the two lounges.

Rudi Birk's Bavarian origins have a key influence on the cuisine – in addition to an English à la carte menu, a selection of traditional Bavarian dishes can be prepared. In 1990 the hotel's 'Restaurant in a Garden' opened, a conservatory dining room with plants, fountain and hand-painted murals, creating a lush setting for dinner. The hosts take credit for inspiring a convivial family atmosphere at this professionally run hotel, which represents good value for money. **Directions: On the A37, eight miles south of Bristol, between Pensford and Clutton. From Bath keep on the A368 right through Chelwood village. Turn left at the roundabout.**

12 M 10

Collin House Hotel

COLLIN LANE, BROADWAY, WORCESTERSHIRE WR12 7PB
TEL: 01386 858354/852544

OWNER: John Mills
CHEFS: Mark Brookes and Anthony Ike

7 rms | 6 ens | SMALL HOTEL

S: £45
D: £88–£96

Believed formerly to have been the home of a wealthy wool merchant, Collin House is a 16th century Cotswold stone house standing in 8 acres of grounds, encompassing gardens, meadows and orchards set amid rolling countryside. It has been carefully restored to retain its original character, with oak beams, inglenook fireplaces where log fires burn on cool evenings, antique paintings and furnishings.

Each of the bedrooms is individual in style and is decorated and furnished to a high standard. All rooms have private bathrooms and 2 have four-poster beds. Collin House has an air of friendly informality, thanks largely to the enthusiasm of proprietor John Mills, who aims to create an ambience akin to that of a weekend house party. Closed 5 days at Christmas.

Collin House has long held a reputation for good English cooking served with flair and the candlelit restaurant, with its exposed timbers, mullioned windows and views over the gardens, provides the perfect setting. A balanced choice of delicious dishes is offered by the à la carte menu while an exceptional variety of bar and garden meals is served at lunchtime. Recommended by many guides.

Places of interest nearby: The Cotswolds, renowned for its picturesque villages and National Trust properties. Stratford-upon-Avon and Cheltenham are also within easy reach.

Directions: Collin House is 1 mile north-west of Broadway on the A44; turn right at Collin Lane.

10 M

For hotel location, see maps on pages 223–229

Leasow House

LAVERTON MEADOWS, BROADWAY, WORCESTERSHIRE WR12 7NA
TEL: 01386 584526 FAX: 01386 584596

OWNERS: Barbara and Gordon Meekings

7 rms | 7 ens

S: £40–£50
D: £50–£60

Leasow House is a traditional Cotswold stone farmhouse dating from the early 1600s. While retaining its 17th century character, Leasow House offers guests every modern comfort, including their own key so that they may come and go as they please. In the library, a complimentary tray of sherry is available for guests to enjoy as they relax with a book. There is a wide range of good eating places in the vicinity to suit all tastes and pockets. Barbara will gladly advise visitors if required.

Bedrooms are spacious, with ensuite bath or shower, and are equipped with tea and coffee making facilities, colour TV and direct-dial telephones. An adjacent barn has been converted to provide two additional en suite rooms – The Bull Pen on the ground floor, suitable for disabled guests, and The Hay Loft, a superior double.

There is ample car parking.

Places of interest nearby: The Cotswolds, Vale of Evesham, Shakespeare country, the cathedral cities of Gloucester and Worcester, Warwick and Sudeley Castles, Blenheim Palace. **Directions: From Broadway, follow B4632 direction Cheltenham. Take the fourth turning on the right signposted Wormington and Dumbleton. Leasow House is the first on the right.**

In association with MasterCard

THE OLD RECTORY

CHURCH STREET, WILLERSEY, NR BROADWAY, WORCESTERSHIRE WR12 7PN
TEL: 01386 853729 FAX: 01386 858061

OWNERS: Liz and Chris Beauvoisin

8 rms | 6 ens

S: £50–£85
D: £60–£95

Built of mellow Cotswold stone the 17th century Old Rectory at Willersey is quietly tucked away at the end of a lane, opposite the 11th century church. With a back-drop of the Cotswold hills and a dry stone wall surrounding the delightful garden, this is truly an idyllic spot. Within the garden a mulberry tree, reputed to have been planted in the reign of Elizabeth I, is laden with fruit each year.

A superb breakfast in the elegant dining room is provided. In the village itself is the 600 year old Bell Inn offering an excellent menu. Locally there are many first class restaurants serving fine wine and food. Owner Liz Beauvoisin is always happy to book these for you.

The immaculate bedrooms are decorated and furnished to a high standard and include TV, tea and coffee making facilities and hairdryers. Non-smoking throughout.

Sports facilities in the locality include racing at Cheltenham, Stratford, Worcester and Warwick and for motor enthusiasts, Prescott Hill Climb (home of the Bugatti Owners' Club). Golf can be enjoyed at Broadway Golf Club and the whole area is paradise for walkers.

Places of interest nearby: Blenheim, Snowshill Manor and Sudeley, Warwick and Kenilworth Castles, Birdland and the model village at Bourton-on-the-Water.

Directions: From Broadway take B4632 (Stratford Road) for 1½ miles. At Willersey turn right into Church Street. The Old Rectory is on the right.

16 M | 8

For hotel location, see maps on pages 223–229

The Thatched Cottage Hotel

16 BROOKLEY ROAD, BROCKENHURST, HAMPSHIRE SO42 7RR
TEL: 01590 623090 FAX: 01590 623479

OWNERS: The Matysik Family

5 rms | 5 ens

D: £80–£110

This enchanting thatched cottage was built in 1627 and only became a hotel in 1991. The Matysik family have over 111 years of hotel experience between them, and this is reflected in the careful transformation that has taken place.

Set in one of the prettiest villages in the heart of the New Forest, modernisation for the comfort of guests has not detracted from its original charm. The beamed lounge is an intimate little area for pre-dinner drinks. The tea garden has canaries, lace table cloths and parasols to create the correct ambience. The bedrooms are all en suite, some with a Turkish steam-shower, another with a four-poster.

An amazing breakfast is available until 11.00 am. The restaurant has light snacks or a full à la carte lunch menu. In the evening exquisite culinary delights are freshly prepared with chefs on show in their open kitchen. A gourmet table d'hôte menu complemented by a selection of fine wines and beverages, set in a unique and casual atmosphere by romantic candlelight.

Places of interest nearby: The New Forest is on the doorstep and Beaulieu to visit close by. Other local activities include mushroom hunting, riding, fishing, sailing and golf. Cookery lessons are available in the low season.

Directions: M27, junction 1, drive south on A337 through Lyndhurst to Brockenhurst, turning right just before the level crossing.

Whitley Ridge Country House Hotel

BEAULIEU ROAD, BROCKENHURST, NEW FOREST, HAMPSHIRE SO42 7QL
TEL: 01590 622354 FAX: 01590 622856

OWNERS: Rennie and Sue Law

13 rms | 13 ens

S: £48–£60
D: £78–£94

Whitley Ridge, once a royal hunting lodge, was built in Georgian style in the late 18th century. It was extended in Victorian times and in more recent years the house has undergone extensive refurbishment, enhancing the appeal of its original Georgian features.

The bedrooms are individually styled and decorated with great care and attention. Chintz curtains frame the long windows and in the bathrooms the use of mahogany, marble and gold fittings recall a gracious age. Public rooms are similarly luxurious and elegant.

Plentiful and interesting cuisine is available in the restaurant, where a table d'hôte menu changes daily. There is also an à la carte menu.

Set in five acres of beautiful and secluded parkland deep in the heart of the New Forest, Whitley Ridge is the perfect setting for a restful holiday. Ancient woodlands, where forest ponies and deer graze undisturbed, are directly accessible from the hotel grounds.

Places of interest nearby: A number of stately homes, including Broadlands and Wilton House, are within easy reach. Also within driving distance are places of interest such as Lord Montagu's Motor Museum, Buckler's Hard and historic Stonehenge. **Directions: M27 junction 1 then A337 to Brockenhurst left at Balmer Lawn Hotel onto B3055 and the Whitley Ridge drive is about one mile on left.**

For hotel location, see maps on pages 223–229

BRADFIELD HOUSE RESTAURANT AND HOTEL

BRADFIELD COMBUST, BURY ST EDMUNDS, SUFFOLK IP30 0LR
TEL: 01284 386301

OWNER: Douglas Green

4 rms | 4 ens | SMALL HOTEL

S: £45
D: £65–£80

Bradfield House, under new ownership, is a friendly, family run hotel with a relaxed atmosphere, where a bright and enthusiastic team offer their guests excellent service. The hotel's bedrooms, which are well decorated and very comfortable, all overlook either the gardens or open countryside. The newly decorated public areas furnished with antiques are bright and cheerful and complemented by beautiful fresh flowers. Open fires help to create a cosy and comfortable atmosphere. Guests and passing travellers can enjoy either an informal bar meal or choose a two or three course lunch or dinner in the elegant restaurant. The cuisine is innovative and well presented and is recommended by all the major guides. **Places of interest nearby:** The lovely old wool town of Lavenham and Long Melford, both of which are renowned antiques centres. Newmarket, the university city of Cambridge, and Bury St Edmunds are within easy reach. **Directions: About four miles south of Bury St Edmunds on the A134 Sudbury Road. Bury St Edmunds is on the A14 (formerly A45), easily reached via M11 or A11.**

New House Farm

LORTON, COCKERMOUTH, CUMBRIA CA13 9UU
TEL: 01900 85404 FAX: 01900 85404

OWNERS: John and Hazel Hatch

3 rms | 3 ens

S: £40–£45
D: £70

Set in 15 acres of lovely gardens and grounds, New House Farm is located in the beautiful Lorton Vale between the villages of Lorton and Loweswater. The name of the house is something of a misnomer as it is neither "new" nor a "farm"!. In fact, the property dates back to the 17th century. Recent and careful renovation revealed many of its original features, such as oak beams and rafters, stone fireplaces and flagged floors.

The spacious, comfortable bedrooms all offer en suite facilities and spectacular views of the surrounding fells. Two separate lounges, both with open fireplaces, provide the ideal environment in which to enjoy the scenery.

In the afternoon, teas with home-made scones and preserves can be enjoyed in the garden, after which guests may like to explore the adjoining fields and woodlands. Hazel produces a fine range of four-course traditional English dinners, including roast pheasant and duckling, Derwent salmon and local trout. AA 5Q premier selected. The Which? hotel guide 1994 Cumbrian Hotel of the Year. **Places of interest nearby:** This is a wonderful location for guests who enjoy walking, ponytrekking, fishing and golf. It is also an ideal base from which to tour the quieter Western lakes. **Directions: From M6 Junction 40 take A66 past Keswick. Turn left onto B5292 to Lorton over the Whinlatter Pass. New House Farm is one mile from Lorton on the left in the middle of the Lorton Vale.**

12

For hotel location, see maps on pages 223–229

Duxford Lodge Hotel and Restaurant

ICKLETON ROAD, DUXFORD, CAMBRIDGESHIRE CB2 4RU
TEL: 01223 836444 FAX: 01223 832271

OWNERS: Suzanne and Ron Craddock

15 rms | 15 ens | SMALL HOTEL

S: £37–£68
D: £70–£89

Duxford Lodge is set in an acre of beautifully tended gardens, situated in the pretty village of Duxford, ideally located for those wishing to explore nearby Cambridge, Thaxted and Saffron Walden. The Imperial War Museum is just a few minutes drive away.

The hotel which is family owned and run has very pretty and comfortable bedrooms, all of which have en suite facilities, colour TV, direct-dial telephone and tea/coffee making facilites. There are four ground floor garden rooms which have four-poster beds and look out over the lawns.

The newly named 'Le Paradis' restaurant has an enviable reputation for its superb cuisine which is an attraction for any gourmet. All types of functions are catered for in the restaurant and the two function rooms, the largest of which can seat 46 people.

Places of interest nearby: The Imperial War Museum containing the largest collection of aircraft in Europe, the historic city of Cambridge and the medieval market towns of Thaxted and Saffron Walden, plus Audley End House. Racing at Newmarket. **Directions: Exit at junction 10 of M11 onto the A505 eastbound. Take the first right off the A505 and continue for half a mile to first T-junction. The hotel is opposite.**

30 M

For hotel location, see maps on pages 223–229

Melbourn Bury

MELBOURN, NR ROYSTON, HERTFORDSHIRE SG8 6DE
TEL: 01763 261151 FAX: 01763 262375

OWNERS: Anthony and Sylvia Hopkinson

3 rms 3 ens

S: £46–£50
D: £74–£80

Set in extensive grounds with a lake and wildfowl, Melbourn Bury is an elegant manor house. It has had only two ownerships since the 1500s. The first owners were the Bishops of Ely and then in 1850, the property was purchased by the ancestors of Sylvia Hopkinson.

Gracious reception rooms are furnished with antiques and fine paintings, while the en suite bedrooms are comfortable and have charming views of the gardens. Fresh flowers and log fires are extra touches which guests will appreciate. Adjoining the library is a 19th century billiard room with a full-size table.

The cuisine is of the highest quality and prepared under the personal supervision of the owners, who will occasionally join guests for dinner. Delicious home cooking encompasses traditional English recipes and continental dishes prepared in cordon bleu style.

Lunches and dinners for up to 22 persons seated; more can be accommodated buffet style – small conferences, receptions and exhibitions. Closed at Christmas & Easter. **Places of interest nearby:** Cambridge, Duxford Air Museum, Audley End, Ely, Wimpole Hall and Hatfield House. **Directions: Turn off A10 to Melbourn. From south, house is on left, 300 yards after turning. From north, house is on right, 1 mile south of village centre traffic lights.**

50 M 8

For hotel location, see maps on pages 223–229

CROSBY LODGE COUNTRY HOUSE HOTEL

HIGH CROSBY, CROSBY-ON-EDEN, CARLISLE, CUMBRIA CA6 4QZ
TEL: 01228 573618 FAX: 01228 573428

OWNERS: Michael, Patricia and James Sedgwick

11 rms | 11 ens | SMALL HOTEL

S: £68–£70
D: £90–£98

Crosby Lodge is a romantic country mansion that has been converted into a quiet efficient hotel without spoiling any of its original charm. Grade II listed, it stands amid pastoral countryside close to the Scottish Lowlands and the Lake District.

Spacious interiors are elegantly furnished and appointed to provide the maximum of comfort. The personal attention of Michael and Patricia Sedgwick ensures that a high standard of service is maintained. All of the bedrooms are beautifully equipped, most with antique beds and half-testers. Two bedrooms are situated in the converted courtyard stables overlooking the walled garden and in these rooms guests are welcome to bring their pet dogs.

In the restaurant, extensive menus offer a wide and varied choice of dishes. Traditional English recipes are prepared along with continental cuisine. Tables are set with cut glass and gleaming silver cutlery and, in keeping with the gracious surroundings, gentlemen are requested to wear a jacket and tie for dinner. Crosby Lodge, with its spacious grounds, is a superb setting for weddings, parties, business and social events. Closed 24 December to 20 January.

Places of interest nearby: Hadrian's Wall, Carlisle Cathedral and Castle, and nine miles from the Scottish Borders. **Directions: From M6 junction 44 take A689 Brampton road for three miles; turn right through Low Crosby. Crosby Lodge is on the right.**

12 M

In association with MasterCard

AYNSOME MANOR HOTEL

CARTMEL, GRANGE-OVER-SANDS, CUMBRIA LA11 6HH
TEL: 015395 36653 FAX: 015395 36016

OWNERS: Tony and Margaret Varley, Chris and Andrea Varley
CHEF: Victor Sharratt

12 rms | 12 ens | SMALL HOTEL

S: £49–£58
D: £84–£104
(including dinner)

In the beautiful Vale of Cartmel, with views of the priory and beyond to the village of Cartmel itself, stands Aynsome Manor, once the home of Wiliam Marshall, Earl of Pembroke. It is an ideal retreat for anyone seeking peace and quiet. Guests can stroll around the grounds or, in cooler months, relax by log fires in the lounges.

The elegant candlelit dining room is the perfect setting in which to enjoy a five-course dinner. The restaurant has an excellent reputation for its home cooking, from delicious home-made soups such as apple, celery and tomato, to main courses such as roast breast of pheasant with smoked bacon and an orange and chestnut sauce. Fresh, local produce is used wherever possible. A high tea is provided for children under five as they are regrettably not allowed in the restaurant for dinner. There are 12 bedrooms, 2 of which are in Aynsome Cottage, across the courtyard.

Places of interest nearby: Aynsome Manor is a perfect base for touring the Lake District. Lake Windermere is 4 miles away. In summer, Holker Hall organises ballooning and vintage car rallies. There is horseracing in Cartmel on Whitsun and August bank holidays and 5 golf courses nearby. Closed 2nd to 26th January. **Directions: Leave M6 at junction 36 and take the A590 signposted Barrow-in-Furness. At end of dual carriageway (12 miles) turn left into Cartmel. The hotel is on the right.**

For hotel location, see maps on pages 223–229

Twitchill Farm Cottages

EDALE ROAD, HOPE, DERBYSHIRE S30 2RF
TEL: 01433 621426

OWNERS: Sarah and John Atkin

4 COTTAGES

Prices from £170–£415 per week.
Special rates available for weekends

Twitchhill Farm Cottages,in the Peak District National Park, offer a perfect retreat for lovers of the countryside. There are four charming self-catering cottages available Ash, Birch, Chestnut and Elm – and all have spectacular views of the stunning Hope Valley. Two of the cottages can accommodate up to eight people each and the other two cottages up to six each. All four are attractively but simply decorated throughout and include antique pine fitted wardrobes and chests of drawers. Each is centrally heated and provided with bed linen, towels, crockery, cutlery, fridge-freezer, colour TV, microwave oven, electric cooker and radio cassette. Natural spring water supplies each cottage.Each cottage has a key to the shared utility room which contains a tumble drier, washing machine, pay phone and additional freezer space. A babysitting service can normally be arranged for a modest additional fee. **Places of interest nearby:** Caves and old mines to explore; The Pennine way to tramp; the following places to visit: Peveril Castle, Chatsworth House, Haddon Hall, The Heights of Abraham, Crich Tramway Museum, Buxton Spa and the famous Blue John Caverns in Castleton. **Directions: Take A625 from Sheffield. Enter the village of Hope and turn opposite the church. Within 1/4 mile take right hand turn marked 'No Through Road'. Follow this road and turn right immediately after railway bridge. The cottages and farm are at the top of this lane.**

20 M

In association with MasterCard

UNDERLEIGH HOUSE

OFF EDALE ROAD, HOPE, DERBYSHIRE S30 2RF
TEL: 01433 621372 FAX: 01433 621372

OWNERS: Barbara and Tony Singleton

5 rms | 5 ens

S: £33–£38
D: £50–£58

Underleigh House is set on a hillside, less than 2 miles from the centre of the ancient Saxon village of Hope in the glorious Peak District National Park. Every bedroom in the house has either a countryside view or one over a lovely garden which in summer displays colourful tubs and baskets, roses and honeysuckle. A full range of modern amenities is available to make guests feel at home, including a colour TV, radio alarm clock, hair dryer, tea and coffee making facilities and a resident teddy bear!

Breakfast and evening meals are served in "house party" style around the scrubbed top kitchen table or the oak refectory table in the stone flagged dining hall. There is a choice of a hearty English breakfast or, for the smaller appetite, a continental breakfast, while an interesting and regularly changing menu is available for the evening.

Half day pony treks are available from the Edale centre for pony treking and there is an abundance of golf courses for the keen golfer. A number of cycle hire centres are nearby for those who wish to enjoy the scenery on wheels. **Places of interest nearby:** Underleigh is centrally located for visiting the historic homes of Chatsworth, Haddon and Hardwick. The historic villages of Hope, Castleton, Hathersage and "Plague" Eyam are all within a five mile radius. **Directions: From Hope take turning opposite church to Edale, one mile on where road bears right take left lane. Underleigh House is 1/3 mile on right.**

en famille | 8 M

For hotel location, see maps on pages 223–229

EASTON COURT HOTEL

EASTON CROSS, CHAGFORD, DEVON TQ13 8JL
TEL: 01647 433469 FAX: 01647 433469

OWNERS: Graham and Sally Kidson

7 rms | 7 ens

S: £60–£65
D: £110–£120
(including dinner)

Easton Court is a 15th century, Grade II listed, thatched Tudor house with many historic connections, particularly literary ones. Both Evelyn Waugh – who wrote *Brideshead Revisited* here – and Patrick Leigh Fermor found inspiration in this rural setting amid the glorious Devon countryside. The sensitive restoration of the hotel has removed none of its old-world charm and period features such as exposed granite walls, oak beams and a great inglenook fireplace, complete with bread oven, have been retained. For those with a literary bent, there is a superb library housing a fascinating collection of old tomes.

The seven tastefully furnished bedrooms have lots of interesting nooks and crannies and offer wonderful rural and moorland views. The menus in the attractive restaurant vary with the seasons and special diets can be catered for by prior arrangement.

Places of interest nearby: Dartmoor's mystery and grandeur lie 'on the doorstep' of the hotel, offering an endless variety of breathtaking walks, while Exmoor, Lynton and the rugged North Devon coast are a short journey away. Castle Drogo, Fernworthy Reservoir and Exeter are among the many other local places of interest. Closed January. **Directions: From Exeter, take the A30. At the first roundabout take the A382 signposted Moretonhampstead.**

CHARLTON KINGS HOTEL

CHARLTON KINGS, CHELTENHAM, GLOUCESTERSHIRE GL52 6UU
TEL: 01242 231061 FAX: 01242 241900

OWNER: Trevor Stuart
MANAGERS: Simon Jones and Christina Gotthard
CHEF: Lee Palmer

14 rms 14 ens

MasterCard VISA AMERICAN EXPRESS S: £39–£64 D: £56–£88

Surrounded by the Cotswold hills, the Charlton Kings Hotel is a building of simple elegance, set in an acre of garden with sweeping lawns and specimen trees. Charlton Kings village itself is a select area on the edge of Cheltenham Spa with its Regency architecture and fashionable shops.

The hotel's bedrooms are decorated in a pleasing style, successfully designed to complement the pine furniture and create a comfortable atmosphere. Some of the rooms are reserved for non-smokers.

The warmly inviting and informal licensed restaurant offers varied and interesting menus to suit all tastes. Of excellent value is the table d'hôte menu, regularly including a roast joint and a vegetarian dish – chacun à son gout! Tea or coffee can be enjoyed in the reception lounge where a leather sofa and comfortable chairs arranged before an open fire provide a cosy spot in which to relax in winter.

Places of interest nearby: Cheltenham Spa, famous for its architecture, festivals and racing, has plenty of theatres, restaurants and historic buildings. Also within easy reach are the Cotswolds, the Wye Valley, Gloucester.
Directions: On the A40 about two miles east of Cheltenham.

20 M

For hotel location, see maps on pages 223–229

HALEWELL

HALEWELL CLOSE, WITHINGTON, NR CHELTENHAM, GLOUCESTERSHIRE GL54 4BN
TEL: 01242 890238 FAX: 01242 890332

OWNER: Mrs Elizabeth Carey-Wilson

6 rms | 6 ens

S: £49.50
D: £79–£82

Halewell is a splendid house, some parts dating from its time as a 15th century farming monastery set in the hills within 50 acres of gardens. The River Coln runs through the grounds and natural springs feed a five acre trout lake on which fly fishing is available..

Elizabeth Carey-Wilson acquired the house in 1971. Since then the interiors have been beautifully restored. There are six large double or twin bedrooms. Two of them are particularly suitable for families and one for a physically disabled guest. All visitors are welcomed as if at a private house party. Breakfast time is flexible: unless necessary after 9 o'clock. Although there are plenty of restaurants in the area for lunch or dinner, guests are invited to enjoy an evening meal at Halewell. Mrs Carey-Wilson prepares a very good set menu and there is a drinks licence for visitors and friends. Since dinner is never served before 8pm, an earlier supper is provided for children. Dogs welcome by prior arrangement.

Places of interest nearby: Cheltenham, Oxford, Blenheim Palace, Bath and Stratford-upon-Avon. Riding can be arranged. **Directions: From Cheltenham–Oxford, leave A40 at Andoversford (A436). Take first left (1/2 mile) to Withington (two miles) – 2nd right in village, 2nd entrance left. From south, leave Cirencester ring road north at only traffic lights (The Whiteway). Go nine miles, 1st right in village, entrance on right.**

en famille | 8 M

For hotel location, see maps on pages 223–229

In association with MasterCard

FROGG MANOR

NANTWICH ROAD, FULLERS MOOR, BROXTON, CHESTER CH3 9JH
TEL: 01829 782629 FAX: 01829 782238

OWNER: John Sykes

6 rms 6 ens

S: £48–£100
D: £65–£130

Frogg Manor is a Grade II listed graceful white Georgian house, situated in nine acres of woods and carefully tended gardens. It is furnished using traditional decor and period furniture to combine modern comfort with the character of its Georgian origins. From its elevated position in the Broxton Hills, the manor affords magnificent views. It offers a haven of rest and and is pervaded by an atmosphere of pure romance.

The bedrooms are creatively decorated, luxuriously furnished and lavishly equipped. Everything is genuine except of course the hundred or more frogs made of straw, ceramic and brass! Comfort is paramount and guests have a choice of cotton or Irish linen sheets.

Traditional English style cuisine, freshly prepared by proprietor John Sykes, is served in the elegant dining room. It is likely to include freshly made soups, savoury garlic mushrooms, rack of local lamb, steak and kidney pie, local beef fillet in various guises and a selection of vegetarian and fat free dishes. A private room is available for small meetings or those who wish to dine in a more intimate atmosphere.

Places of interest nearby: Chester, with its timbered houses and Roman remains, the only completely walled city still left in Britain. **Directions: From Chester take A41 towards Whitchurch, then A534 towards Nantwich – hotel is on right approx ¾ mile.**

25 M 5

For hotel location, see maps on pages 223–229

Higher Huxley Hall

HUXLEY, CHESTER, CHESHIRE CH3 9BZ
TEL: 01829 781484 FAX: 01829 781142

OWNERS: Pauline and Jeremy Marks

3 rms | 3 ens

S: £35–£40
D: £60–£70

Mention is made of the land at Huxley in the *Domesday Book* of 1086, at which time there stood a construction of fortified sandstone on the site of the present-day Higher Huxley Hall. That basic edifice was updated and extended by successive generations through the centuries – to become the impressive establishment it is today, complete with one of the most recent modifications: a 40ft by 20ft heated indoor swimming pool.

Guests are assured of a warm welcome at the home of Pauline and Jeremy Marks, and of a memorable stay in this historical building not far from the Welsh border. The prettily furnished and comfortable bedrooms are all on the second floor, with en suite facilities and views across the 220 acres of surrounding gardens and farmland. The Hall has been designated a no smoking area throughout.

A seven course set dinner menu may include a variety of delicious game and fish dishes, followed by exquisite desserts and coffee with mints – by prior arrangement.

Places of interest nearby: There is plenty to discover in the historic city of Chester, plus Beeston and Peckforton Castles and, slightly further away, Wales. **Directions: From M6 junction 16 head to Chester A500/A51. After Tilstone Fearnall traffic lights turn left on to A49. About $^3/_4$ mile on, turn right to Huxley, then second left, passing Farmers Arms to T-junction. Turn left and the Hall drive is immediatly on the right.**

en famille | 10 M

THE MALT HOUSE

BROAD CAMPDEN, GLOUCESTERSHIRE GL55 6UU
TEL: 01386 840295 FAX: 01386 841334

OWNERS: Nick and Jean Brown
CHEF: Julian Brown

7 rms 7 ens

S: £48–£65
D: £65–£88
Suites: £80–£105

Nick and Jean Brown have achieved a blend of warm, relaxed and yet professional service, welcoming guests as part of an extended house party. The idyllic surroundings of The Malt House, a beautiful 17th century Cotswold home in the quiet village of Broad Campden, further enhance the congenial atmosphere.

Rooms, including a residents' sitting room, combine comfortable furnishings with antiques and displays of fresh flowers. Most bedrooms overlook the wide lawns which lead to a small stream and orchard beyond. All of the recently refurbished rooms are individually decorated and have an en suite bathroom. The Windrush Suite has an 18th century four-poster bed and a family suite is also available.

Dinner is served six days a week. The proprietors' son Julian is a highly accomplished chef who uses many ingredients from the kitchen gardens to prepare a table d'hôte menu, accompanied by a choice selection of wines. The English breakfasts are equally good.

The Malt House has earned a Highly Commended award from the English Tourist Board. Special breaks are on offer throughout the year – details are available on request. **Places of interest nearby:** Hidcote Manor Gardens (N.T), Chipping Camden Church, The Cotswolds, Cheltenham, Stratford-upon-Avon, Oxford and Bath. **Directions: The Malt House is in the village of Broad Campden which is just one mile from Chipping Campden.**

en famille 10 M 5

For hotel location, see maps on pages 223–229

Cotswold Park

WOODMANCOTE, CIRENCESTER, GLOUCESTERSHIRE GL7 7EL
TEL: 01285 831414

OWNERS: Nicky and Ian Wasserman

3 rms | 1 ens

S: £35
D: £60

This 18th century Cotswold house has some of the most spectacular views to be found in Gloucestershire. Set in its own park with a classical garden made up of borders and lawns, its aura is serene.

The interior has its own unique charm and elegance, giving it a most warm welcome to any guest – antique furniture, log fires and rooms filled with scented flowers. The three bedrooms, one with en suite bathroom and the other two with private bathrooms, cater for every comfort that a guest might need. Dinner menus are seasonal, made up from the organic kitchen garden. Individual needs may be catered for with prior notice. A continental breakfast is served in the breakfast room.

Places of interest nearby: Ideally situated for touring the Cotswolds, Cirencester with Roman sights, Georgian Cheltenham spa, Stratford, Warwick, Oxford and Bath. The area boasts many gardens to visit. For those whose interests are more active you may enjoy riding, racing, polo or walking. The water parks nearby offer all sports and bird watching. Also available are clay shooting, fishing and golf. **Directions: From Cirencester take the A417 towards Gloucester, approx six miles at the cross-road turn right signposted Woodmancote. Follow the hill to the top where gates and stone pillar on the right mark the entrance.**

10 M

HINTON HOUSE

ABLINGTON, CIRENCESTER, GLOUCESTERSHIRE GL7 5NY
TEL: 01285 740233 FAX: 01285 740282

OWNER: George Cooper

3 rms | 1 ens

S: £32–£40
D: £60–£70

This 18th century house, on the edge of a small village, has been sympathetically restored by its interior designer owner. It is set in two acres of beautiful gardens reflecting its occupation by the noted garden designer, Rosemary Verey, in the 1950s. The location is ideal for touring the Cotswolds.

The three bedrooms are country house style. One is en suite and the other two share an adjacent bathroom. The drawing room is extremely elegant, with antique furniture and a peaceful colour scheme. The reception rooms are filled with flowers.

Dinner menus are seasonal, with a continental influence, cooked by the owner. Most guests prefer eating en famille.

Places of interest nearby: Historic Roman Cirencester and more modern Cheltenham are both an easy drive, and Rosemary Verey's famous gardens at Barnsley are two miles away. England's best preserved Roman Villa is at Chedworth. Active guests may enjoy riding, polo, water sports and hot air ballooning. **Directions: Leave Cirencester on B4425 for Burford, two miles past Barnsley turn left, signed Winson & Ablington. After 3/4 mile turn right into Ablington, pass turning on left signed Northleach– Cheltenham, take next left turning, an unmarked lane. Hinton House is 100 yards on right, entering through the stables.**

en famille

Foxdown Manor

HORNS CROSS, NR CLOVELLY, NORTH DEVON EX39 5PJ
TEL: 01237 451325 FAX: 01237 451525

OWNERS: John and Helen Coleson

6 rms | 6 ens | SMALL HOTEL

S: £65–£76
D: £110–£140
(including dinner)

Foxdown Manor is delightfully situated only 2 miles from the sea, within 20 acres of gardens and woodland, midway between Bideford and Clovelly. Guests are drawn back again and again by the beauty of the setting, the country house ambience and the warmth with which all guests are welcomed by resident proprietors John and Helen Coleson. The Victorian manor house is filled with period furniture, while crackling fires add to the cosy atmosphere during the winter months.

The bedrooms in the main building are all en suite and two have four-poster beds. The old stone stables, which extend from the house, have been converted into several self-catering cottages which are all fully equipped and are ideal for guests who prefer more independence but who also wish to enjoy the hotel's facilities. A wide choice of dishes is offered on the menu and served in the elegant Victorian dining room and conservatory. There is a heated outdoor swimming pool, indoor spa pool, sauna, all-weather tennis court and an 18-hole putting green.
Places of interest nearby: Fishing, golf and sailing are available and shooting breaks (game and clay) can be arranged. Foxdown is well placed for exploring North Devon and Cornwall, and visiting Arlington Court (N.T), Exmoor and Doone Valley, the legendary home of Lorna. **Directions: Exit M5 junction 27. The Manor is 6 miles west of Bideford on the A39.**

THE BAUBLE

HIGHAM, COLCHESTER. ESSEX C07 6LA
TEL: 01206 337254 FAX: 01206 337263

OWNERS: Nowell and Penny Watkins

3 rms | 3 ens

S: £20–£25
D: £40–£45

The Bauble is ideally placed for tourists visiting East Anglia and for business people with interests in Ipswich and Colchester. Set in the heart of Constable country, this delightful 16th century property is surrounded by 1½ acres of lovely gardens. The house been carefully renovated to retain its Tudor character while offering every modern amenity.

The accommodation is both attractive and comfortable throughout. The three bedrooms are bright, pretty and equipped with colour television, radio, tea and coffee facilities and a hairdryer. In winter, the guests' sitting room is enhanced by a log fire. Antiques decorate every room in the house and books and magazines are freely available for guests to enjoy. The Bauble serves a good breakfast. For the evenings there are excellent restaurants nearby.

Guests are invited to relax in the gardens, play tennis, or swim in the heated pool.

Places of interest nearby: Newmarket, Cambridge, Norwich, Aldeburgh, Snape Maltings, Minsmere Bird Sanctuary and various coastal resorts are all within an hour's drive. Dedham, Beth Chatto's gardens, Colchester Castle, Lavenham and Gainsborough's House in Sudbury are all close by. **Directions: Higham is on the B1068 which runs from A12 to Stoke-by-Nayland. The house is through the village immediately over the bridge over the river on the left.**

For hotel location, see maps on pages 223–229

Hockley Place

FRATING, COLCHESTER, ESSEX CO7 7HF
TEL: 01263 70382 FAX: 01263 708101

OWNERS: Helen and Humphrey Bowles

3 rms | 3 ens

S: £30
D: £60

Hockley Place is renowned for its rhodendendron walk, in full bloom in May and June, just part of the lovely five acres of parkland, apple orchards and farmland surrounding this 'Lutyens' style house, where no smoking is permitted.

The interior reflects the hostess's talents as an artist, with her paintings around the house. The kitchen is equally creative, as she is also a superb cook, using prime local ingredients for the delicious five-course dinner served in the beamed dining room – and breakfast is substantial. The wine list is limited but inexpensive.

The charming bedrooms will delight tall guests, for there are extra long beds! Francophiles will enjoy French TV as well as Sky and the ususal UK channels.

Relaxation facilities include a gymnasium, heated pool and croquet lawn. Highly rated by other guides. **Places of interest nearby:** Mystical Constable country, the Essex coastline and Colchester with its Norman Castle and Roman Walls. Beth Chatto's gardens are just three minutes' drive away. Felixstowe, Ipswich, and, beloved of many artists, Dedham, Flatford Mill and Lavenham are all very accessible. **Directions: Take A133 from Colchester (signed Frinton), turn right at Frating Hill into Church Road. Hockley Place is one mile on the right, two miles from the Harwich Trunk Road.**

In association with MasterCard

BESSEMER THATCH

BERRYNARBOR, NR COMBE MARTIN, NORTH DEVON EX34 9SE
TEL: 01271 882296

OWNERS: Les and Heather Levey

6 rms | 6 ens | SMALL HOTEL

S: £40
D: £50–£80

Bessemer Thatch is a delightful old house in one of the prettiest villages in Devon, only a mile from the sea between Combe Martin and Ilfracombe on the northern edge of Exmoor. As a base for touring the area or as a secluded retreat, it is the perfect spot. With no pets, nor children under 16 to create their respective holiday problems, the genuinely wonderful atmosphere in the house and its enclave are ideal for those in search of a quiet holiday.

The building dates from the 17th century Three bedrooms have balconies overlooking the garden – a setting of unique character – and there are two ground floor garden rooms. The proprietors, Les and Heather Levey, are friendly hosts who set themselves exceptionally high standards and the house is beautifully furnished. Every bedroom has colour TV, direct-dial telephone, clock-radio, hairdryer and tea and coffee making facilities. There are electric blankets in winter for those who need even more warmth than the central heating.

The dining arrangements, as one would expect in such a place, are excellent.

Places of interest nearby: Arlington Court, Rosemoor Gardens, 'Lorna Doone', the North Devon coast, Exmoor.
Directions: Off A399 three miles east of Ilfracombe.

For hotel location, see maps on pages 223–229

GLENVIEW

6 MEADOWFIELD ROAD, STOCKSFIELD, NORTHUMBERLAND NE43 7QX
TEL: 01661 843674

OWNER: Kenneth Harrison

3 rms | 1 ens

VISA — S: £25–£35 D: £40–£60

Glenview is Kenneth Harrison's Victorian family home, set in 3½ acres of lovely gardens and woodlands.

The bedrooms, which are tastefully decorated and furnished, are comfortable and provide every modern comfort. One of them even includes a large Jacuzzi bath.

Dinner is taken in the formal dining room, where guests are seated around an elegant candlelit table. The interesting menu offers well prepared food, often including home smoked wild salmon caught by Kenneth himself. The house is unlicensed, so guests are invited to bring their own wine.

Within the house and grounds there is an indoor heated swimming pool, games room and croquet lawns. There are also many leisure opportunities in the near vicinity, including golf, horse riding and fishing on the River Tyne. The woodland walks offer guests occasional sightings of foxes, badgers and deer.

This is a no smoking establishment.

Places of interest nearby: Hadrian's Wall, Keilder Reservoir, Beamish Historical Museum, and the lively city of Newcastle. **Directions: From A69 Newcastle to Hexham Road take the B6309 into Stocksfield. Turn left at T junction by station. Go through the village, past a school on the left and take second right into Cadehill Road. Road bends to left and becomes Meadowfield Road and Glenview is the third house on the right.**

en famille | 10 M | 8

For hotel location, see maps on pages 223–229

WARK FARM HOUSE

WARK, CORNHILL-ON-TWEED, NORTHUMBERLAND TD12 4RE
TEL: 01890 883570

OWNERS: David and Sheila Hogg

2 rms | 1 ens

S: £30
D: £50–£60

Half way between Edinburgh and Newcastle, turn off at Cornhill-on-Tweed and find this delightful farm house, just 200 yards from the south bank of the River Tweed.

David and Sheila welcome guests into their spacious and comfortable home, with a log fire in the sitting room and superb views of the Cheviots. The Farm House has two spacious twin bedded rooms, one en suite with its own private sitting room and the other with a private bathroom and nearby shower room.

Residents have a choice of eating in the dining room or less formally in the breakfast room. The arrangements for dinner are flexible. The menu often includes salmon from the Rivers Tweed or Till. Interesting dishes are offered to vegetarians. Wark Farm House is licensed, so there is a choice of selected wines. This is a no smoking house.

Fishermen are well catered for, with a drying room and freezer facilities – day tickets being available from local angling associations for both river and lake fishing. Excellent golf can be found at Coldstream and Kelso, and riding is another popular local pursuit.

Places of interest nearby: Holy Island, Bamburgh Castle, Floors Castle and the site of the Battle of Flodden – history abounds. **Directions: Leave the A1 at Berwick-on-Tweed, taking the A698 to Cornhill-on-Tweed then the B6350 into Wark. The Farm House is the first big white house on the right.**

en famille | 12 M

For hotel location, see maps on pages 223–229

LEUSDON LODGE HOTEL

LEUSDON, POUNDSGATE, NR ASHBURTON, DEVON TQ13 7PE
TEL: 01364 631304 FAX: 01364 631599

OWNERS: Ivor and Miranda Russell

7 rms | 7 ens | SMALL HOTEL

S: £30–£50
D: £60–£100

Built in the 19th century, Leusdon Lodge is situated in an elevated position in the Dartmoor National Park, with commanding views over the surrounding countryside. The location is a haven of peace, with farmland and wooded valleys all around, seven miles from the town of Ashburton. The house is comfortably furnished and has the feel of a family home, with attractive fabrics, interesting pictures and antiques. A log fire burns in the sitting room in winter and there is also a bar where guests enjoy a drink.

The seven bedrooms, all with ensuite bathrooms, are decorated to a high standard. Top-quality beds, combined with the Devon air, ensure a good night's sleep. In the panelled dining room, great care is taken with the preparation of the menus, which change daily and offer several choices at each course. Quality local produce, including vegetables from the kitchen garden, is used. Special diets are catered for. The wine list features both New World and European wines. Special breaks are available.
Places of interest nearby: Walking on the open moor, riding, fly fishing, golf, racing at Newton Abbot and Haldon, Iron Age and prehistoric sites, houses and gardens such as Castle Drogo, Knightshayes and Killerton. **Directions: Leave A38 at Pear Tree Cross exit near Ashburton, take B3357 following signs for Princetown. Go through village of Poundsgate, turning right at top of hill, signposted Leusdon, then first right and right again.**

For hotel location, see maps on pages 223–229

In association with MasterCard

MOOR VIEW HOUSE

VALE DOWN, LYDFORD, DEVON EX20 4BB
TEL: 0182 2820 220

OWNERS: David and Wendy Sharples
CHEF: Wendy Sharples

4 rms | 4 ens | SMALL HOTEL

S: £45–£55
D: £90–£105
(including dinner)

Originally built as a farmhouse in 1869, it was not until the early 1980s that this attractive house was converted into a small hotel and restaurant. The property faces Dartmoor from the front, while to the rear are spectacular views across the Devon countryside. Wonderful pictures of the landscape are lit by the setting sun.

Always putting their guests' comfort first, the Sharples family has created a friendly hotel with a genuinely relaxing ambience. The reception rooms reflect the cheery glow of open fires, and tasteful furnishings are a feature throughout. A Victorian decorative theme characterises the well-appointed bedrooms.

Sparkling crystal, bone china and gleaming silver in the dining room ensure that each meal is a special occasion. The daily four-course dinner menu embodies traditional country-style recipes such as rabbit and celery pie, venison in red wine, and duck with gooseberry sauce. Sunday lunch and Devon cream teas are a speciality, while a marquee is available for weddings and private gatherings. **Places of interest nearby:** Lydford Gorge and Castle, Tavistock, Clovelly and Exeter. **Directions: From Exeter take A30 Okehampton bypass to Sourton Cross. Then take A386 signposted to Tavistock; Moor View's drive is situated four miles along on the right.**

For hotel location, see maps on pages 223–229

MAISON TALBOOTH

STRATFORD ROAD, DEDHAM, COLCHESTER, ESSEX CO7 6HN
TEL: 01206 322367 FAX: 01206 322752

OWNERS: The Milsom Family
MANAGER: Marian Barwell

10 rms | 10 ens | SMALL HOTEL

S: £85–£110
D: £105–£140

In the north-east corner of Essex, where the River Stour borders with Suffolk, is the Vale of Dedham, an idyllic riverside setting immortalised in the early 19th century by the paintings of John Constable. One summer's day many years later, in 1952, the young Gerald Milsom chanced to visit the Talbooth tea room and soon afterwards took the helm at what would develop into Le Talbooth Restaurant.

Business was soon booming and the restaurant built itself a reputation as one of the best in the country. By 1969 Gerald had branched out, and Maison Talbooth was created in a nearby Victorian rectory, to become, as it still is, a vanguard of England's small country house hotels. Indeed, in 1982 Gerald Milsom was a founder member of the Pride of Britain group.

Maison Talbooth has ten spacious guest suites which all have an air of quiet luxury. Every comfort has been provided. Breakfast is served in the suites. Le Talbooth Restaurant is a pleasant ½ mile stroll or a courtesy car can drive you – first-class cuisine is served.

Places of interest nearby: For art lovers Flatford Mill, Gainsborough's House. Alfred Mannings House (which is open May–October). It is a good area for antique collectors and also for gardeners, Beth Chatto's garden for instance. It's an excellent centre for walking, golf and sailing. **Directions: Dedham is about a mile from the A12 between Colchester and Ipswich.**

35 M

For hotel location, see maps on pages 223–229

SALISBURY HOUSE

VICTORIA ROAD, DISS, NORFOLK IP22 3JG
TEL: 01379 644738 FAX: 01379 644738

OWNERS: Barry and Sue Davies

3 rms | 2 ens

S: £39–£50
D: £59–£70

This impressive Victorian house is set in pleasant, mature gardens on the edge of Diss, described as 'the perfect market town' by the late Sir John Betjeman. Salisbury House has established an enviable reputation for its individual style of cooking and cellar of 200 wines. The à la carte menu changes monthly to take advantage of the best seasonal produce.

Making a selection from the menu in the non smoking restaurant will whet anyone's appetite; rabbit and leek terrine with apple and hazelnut vinaigrette, medley of seafood with a creamy Noilly Prat and tarragon sauce, baked medallions of monkfish served with a red wine sauce and roasted garlic, hot blackcurrant and sloe gin pancakes with vanilla ice cream and, to finish off, coffee and home-made petit fours.

The decoration is principally Victorian and in each individually styled bedroom fresh flowers and pot-pourri add a welcoming touch. During the summer months, guests can sip their drinks in the large conservatory overlooking a pretty garden complete with walled patio, croquet lawn, summer-house and a duck pond graced by a weeping willow. A private room is available for boardroom meetings and private dining. Closed at Christmas and for 2 weeks in August.

Places of interest nearby: Newmarket, Snetterton motor circuit, Norwich, Thetford, Bury St Edmunds, Ipswich and the coast. **Directions: On the A1066 Victoria Road, ¼ mile outside town centre of Diss. The A143 and A140 feed into the A1066.**

18 M

For hotel location, see maps on pages 223–229

YALBURY COTTAGE HOTEL

LOWER BOCKHAMPTON, DORCHESTER, DORSET DT2 8PZ
TEL: 01305 262382 FAX: 01305 266412

OWNERS: Heather and Derek Furminger

8 rms | 8 ens

S: £41–£44
D: £62–£68

Yalbury Cottage Hotel is a lovely thatched property dating back around 300 years. Family run, it offers guests a warm welcome and a friendly, personal service in an atmosphere of peace, relaxation and informality.

The eight spacious bedrooms are all attractively decorated and furnished and offer well appointed bathrooms en suite. Each offers a full range of facilities, including colour television, hairdryer and tea and coffee facilities.

A comfortable lounge, complete with large inglenook fireplace and low, beamed ceilings, is the perfect place to relax before dinner. The proprietors pride themselves on the high standard of cuisine served in the beautiful dining room. A good variety of imaginative dishes is always available, for example, paupiette of cod filled with crab on a mustard sauce, rack of lamb with a honey and rosemary sauce, local calves liver with a redcurrant and thyme sauce or vegetable Wellington with a pesto sauce. A selection of carefully chosen wines is available to complement any meal.

Places of interest nearby: Thomas Hardy's birthplace, Athelhampton House, Parnham House, Abbotsbury Swannery, Corfe Castle and Sherborne Castle. Yalbury Cottage is an excellent centre from which to explore Dorset, with its superb walking country, pretty villages and magnificent coastline. **Directions: Lower Bockhampton is one mile south of A35 between Puddletown and Dorchester.**

8 M

WALLETT'S COURT

WEST CLIFFE, ST MARGARET'S-AT-CLIFFE, DOVER, KENT CT15 6EW
TEL: 01304 852424 FAX: 01304 853430

OWNERS: Chris and Lea Oakley

9 rms 9 ens

S: £45–£60
D: £55–£75

The Doomsday Book records this listed Grade II house as 'The Manor of Westcliffe'. It was transformed into this lovely hotel by the Oakley family who discovered it in ruins in the late 70s. Wallett's Court invites relaxation, either strolling in the extensive gardens, collapsing into the large leather sofa listening to the tick of the grandfather clock or enjoying the view from the conservatory.

There are large bedrooms in the main house, some with four-posters and others are in a converted barn, with names such as the Dairy or Stable. All are comfortable and well-equipped.

The Chef-Patron, Chris Oakley, puts history into the restaurant with a Jacobean flavour to the menus, which change every month. Try the Huntsman's Platter, local monkfish, Kentish lamb and syllabub. The wine list is long, mostly French, and there is a good selection of half-bottles, all acceptably priced. Breakfast is another feast, with farm eggs, sausages made by the nearby butcher, and homemade preserves. Awarded 3 AA Rosettes.

Places of interest nearby: Guests enjoy walking on the cliff tops to St Margarets Bay, exploring the Cinque Ports and playing golf on the nearby championship courses. Some visitors drive 10 miles to the Channel Tunnel for a day in France! **Directions: From the A2 roundabout immediately north of Dover take the A258 signposted Deal. After one mile turn right and the Court is on the right.**

20 M

For hotel location, see maps on pages 223–229

The Woodville Hall

TEMPLE EWELL, DOVER, KENT CT16 1DJ
TEL: 01304 825256 FAX: 01304 825256

OWNER: Mr A.D.M. Allen
MANAGERS: Sue and Roger Westoby

3 rms | 3 ens

Suites: from £85

The owners justifiably boast that this is one of the most beautiful small hotels in the world. One cannot believe that this magnificent residence, only recently opened to the public, standing in 40 acres of secluded parkland, is a short drive from Dover and the Channel Tunnel.

The accommodation is absolutely superb, three spectacular suites which are all furnished most luxuriously in the greatest detail.

The ambience throughout the entire house reflects the gracious Georgian era, with silver and highly polished antiques, oil paintings and marvellous flowers. The private meeting rooms, discreetly and appropriately equipped, are very impressive, and Directors' lunches can be arranged. Hospitality is of the highest standards, immaculate service, haute cuisine beautifully presented with interesting wines and champagnes. Other than for house-parties dinner is generally served in the suites.

Places of interest nearby: When not enjoying the extensive grounds with its ancient woodland guests can visit nearby nature reserves, Dover Castle and Hellfire Corner, the Battle of Britain Museum, the Old Town Gaol, the White Cliffs Experience and Walmer Castle, or, further afield, Canterbury Cathedral. **Directions: Take A2 from Dover and at the second roundabout turn left. At the bottom of the hill turn right towards Lydden. Continue for one mile and the hotel is on your right.**

25 M

Rectory House

FORE STREET, EVERSHOT, DORSET DT2 0JW
TEL: 0193583 273

OWNER Mrs Chris Walford

6 rms | 6 ens

S: £40–£60
D: £60–£75

Rectory House is an 18th century listed building of great charm, situated in the quiet and unspoiled Dorset village of Evershot in an area made famous by Thomas Hardy's *Tess of the D'Urbevilles*. Rectory House offers the utmost comfort with well-proportioned bedrooms, two of which are located in the main house with four cottage-style rooms in the converted stables. Each bedroom has its own en suite bathroom, with fresh flowers and home-made shortbread adding a welcoming touch.

In the guests' dining room, the emphasis is on wholesome home cooking. Hearty breakfasts include bread baked in the village bakery and locally made sausages. Dinner is served most evenings – and good evening meals are also available locally. A log fire creates a cheery glow in the lounge during the winter months.

Rectory House is Highly Commended by the RAC and English Tourist Board, and has been awarded 4 Qs by the AA. Closed at Christmas and New Year.

Places of interest nearby: Evershot is surrounded by lovely walking country – Melbury Park at Melbury Osmond, Dorchester *(Hardy's Casterbridge)* Sherborne Castle, Kingston Lacy, Parnham House, Forde Abbey, Abbotsbury, the Cerne Giant and Yeovilton Air Museum are within driving distance. **Directions: Evershot is off the A37 Yeovil–Dorchester road. On entering the village, Rectory House is on the right.**

For hotel location, see maps on pages 223–229

The Mill at Harvington

ANCHOR LANE, HARVINGTON, EVESHAM, WORCESTERSHIRE WR11 5NR
TEL: 01386 870688 FAX: 01386 870688

OWNERS: Simon and Jane Greenhalgh

15 rms | 15 ens | SMALL HOTEL

S: £54
D: £85

From the first glimpse of Simon and Jane Greenhalgh's elegant brochure one is aware that The Mill at Harvington is going to be very special. This delightful small country house hotel set on the bank of the Avon is in the heart of England with easy access to the West Country, Wales and, of course, Shakespeare country.

Once inside the welcoming and graceful reception rooms, which are brightened by big log fires in the winter, looking out over the extensive gardens and the river, the high standards of hospitality and service are evident. The en suite bedrooms are beautifully furnished and equipped with all the modern comforts including hairdryers, mineral water, colour television, tea and coffee facilities and telephone.

A modestly priced but excellent wine list accompanies the appetising menu which makes maximum use of local and seasonal produce, fish and game (there are also light lunches on the Terrace), reflecting the owners' belief that dining well must be high on the agenda for a successful visit. Guests can only take away memories of spectacular countryside, superb meals, immaculate service, charming surroundings and perfect hosts. **Directions: The Mill is signposted from the B439 at Harvington, 4 miles NE of Evesham, 10 miles SW of Stratford-upon-Avon.**

In association with MasterCard

THE LORD HALDON HOTEL

DUNCHIDEOCK, NR EXETER, DEVON EX6 7YF
TEL: 01392 832483 FAX: 01392 833765

OWNERS: Michael and Simon Preece

19 rms 19 ens

S: £38–£54
D: £59–£79

Ideally situated amid rolling Devon countryside between the historic cathedral town of Exeter and the coast lies this imposing country house.

The present building is a fragment of the huge mansion that once stood in this marvellous location, built in 1737. However, the beautiful views planned by Capability Brown can still be enjoyed, as can the peace and tranquillity of this quiet part of Devon.

All the bedrooms are decorated in an individual style, the majority enjoying picturesque rural views, and there are family rooms and four-poster suites for the romantic at heart.

Meals are served in the Chandelier Restaurant, a superb setting to enjoy only the freshest of seasonal produce. Special diets can also be catered for and picnics can be provided on request.

Places of interest nearby: The Maritime Museum at Exeter, Haldon Forest, (designated SSSI) perfect for ornithologists and photographers, and the moorland beauty of Dartmoor, are all just a short drive away from the hotel. **Directions: Exit junction 31 of the M5 and leave the dual carriageway at the first available exit signed Marsh Barton and Exeter. Take the first exit at the roundabout signed Ide and then follow local signs for Ide and Dunchideock.**

300 M

For hotel location, see maps on pages 223–229

THE CROWN HOTEL

EXFORD, EXMOOR NATIONAL PARK, SOMERSET TA24 7PP
TEL: 01643 831554/5 FAX: 01643 831665

OWNERS: Mike Bradley and John Atkin
MANAGER: Tony Gable
CHEF: Simon Whitley

17 rms | 17 ens | SMALL HOTEL

S: £60–£75
D: £120–£130
(including dinner)

This coaching inn, almost three hundred years old, in the Exmoor National Park is surrounded by stunning countryside, from coastline to valleys, streams and moorland, populated with red deer, ponies, amazing birdlife and salmon.

The hotel has been completely refurbished, to the highest standards of elegance and comfort. Guests can enjoy its comfort in every season – its coolness in summer, its warmth in winter.

The bedrooms, all en suite, have been beautifully decorated and are well-equipped with modern necessities.

There is a lively bar, patronised by the locals, for drinks or informal meals ordered from the extensive menu, or guests may prefer an apéritif in the lounge before entering the delightful dining room for a beautifully presented evening meal from the set menu. There is also an à la carte selection of marvellous fish dishes. Good wines complement the meal.

Places of interest nearby: Exford is a renowned fishing centre on the River Exe. Fly fishing (and tuition) in local rivers, riding over the moor and clay pigeon shooting can be arranged. Order a packed lunch and walk the moor or visit Lynmouth and Porlock. **Directions: Exit M5, junction 27. Drive eight miles down the A361, then take the A396 to Wheddon Cross, where Exford is signposted.**

16 M

For hotel location, see maps on pages 223–229

FENNY DRAYTON (Leicestershire)

In association with MasterCard

WHITE WINGS

QUAKER CLOSE, FENNY DRAYTON, NR NUNEATON, LEICESTERSHIRE CV13 6BS
TEL: 01827 716100 FAX: 01827 717191

OWNERS: Ernest and Josephine Lloyd

3 rms | 2 ens

S: £50
D: £70

White Wings is set in the village of Fenny Drayton, which is mentioned in the Doomsday Book and is the birthplace of George Fox, the founder of the Religious Society of Friends (Quakers).

This lovely family home provides peaceful and informal accommodation with spacious and traditionally furnished rooms. The well appointed bedrooms all offer private facilities, colour TV and views of the luxuriant garden.

Breakfast is served in the roomy kitchen overlooking the outdoor heated swimming pool. Dinner is available by prior arrangement and is served in the elegant dining room. Afterwards guests are invited to relax in the library or the conservatory and to enjoy the use of the Steinway grand piano or the full-size billiard table.

The surrounding villages and towns offer plenty of entertainment, including music, opera, ballet, theatre and exhibitions. For the active, there are golf courses and opportunities for fishing, canal trips and indoor skiing.

Places of interest nearby: Fenny Drayton is an excellent centre from which to visit Stratford-upon-Avon, Warwick, Kenilworth and Leicester, with their ancient castles, historic houses, museums and art galleries. Close by is the village of Twycross with its zoo housing a famous collection of primates. **Directions: On the A444 from Nuneaton, turn left into George Fox Lane (becoming Old Forge Road) and right into Quaker Close.**

en famille

For hotel location, see maps on pages 223–229

LIONS COURT RESTAURANT AND HOTEL

29 THE HIGH STREET, FORDINGBRIDGE, NEW FOREST, HAMPSHIRE SP6 1AS
TEL: 01425 652006 FAX: 01425 657946

OWNERS: Michael and Jenny Eastick
CHEF: Danny Wilson

6 rms | 6 ens | SMALL HOTEL

S: £40
D: £60–£75
Suite: £95

Lions Court is a charming 17th century family run hotel and restaurant with delightful gardens extending to the River Avon. Set in the centre of historic Fordingbridge, on the edge of the New Forest with all its amenities and rural pursuits. A wealth of oak beams and log fires creates a classic English atmosphere in which to enjoy a honeymoon, weekend break or business trip. Guests are guaranteed a warm welcome and friendly service. There are six en suite bedrooms, one with a four-poster bed and also a family apartment. All are pleasantly decorated and furnished.

A varied table d'hôte luncheon menu represents good value for money, while the à la carte restaurant, featuring fresh seasonal local produce, has a reputation for excellent cuisine in a relaxed atmosphere. Its menu includes tempting dishes such as panfried pork tenderloin, served with sweet peppers and black bean sauce and roasted loin of venison, served with juniper berries and a ragout of vegetables and port wine. There is also a vegetarian selection. Awarded 2 AA Rosettes for their cuisine.

Sporting facilities nearby include fishing, golf and horse riding. The hotel is closed for two weeks in January.

Places of interest nearby: Lions Court is ideally placed for the cathedral cities of Salisbury and Winchester, also Bournemouth, Broadlands and Stonehenge. **Directions: Fordingbridge is midway between Salisbury (11 miles) and Ringwood (5 miles) on the A338.**

12

CHIPPENHALL HALL

FRESSINGFIELD, EYE, SUFFOLK IP21 5TD
TEL: 01379 588180/586733 FAX: 01379 586272

OWNERS: Barbara and Jakes Sargent

3 rms | 3 ens

MasterCard VISA
S: £46–£52
D: £55–£62

The present manor is a listed Tudor building, although its origins date from Saxon times and is referred to in the *Domesday Book* as Cybenhalla. Secluded at the end of a long leafy drive, the hall enjoys a setting of rural tranquillity amid seven acres of lawns, trees, ponds and gardens.

Every evening, by arrangement, a superb candle-lit dinner is prepared by your hostess and served in convivial surroundings. Proprietors Barbara and Jakes Sargent pride themselves in offering a fine choice of reasonably priced wines from the cellar to complement your meal. A seat beside the copper-canopied inglenook fire in the Shallow End bar room is the ideal place to enjoy pre-dinner drinks.

The house is heavily-beamed throughout, including the en suite bedrooms which are named after relevant historical associations. During the summer, guests can relax by the heated outdoor swimming pool which is set in the rose-covered courtyard. With attentive service, good food and wine, it is not surprising to learn that Chippenhall Hall is ETB Highly Commended.

Places of interest nearby: Snape Maltings, Minsmere Bird Sanctuary, the Otter Trust at Earsham and the towns of Bury St Edmunds and Norwich. **Directions: One mile outside Fressingfield on the B1116 to Framlingham.**

For hotel location, see maps on pages 223–229

STANHILL COURT HOTEL

STANHILL ROAD, CHARLWOOD, NR HORLEY, SURREY RH6 0EP
TEL: 01293 862166 FAX: 01293 862773

OWNERS: Blendhome Ltd
MANAGING DIRECTOR: Antonio Colas

13 rms | 13 ens

D: £69–£150

Built in 1881 in the Scottish Baronial style, Stanhill Court Hotel is set in 35 acres of ancient wooded countryside and offers spectacular views over the North Downs. It boasts an original Victorian walled garden and amphitheatre and retains all the charm of yesteryear.

The hotel is traditionally furnished to provide an intimate, warm and comfortable atmosphere, with rich pitch pine panelling evident throughout the hall, minstrels gallery and barrel roof. There is a wide choice of bedrooms, all decorated and furnished to the same high standards and offering a full range of facilities.

A superb à la carte restaurant offers a menu which is international in flavour and complemented by an excellent range of regional and vintage wines. A choice of vegetarian dishes is always included and old style, friendly personal service is guaranteed.

Versatile conference facilities include small meetings rooms and a choice of five function rooms. Stanhill Court is also an excellent venue for wedding receptions, family celebrations and social gatherings.

Places of interest nearby: Leonardslee, High Beeches, Nymans and Wakehurst Place. **Directions: Charlwood is north west of the airport and reached off the M23/A23 via Hookwood or Lowfield Heath. Go through Charlwood and follow signs towards Newdigate. The hotel is on the left.**

180 M

For hotel location, see maps on pages 223-229

THE OLD RECTORY

GISSING, DISS, NORFOLK IP22 3XB
TEL: 01379 677575 FAX: 01379 674427

OWNERS: Jill and Ian Gillam

3 rms | 3 ens

S: £36–£42
D: £48–£58

This handsome Victorian Rectory stands surrounded by three acres of sweeping lawns and woodland on the edge of the peaceful hamlet of Gissing. The tranquility of the setting is extended to the interior which is beautifully appointed to ensure a comfortable and restful break from the bustle of the outside world.

The bedrooms are large and individually decorated with imagination attaining the highest standards. All have lavishly equipped en suite or private bathrooms.

The comfortable drawing room looks out over the terraces and lawns and has the added warmth of a log fire in the winter. Guests are invited to play a game of croquet on the lawns in the summer, swim in the indoor pool or simply relax on the south facing terrace.

A four-course candle-lit dinner is available by prior arrangement. There are many interesting local pubs and restaurants at which to eat if guests prefer to go out. Copious breakfasts are provided with locally produced bacon and sausages as well as Scottish kippers being a favourite.

Places of interest nearby: The picturesque seaside town of Southwold, Norwich, the market town of Diss, Bressingham Gardens and the Otter Trust at Earsham.

Directions: Take A140 towards Norwich. Turn left towards Burston and Shimpling, cross level-crossing and turn right to Gissing. At Gissing turn right just before church (Rectory Road).

12 M | 8

For hotel location, see maps on pages 223–229

The Wind In The Willows

DERBYSHIRE LEVEL, GLOSSOP, DERBYSHIRE SK13 9PT
TEL: 01457 868001 FAX: 01457 853354

OWNERS: Anne Marsh and Peter Marsh
CHEF: Anne Marsh

11 rms | 11 ens | SMALL HOTEL

S: £55–£75
D: £66–£95

"Not so much an hotel, more a delightful experience" said a guest recently of this charming small hotel where guests will discover a convivial combination of friendliness and professionalism. The hotel has benefited from the continuity provided by proprietors Anne and Peter Marsh, a mother and son team who have been running The Wind in the Willows for over 12 years. Each year has seen a careful upgrading of the interior and in 1994, 3 more stylish bedrooms and conference room..

Set in the marvellous scenery of the Peak District National Park and the Pennine Hills, the totally relaxed atmosphere of this early Victorian house is further protected by the 5 acres of land and gardens on three sides and the Park and golf course on the other. In recognition of its high standards, the hotel won the 1991 RAC Best Small Hotel in the North of England Award.

Home-cooking at its best is served in a private dining room. The pretty bedrooms have interesting individual features and all have private shower/bathrooms: the Erika Louise room has an attractive Victorian bathroom. Riding, pot-holing and gliding can all be arranged locally. **Places of interest nearby:** Glossop itself, a historic town mentioned in the *Domesday Book*, Peak District National Park, Derwent and Ladybower Reservoirs and the Pennines. **Directions: One mile east of Glossop on the A57, 400 yards down the road opposite the Royal Oak.**

16 M | 8

For hotel location, see maps on pages 223–229

WHITE MOSS HOUSE

RYDAL WATER, GRASMERE, CUMBRIA LA22 9SE
TEL: 015394 35295 FAX: 015394 35516

OWNERS: Peter and Susan Dixon

6 rms | 6 ens | SMALL HOTEL

MasterCard VISA

S: £74–£87
D: £128–£174
(including 5-course dinner)

Set in a fragrant garden of roses and lavender, White Moss House was once owned by Wordsworth, who often rested in the porch here between his wanderings. Built in 1730, it overlooks beautiful Rydal Water. Many famous and interesting walks through fells and lakeland start from the front door. Guests have free use of the local leisure club and swimming pool and free fishing on local rivers and lakes.

It has been described by a German gourmet magazine as 'probably the smallest, most splendid hotel in the world'. Proprietors Peter and Susan Dixon have created an intimate family atmosphere with a marvellous degree of comfort and attention to detail.

The five bedrooms in the main house and the two in the Brockstone Cottage Suite are individually furnished, and all have lake views. Chef Peter Dixon has won international acclaim for his culinary skills including 2 AA rosettes and a Red Star. The restaurant is deservedly famous for food prepared with imagination and style – 'the best English food in Britain', said *The Times* – and offers an extensive wine list of over 300 bins.

Closed early December to early March.

Places of interest nearby: Dove Cottage and Rydal Mount (Wordsworth's houses) are both one mile away. **Directions: White Moss House is off the A591 between Rydal Water and Grasmere, on the right as you drive north to Grasmere.**

20 M

For hotel location, see maps on pages 223–229

THE OLD RECTORY

GREAT SNORING, FAKENHAM, NORFOLK NR21 OHP
TEL: 01328 820597 FAX: 01328 820048

OWNERS: Rosamund and William Scoles

6 rms 6 ens

S: £68
D: £87

The Old Rectory, a former manor house, stands in $1^1/_2$ acres of walled gardens amid the unspoilt countryside of North Norfolk. It is believed to date back to 1500, when it was the seat of Sir Ralph Shelton. The house was originally hexagonal and the south east façade has stone mullioned windows bordered with frieze designs in terro-cotta tiles. Development and restoration work during the Victorian era accounts for its present day appearance.

The timeless tradition of the Old Rectory's décor and furnishings create an ambience of bygone days, with fresh flowers adding a homely touch to the surroundings. Each bedroom has a private bathroom, colour television and direct dial telephone.

Full English breakfast is served in the dining room and luncheon hampers are provided on request. Traditional English cuisine is a speciality.

For those who like to be cosseted, without the restrictions associated with traditional hotel service, the Sheltons cottage apartments are available. These are serviced and self contained providing guests complete privacy in delightful surroundings. The house is closed from 24-27 December.

Places of interest nearby: Norfolk coast, nature reserves, Sandringham and Walsingham. **Directions: Great Snoring is 3 miles north-east of Fakenham from the A148 King's Lynn–Cromer road.**

12 M

ABBOTS OAK

GREENHILL, COALVILLE LE67 4UY
TEL: 01530 832 328 FAX: 01530 832 328

OWNERS: Bill, Audrey and Carolyn White

4 rms | 2 ens

S: £50–£55
D: £65–£70

This Grade II listed building is on the edge of Charnwood Forest, with 19 acres of gardens, woodland and unusual granite outcrops where guests can stroll or play croquet and tennis. Being in the heart of Quorn country, stables are available for visitors' horses in the hunting season.

Inside is the most spectacular carved oak panelling and stained glass – indeed the staircase goes to the top of the tower from where it is possible to look out at over five counties.

The house has four bedrooms available for the use of guests', two of which are en suite. There is a gorgeous drawing room and elegant dining room. Dinner is served en famille by candlelight. The menu is therefore not extensive and the wine list short but good. After dinner enjoy a game of snooker in the superb billiard room. A traditional Sunday lunch is available. It is not really suitable for children under twelve.

Places of interest nearby: Mid-week it is ideal for businessmen with meetings in Loughborough or Leicester. There is excellent golf nearby and shooting can be arranged. Further afield are Stratford-upon-Avon, Warwick Castle and Rutland Water. **Directions: Leave the M1 at junction 22, taking B587 through Copt Oak to Whitwick. Abbots Oak is 1¼ miles on opposite the Bulls Head inn.**

en famille | 10 M | 12

For hotel location, see maps on pages 223–229

THE MANOR

NEWLANDS CORNER, GUILDFORD, SURREY GU4 8SE
TEL: 01483 222624 FAX: 01483 211389

OWNER: Peter Davies
GENERAL MANAGER: David Hill

19 rms | 19 ens | SMALL HOTEL

S: £60–£69.50
D: £70–£80.50

Only a few mioles from both Heathrow and Gatwick, set in nine acres of parkland, The Manor was a prestigious residence set in one of Surrey's most spectacular areas of natural beauty, making it ideal for business and for pleasure.

Heading an experienced and professional team, the resident owner, Peter Davies, will welcome you to his country house, built in 1870 as a retreat for the Bloomsbury set. Incorporating two of the finest function rooms, you will not find a better venue for conferences, banqueting, dances, meetings or weddings.

All nineteen bedrooms have en suite facilities and feature colour television, direct-dial telephone, tea and coffee making facilities as well as a trouser press and hairdryer.

The proprietor, chef and general manager have collaborated to produce the finest menus for the newly refurbished Squires Bar and Restaurant. Excellent bar meals are available at lunch or in the evening, with the main restaurant offering traditional and more unusual cuisine, complemented by a comprehensive wine list.

Places of interest nearby: Clandon Park, Polesden Lacey and Hatchlands. The Royal Horticultural Society gardens at Wisley, Brooklands Museum at Weybridge. Guests can enjoy the superb walks and views from Newlands Corner.

Directions: Ten minutes south from junction 10 of the M25. The Manor is located on the A25 just east of its junction with the A246.

130

For hotel location, see maps on pages 223–229

In association with MasterCard

CHASE LODGE

10 PARK ROAD, HAMPTON WICK, KINGSTON-UPON-THAMES, SURREY KT1 4AS
TEL: 0181 943 1862 FAX: 0181 943 9363

OWNERS: Nigel and Denise Stafford-Haworth

9 rms | 9 ens | SMALL HOTEL

S: £48
D: £62–£107

Chase Lodge is situated in Hampton Wick, adjacent to Bushy Park, in a conservation area of outstanding architectural and historical merit. Indeed, it is an ideal touring centre for places of historical interest such as Kew Gardens, Hampton Court Palace, Richmond Theatre and Royal Windsor.

Its proximity to so many major events makes Chase Lodge a popular choice for good accommodation. The Wimbledon Tournament, the Oxford and Cambridge Boat Race, racing at Kempton, Epsom, Ascot and Sandown, rugby at Twickenham and summer regattas at Kingston and Richmond are among the attractions within easy reach.

Originally built in 1870, Chase Lodge is a very successful small hotel, run with style and personality by proprietors Nigel and Denise Stafford-Haworth. The interiors have been designed to a high standard with well-chosen items of furniture and striking fabrics. The bedrooms, although not large, are beautifully appointed.

Private parties and functions can be accommodated. **Places of interest nearby:** Hampton Court, Windsor Castle and Richmond Park. **Directions: From the centre of Kingston take the A308 towards Hampton Court. Just after Kingston bridge is the Hampton Wick roundabout; take the White Hart exit into High Street (A310), the left at The Forresters into Park Road.**

30 M

For hotel location, see maps on pages 223–229

THE WHITE HOUSE

10 PARK PARADE, HARROGATE, NORTH YORKSHIRE HG1 5AH
TEL: 01423 501388 FAX: 01423 527973

OWNER: Jennie Forster

10 rms | 10 ens | SMALL HOTEL

S: £68–£80
D: £85–£125

The White House enjoys a superior location overlooking the Stray, 200 acres of parkland just a few minutes from the town centre. Guests will discover a unique, timeless residence in which luxury and comfort have blended with informality. The proprietor, Jennie, had an interior design business prior to the hotel and has used her skills to create a comfortable and relaxed atmosphere with antique furniture and memorabilia. The en suite bedrooms are individually furnished with designer fabrics and pastel tones, together with all the facilities one would expect from a hotel of this quality.

The Venetian Room Restaurant offers a wide variety of exquisite and orginal dishes and diners may select from a list of fine wines. After dinner, retire to the library where a selection of games and cards are kept.

Some of the many awards the hotel has achieved in the past four years are 'Which?' County Hotel of the Year, A.C.E. Best Small Hotel 1995, AA two Rosettes for cuisine, RAC Restaurant and Hospitality awards.

Places of interest nearby: Harrogate is a spa town with its own Turkish bath, beautiful parks and gardens and there are numerous shops of distinction with an abundance of antique shops. Other attractions nearby include Fountains Abbey, Harewood House and the Yorkshire Dales.

Directions: The White House is situated on The Stray and is set back from the A59.

50 M

ROOKHURST GEORGIAN COUNTRY HOUSE HOTEL

WEST END, GAYLE, HAWES, NORTH YORKSHIRE DL8 3RT
TEL: 01969 667454 FAX: 01969 667454

OWNER: Iris Van der Steen

5 rms | 4 ens | SMALL HOTEL

S: £60
D: £90–£120
(including dinner)

Nestling in the midst of Wensleydale, the front gate of this part-Georgian, part-Victorian country house opens onto the 250 mile-long Pennine Way. Visitors to Rookhurst are welcomed as friends by proprietress Iris Van der Steen. The cosy oak-beamed Georgian bedrooms and more spacious Victorian bedrooms are furnished with half-tester or four-poster beds: the Bridal Suite and master four-poster rooms are particularly ornate. Smoking is not permitted in the bedrooms or the dining room.

Iris specialises in traditional home-cooked English dishes, made with fresh produce. Dinner in the restaurant is a candle-lit ceremony at 7.30pm, whatever the time of year.

A wood-burning stove creates a snug atmosphere in the sitting room and bar, where guests can relax with a drink. The hotel is closed during January.

Places of interest nearby: Rookhurst makes an ideal base for exploring Herriot country – the Yorkshire Dales are a delight for both serious walkers and strollers. Nearby is the Carlisle to Settle railway and you can be collected from Garsdale Station. Just round the corner is the Wensleydale Creamery. **Directions: Take A684 Sedbergh–Bedale road. At Hawes take Gayle Lane to Gayle. At the top of the lane turn right and the hotel is 300 yards further on the right.**

10 M | 12

For hotel location, see maps on pages 223–229

Tregildry Hotel

GILLAN, MANACCAN, HELSTON, CORNWALL TR12 6HG
TEL: 01326 231378 FAX: 01326 231561

OWNERS: Huw and Lynne Phillips

10 rms | 10 ens

S: £45–£50
D: £90–£100
(including dinner)

Tregildry Hotel stands in four acres of lovely grounds and enjoys a spectacular setting overlooking Gillan Creek, the Helford River and Falmouth Bay. To the south is the dramatic and beautiful landscape of the Lizard Peninsula. Huw and Lynne Phillips, the successful former owners of Quarry Garth Country House Hotel and Restaurant in The Lake District, have recently taken over the hotel and totally refurbished it to the highest standards.

Each of the ten tastefully decorated bedrooms has an en suite bathroom and most offer stunning views of this tranquil corner of Cornwall. A spacious and comfortable lounge provides the perfect leisured environment.

The main theme in the elegant restaurant is Anglo French, with excellent food complemented by an imaginative wine list. In the summer months, à la carte alfresco barbecues are held on the sun terrace.

The area has been designated one of Outstanding Natural Beauty. Riding, golf, fishing trips and sailing tuition are all available and the coastal footpath near the hotel makes an ideal starting point for exploring the coast or creeks with their huge variety of wildlife.

Tregildry Hotel is closed from November to March.

Places of interest nearby: Frenchman's Creek, Lizard Peninsula. **Directions: From Helston join A3083 towards Lizard and take first left for St Keverne. Follow signs for Manaccan and then Gillan.**

In association with MasterCard

NANSLOE MANOR

MENEAGE ROAD, HELSTON, CORNWALL TR13 0SB
TEL: 01326 574691 FAX: 01326 564680

OWNERS: John and Wendy Pyatt

7 rms | 6 ens | SMALL HOTEL

S: £45–£55
D: £70–£120

On an enviable site in the beautiful Loe Valley, Nansloe is a fine Georgian Manor which was built in 1735 and extended in 1900. It stands in four acres of garden, surrounded by farmland and woods.

Each of the comfortable bedrooms has a charm of its own and all offer country views and every modern convenience. The elegant Georgian dining room overlooks the croquet lawn and, on chilly evenings, is warmed by a homely fire.

The Manor has earned an excellent reputation for its imaginitively prepared food. Menus change daily and all the dishes make use of local produce wherever possible. Desserts are accompanied by bowls of Cornish clotted cream! Fresh fish comes from the sea.

Places of interest nearby: Helston, the home of the floral dance, annually on May 8th, is an ideal centre from which to enjoy wonderful walks, the many gardens and a stunning coastline. Sporting activities are within easy reach. The Manor's owners are happy to suggest sightseeing trips to suit the weather and season. **Directions: At the end of a well signed drive some 300 yards from junction of A394 from Falmouth and A3083 to the Lizard.**

THE STEPPES

ULLINGSWICK, NR HEREFORD, HEREFORDSHIRE HR1 3JG
TEL: 01432 820424 FAX: 01432 820042

OWNERS: Henry and Tricia Howland

6 rms 6 ens

S: £45
D: £70

A Grade II listed 17th-century yeoman's house, The Steppes is located in Ullingswick, a *Domesday Book* hamlet set in the Wye Valley. The gleaming whitewashed exterior conceals a host of original features. Cobble and flag-flooring, massive oak timbers and an inglenook fireplace were part of the ancient dairy and cider-making cellars, which form the splendid cellar bar and lounge.

The singular ambience of the house has been applauded by *The Sunday Telegraph*, *The Guardian* and *The Independent* newspapers – all of which praise the enthusiasm and hospitality of owners Henry and Tricia Howland and, in particular, Tricia's cooking. The candle-lit dinners are compiled from medieval recipes, revived local dishes, Mediterranean delicacies and French cuisine. The interesting breakfast menu is complemented by generous service. Exceptionally high standard en suite accommodation is provided in either the Tudor Barn or Courtyard Cottage, both located within the grounds. Closed for two weeks before Christmas and three weeks after New Year.

Places of interest nearby: River Wye (for salmon fishing), Black Mountains, Malvern Hills (Elgar's birthplace), Welsh Marches, Gloucester and Worcester. Riding can be arranged. **Directions: One mile off the A417 Gloucester–Leominster road, signposted Ullingswick.**

12

DALE HEAD HALL LAKESIDE HOTEL

THIRLMERE, KESWICK, CUMBRIA CA12 4TN
TEL: 017687 72478 FAX: 017687 71070 FREEPHONE: 0800 454166

OWNERS: Alan and Shirley Lowe and family

9 rms | 9 ens | SMALL HOTEL

S: £87
D: £98–£158
(including dinner)

On the shores of Lake Thirlmere, surrounded by lush woodland, stands this glorious 16th century house. The lawns sweep towards the water, where fishing, sailing, canoeing and beautiful lakeside walks are all to be enjoyed. The tranquillity of the location is unsurpassable, since the house stands alone on the lakeside.

Alan and Shirley Lowe and their family offer exceptional accommodation and service, and are working towards restoring the 16th century authenticity of the house. The bar and lounge are delightful and most bedrooms have lake views.

The five-course table d'hôte dinner is served in the beamed dining room, which has an inglenook fireplace. The food is fresh, imaginatively prepared and there is a good choice of fine wines. Every dish is home-made, using vegetables and herbs from the Victorian kitchen garden.

If you are planning an excursion, ask for one of the hotel's delicious packed lunches. Special breaks available.

Places of interest nearby: All the splendours of the Lake District: Helvellyn is on the doorstep and Borrowdale is close by. **Directions: On the A591, halfway between Keswick and Grasmere. The hotel is situated along ¼ of private driveway overlooking Lake Thirlmere.**

For hotel location, see maps on pages 223–229

SWINSIDE LODGE HOTEL

GRANGE ROAD, NEWLANDS, KESWICK, CUMBRIA CA12 5UE
TEL/FAX: 017687 72948

OWNER: Graham Taylor

9 rms | 9 ens | SMALL HOTEL

S: £60–£76
D: £105–£135
(including dinner)

Swinside Lodge, situated at the foot of Catbells, is a Victorian lakeland house, surrounded by hills, valleys and woodland, and close to the shores of Derwentwater.

The house has nine attractive and thoughtfully decorated en suite bedrooms, each offering a high degree of comfort and equipped with colour TV, radio, hairdryer, tea making facilities plus a wealth of extras.

Begin your day with a hearty Cumbrian breakfast and later return to the comfort of the charming sitting rooms before enjoying your five-course dinner in the intimate candle-lit dining room. Menus change daily and a typical meal could include bavarois of smoked trout with cucumber salad, a delicious soup with home-baked rolls followed by roast best end of local lamb with a herb crust and rosemary sauce with freshly cooked vegetables. A choice of puddings is followed by a variety of British farmhouse cheeses and coffee.

An AA Red Star hotel with 2 Rosettes for food and ETB 3 Crown De Luxe, Swinside Lodge is non-smoking and unlicensed but guests are welcome to bring wine of their own choice. Closed from mid-December to mid-February.

Places of interest nearby: Keswick Pencil Museum, Castlerigg Stone Circle, Wordsworth's birthplace, excellent walks from the house. **Directions: M6 junction 40 take the A66 bypassing Keswick – over main roundabout – take second left. Go through Portinscale towards Grange; hotel is two miles further on the right.**

THE GRANGE COUNTRY HOUSE HOTEL

MANOR BROW, KESWICK-ON-DERWENTWATER, CUMBRIA CA12 4BA
TEL: 017687 72500

OWNERS: Duncan and Jane Miller

10 rms | 10 ens | SMALL HOTEL

S: £54–£61
D: £88–£102
(including dinner)

Standing in its own secluded grounds, The Grange commands views over Keswick-On-Derwentwater and the surrounding fells. The imposing lakeland house dates from the 1840s and is furnished with numerous antiques. The bedrooms all have en suite bathrooms or showers and some have romantic half-tester beds.

The award-winning restaurant has a varied menu which may include crab and asparagus tart and coronation chicken with Waldorf salad followed by a wonderful home-made soup, duck breast with a red plum sauce or medallions of pork fillet with apple and cider. Tempting sweets include hot puddings like spiced apple tart with an almond crunch top or mango and passion fruit crême brulée. The wine list includes labels from Europe, Australia and South America.

The hotel also has a cocktail bar, a quiet reading lounge and a coffee lounge. The garden is lovely. Closed mid-November to mid-March.

Places of interest nearby: Many spectacular walks are to be had across the fells. Local attractions include numerous National Trust Properties, the Castlerigg Stone Circle, Mirehouse, Wordsworth's Dove Cottage, the Pencil Museum and all the beauties of the Lake District. **Directions: Leave M6 at junction 40. Take A66 into Keswick then go left on to A591 to Windermere for 1/2 mile. Take first right, hotel 200 yards on right.**

For hotel location, see maps on pages 223–229

HIPPING HALL

COWAN BRIDGE, KIRKBY LONSDALE, CUMBRIA LA6 2JJ
TEL: 015242 71187 FAX: 015242 72452

OWNERS: Ian Bryant and Jocelyn Ruffle

7 rms | 7 ens

S: £63
D: £79

Hipping Hall is a 17th century countryhouse set in four acres of walled gardens on the Cumbria/Yorkshire borders, and therefore an ideal centre from which to tour both the Lake District and Yorkshire Dales.

All five double rooms and two cottage suites are well-equipped with own bathrooms and most are furnished with antiques. Guests help themselves to drinks from a sideboard in the conservatory before dining together in a very informal dinner-party style at a large table in the Great Hall, looked after by the owners Ian Bryant and Jocelyn Ruffle. All dishes are freshly prepared by Jocelyn from home and local produce. Dinner is a set five-course menu (but with alternatives including vegetarian dishes by prior request), served with three wines (optional) selected by Ian for that particular menu.

As well as accommodating individual guests, Ian and Jocelyn arrange private house parties for 5–7 couples, either for groups of family or friends celebrating anniversaries or for companies entertaining clients. Open from March to November, also during winter for groups. **Places of interest nearby:** The Lake District, The Yorkshire Dales, The Settle to Carlisle Railway, Brontë country, Sizergh Castle. **Directions: Hipping Hall lies on the A65, two miles east of Kirkby Lonsdale towards Settle & Skipton, eight miles from M6 junction 36.**

10 M 12

For hotel location, see maps on pages 223–229

In association with MasterCard

THE GREAT HOUSE RESTAURANT AND HOTEL

MARKET PLACE, LAVENHAM, SUFFOLK CO10 9QZ
TEL: 01787 247431 FAX: 01787 248007

OWNERS: Mr and Mrs Regis Crepy

4 rms | 4 ens | SMALL HOTEL

MasterCard VISA AMERICAN EXPRESS S: £50–£75 D: £68–£88

The Great House is set in the heart of one of England's finest medieval towns, beside the old market square away from the traffic. Built in the 14th and 15th centuries, has an imposing Georgian façade added in the 1700s and today retains all the character of a past era. In the 1940s it was home to the poet Stephen Spender.

In 1985 The Great House was converted to a restaurant, with the spacious bedrooms added a year later. All have full suites and are furnished with interesting antiques. Families with children are particularly welcome.

The French patron has established an excellent reputation for the restaurant, which features a historic carved Bressemer beam over a massive inglenook. Creative French cuisine is complemented by excellent service from professional staff. There is a choice of food from Bistro, à la carte and table d'hôte menus.

A paved York-stone courtyard, decorated with a mass of colourful baskets during the summer months, is the ideal place to enjoy a sunny luncheon or "al fresco" dinner on warm evenings.

Places of interest nearby: Lavenham, Guildhall and Little Hall Museums, St Peters & St Pauls Church, The Priory & Gardens, Crooked House, Kentwell Hall, Long Melford Hall and antique shops, Constable and Turner country, Bury St Edmunds and Cambridge. **Directions: From the A134 take the A1141 Hadleigh road.**

20 M

For hotel location, see maps on pages 223–229

Lower Bache

KIMBOLTON, NR LEOMINSTER, HEREFORDSHIRE HR6 OER
TEL: 01568 750304

OWNERS: Rose and Leslie Wiles

3 rms | 3 ens

S: £29.50
D: £49

Just 4 miles from historic Leominster, Lower Bache lies in 14 acres of a gentle Herefordshire valley. This substantial 17th century stone farmhouse has been restored by Rose and Leslie Wiles. While retaining its exposed stone walls, wealth of oak beams and flagstone flooring, it incorporates all the comforts of modern living. ETB Highly Commended. Accessed by an external, stone stairway, the three en suite bedrooms are furnished in a charming cottage style. Each bedroom has its own private sitting room. Watercolours, original prints, plants, books and ornaments create an atmosphere of quality and comfort. With its vaulted ceiling and original cider press, the dining room is unique. Rose and Leslie are acclaimed gourmet cooks: the four-course table d'hôte is superb value. Bread, ice-cream, sausages and preserves are all home-made; fish, game and poultry are smoked on the premises and most of the vegetables are grown organically in the garden. The breakfast menu offers an exceptional choice including laverbread oatcakes, kedgeree, sautie bannocks, floddies and scrambled eggs with smoked salmon.

Places of interest nearby: Welsh Marches, Ludlow, Tenbury Wells, Hereford, Worcester and Hay-on-Wye.

Directions: Kimbolton village is 2 miles north-east of Leominster (which is off the A49). Lower Bache is signposted at the top of the hill on the Leysters road.

For hotel location, see maps on pages 223–229

LIFTON (Sprytown)

THE THATCHED COTTAGE COUNTRY HOTEL AND RESTAURANT

SPRYTOWN, LIFTON, DEVON PL16 0AY
TEL: 01566 784224 FAX: 01566 784334

OWNERS: Garth and Rita Willing and Victoria Bryant and Janet Purr

5 rms | 5 ens | SMALL HOTEL

S: £35–£45
D: £70–£90

Nestling on the edge of Dartmoor in $2^1/_2$ acres of landscaped gardens, The Thatched Cottage Country Hotel & Restaurant is just 1 mile from the Saxon village of Lifton. The bedrooms are situated in a converted stable block a few yards from the main thatched house. All rooms are decorated in a charming cottage style and have lovely views of the surrounding countryside.

The 16th century thatched cottage houses the restaurant, where a leisurely breakfast is served until 10am. The restaurant has been awarded two stars and a rosette by the AA for food and service. The menu which changes regularly plus an extensive wine list offers a varied and imaginative choice for the gourmet.

The lounge, with its inglenook fireplace, comfortable armchairs and cosy atmosphere, is the ideal place to enjoy apértifs, after-dinner coffee, liqueurs and petits fours.

The premises are unsuitable for very young children.

Places of interest nearby: Well placed for exploring Exmoor, Bodmin Moor and Dartmoor. This is an area rich in sites of historical, architectural and archaeological interest. **Directions: From Exeter follow A30 for about 35 miles. Leave A30 at Stowford Cross. At the top of the slip road at the T-junction turn left (the hotel is signposted) and travel to Sprytown Cross, straight across, the hotel drive is 100 yards on right.**

For hotel location, see maps on pages 223–229

WASHINGBOROUGH HALL

CHURCH HILL, WASHINGBOROUGH, LINCOLNSHIRE LN4 1BE
TEL: 01522 790340 FAX: 01522 792936

OWNERS: Mary and Brian Shillaker

12 rms | 12 ens | SMALL HOTEL

S: £52–£62
D: £72–£84

This listed Georgian Manor House is set in three acres of secluded grounds, containing many mature trees and some wonderful displays of fuchsias and begonias. There is also a large lawned area where guests can play croquet.

The individually and prettily furnished bedrooms offer a full range of modern comforts, with some including a four-poster bed or spa bath.

A good selection of real ales is served in the bar, while the Wedgwood Dining Room overlooks the garden and provides the perfect setting for a meal. The imaginative menu caters for all tastes and is complemented by an extensive list of carefully selected wines. RAC Restaurant Award 1994 and RAC Hospitality, Comfort and Restaurant Award. Guests at Washingborough Hall have access to the Canwick Golf Club and hard tennis courts. **Places of interest nearby:** The city of Lincoln is just two miles away and has a magnificent 11th century cathedral and castle. A short drive away is the beautiful rolling countryside of the Lincolnshire Wolds with many unspoilt villages and market towns to visit. Aircraft buffs should head for The Battle of Britain Memorial Flight, The Aviation Heritage Centre and The Newark Air Museum. **Directions: From Lincoln take the B1188 towards Branston and then turn left onto the B1190 towards Bardney. Turn right (approx two miles) opposite telephone box. The Hall is 200 yards on the left.**

50 M

ALLHAYS COUNTRY HOUSE

TALLAND BAY, LOOE, CORNWALL PL13 2JB
TEL: 01503 272434 FAX: 01503 272929

OWNERS: Brian and Lynda Spring

7 rms | 5 ens

S: £28–£36
D: £56–£72

Set in its own gardens, just a few minutes' walk from the sea, Allhays stands on a gently sloping hillside overlooking Talland Bay. Situated between Looe and the fishing village of Polperro, it lies on a spectacular stretch of rugged coastline, much frequented by smugglers for many years. As a quiet retreat, Allhays is as attractive to those who wish to relax in comfort as it is to guests with a more energetic holiday in mind. Allhays is closed 24 December to 7 January.

The bedrooms, most of which offer magnificent views, have a radio alarm, tea/coffee making facilities and electric over-blankets for the out-of-season months. Until the arrival of summer a log fire blazes in the lounge, where drinks are served from the bar.

This corner of Cornwall is a living larder of wholesome produce – early vegetables, dairy cattle, Cornish cream, farmhouse cheese, garden herbs, soft fruits and fresh seafood are all made use of by chef-patronne, Lynda Spring. Food is cooked with an Aga in the traditional way, using recipes that have become an integral part of West Country life, and she has been awarded an AA Rosette for her cuisine.
Places of interest nearby: Miles of walking along National Trust coastline, quaint fishing villages and the smugglers museum of Polperro. Water sports, riding and golf can be arranged locally. **Directions: From Looe take the A387 signposted to Polperro. After approximately 2 miles you will see Allhays signposted on the left-hand side.**

For hotel location, see maps on pages 223–229

COOMBE FARM

WIDEGATES, NR LOOE, CORNWALL PL13 1QN
TEL: 01503 240223

OWNERS: Alexander and Sally Low

9 rms 9 ens

S: £20–£26
D: £40–£52

Coombe Farm was originally part of a large estate and the house was built in 1928 for a nephew of the landowner. It enjoys magnificent views down an unspoilt wooded valley to the sea and is set in $10^1/_2$ acres of lawns, meadows, woods, streams and ponds.

A warm, friendly and relaxed atmosphere pervades the house, which has been carefully furnished with antiques and paintings. Open log fires in the winter months add to the sense of comfort and cosiness. All the bedrooms offer lovely country views and are cheerfully decorated and centrally heated.

A full English breakfast is served at Coombe Farm and in the evening a four-course dinner is available in the lovely candlelit dining room. The traditional menu is changed daily and vegetarians are well catered for.

There are over three acres of lawns where guests are invited to soak up the sun, play croquet or swim in the heated outdoor swimming pool and there is a snug stone outhouse for snooker and table tennis. The farm is closed from 1 November to 1 March.

Places of interest nearby: Coombe Farm is an ideal centre for visiting all parts of Cornwall and most of Devon – The Coastal Path, fishing villages, coves and beaches. Dartmoor and Bodmin Moor, and many superb National Trust houses and gardens. **Directions: B3253 road just south of Widegates village, $3^1/_2$ miles east of Looe.**

For hotel location, see maps on pages 223–229

THE BRAKES

DOWNTON, NR LUDLOW, SHROPSHIRE SY8 2LF
TEL: 01584 856485

OWNERS: Tim and Tricia Turner

3 rms | 3 ens

S: £25
D: £45

Built in 1830 as a farmhouse, and standing in a beautiful garden where one can play croquet or badminton, this small country house has a friendly and relaxing ambience. It is surrounded by beautiful countryside.

The house has been carefully modernised with central heating throughout. The establishment has a residents' licence enabling guests to enjoy an apéritif in the charming lounge before indulging in one of Tricia's excellent dinners, no doubt accompanied by a bottle of wine from the short but well-chosen wine list.

There are three very individual double bedrooms, all en suite and with colour television and pleasant views over the garden. Fax/phone facilities are available on request. Children over 13 welcome. Small business parties catered for with additional accommodation in an adjoining cottage to make a business meeting a real treat.

Places of interest nearby: Ludlow is only a few miles away, famous both for its history and for its races. Golf, fishing and riding are available and walkers will enjoy Offa's Dyke and the Long Mynd nearby. **Directions: The Brakes is six miles north of Ludlow. Leave the A49 onto A4113 signed Knighton/Leintwardine. Turn left again at signpost to Downton Castle. It is very accessible from Shrewsbury, Bridgnorth, Kidderminster and Hereford.**

13

For hotel location, see maps on pages 223–229

Delbury Hall

DIDDLEBURY, CRAVEN ARMS, SHROPSHIRE SY7 9DH
TEL: 01584 841267 FAX: 01584 841441

OWNERS: Patrick and Lucinda Wrigley

3 rms | 1 ens

S: £50
D: £70–£80

Delbury, built in 1753 and probably Shropshire's most beautiful Georgian mansion, faces south across water meadows to medieval Ludlow, with a backdrop of the Clee Hills and the Wenlock Edge. Approached through 80 acres of landscaped parkland, the house is in a tranquil setting, surrounded by flower-filled gardens and overlooking a lake with ornamental ducks.

Delbury is a family house with bedrooms available for guests, one with a four-poster, one with a half-tester, all with private bathrooms (one en suite) and all recently restored to a high standard. The large entrance hall has the original oak staircase, leading up to a first floor gallery on three sides and there is a large drawing room and sitting rooms for guests' use.

Guests dine at one large table in the dining room, where Patrick, an enthusiastic cook, who has completed an advanced course at Leith's School of Food and Wine in London, serves the finest home produced food; smoked salmon from the house smoker, home cured prosciutto, fresh vegetables from the walled garden, eggs, Jersey milk and hand-churned butter from the home farm.

Places of interest nearby: Ludlow Castle. Offa's Dyke (built centuries ago to fend off the Welsh), Stokesay Castle, a 13th century manor house five miles away, and the Severn Valley Steam Railway. **Directions: On the B4368 between Craven Arms and Much Wenlock.**

For hotel location, see maps on pages 223–229

LITTLE OFFLEY

HITCHIN, HERTFORDSHIRE SG5 3BU
TEL: 01462 768243 FAX: 01462 768243

OWNERS: Martin and Lady Rosemary French

3 rms

S: £40
D: £60

Set in 800 acres of farmland in the Chiltern Hills, Little Offley is a beautiful 17th century house with wonderful views over the garden and surrounding countryside. One complete wing of the house has been set aside for guests, and provides a quiet haven comprising a large drawing room with a listed carved fireplace, dining room, 3 double bedrooms and 2 bathrooms. The rooms are spacious and comfortable and there is an outdoor swimming pool and croquet lawn available for guests' use in summer.

Accommodation is offered on a bed-and-breakfast basis, although dinner can be provided by arrangement. Lunch and dinner for larger groups can be provided, as can meetings, small exhibitions and receptions. Alternatively, there are 5 pubs – 4 of them with excellent restaurants – in the nearby village of Great Offley, $1^1/_2$ miles away. Guests may leave their car at the house when flying from Luton Airport.
Places of interest nearby: Little Offley is an ideal touring base from which to visit Hatfield House, Luton Hoo and Whipsnade Zoo, Woburn Abbey and Cambridge. The nearest town is Hitchin, which has large open-air markets on Tuesdays and Saturdays. London is 30 minutes by train. **Directions: Take A505 Luton–Hitchin road. At Great Offley, turn off for Little Offley.**

12 M

For hotel location, see maps on pages 223–229

THE GORDLETON MILL HOTEL

SILVER STREET, HORDLE, NR LYMINGTON, HAMPSHIRE SO41 6DJ
TEL: 01590 682219 FAX: 01590 683073

OWNER: William F. Stone
MANAGER: Toby Hill

7 rms | 7 ens | SMALL HOTEL

S: from £97
D: from £103

Hidden in the countryside between the New Forest National Park and the sea lies an ivy-clad 17th century Water Mill, now privately owned and sympathetically renovated to make a seven bedroomed luxury hotel. It is set in 5½ acres of landscaped, natural garden, with woods, fields, millpond, sluice gates, rustic bridges and lily pond creating a perfect riverside retreat.

Gordleton Mill is renowned too for the gastronomique delights of Toby Hills' nationally acclaimed 'Provence Restaurant', which has won a star from Egon Ronay and three stars from the AA for its excellent food. Also rated AA Best New Hotel in the South 1991.

This idyllic hotel boasts seven exquisitely furnished bedrooms all en suite including whirlpool baths and showers along with luxury towelling robes, flowers, bottled water, fruit and a complimentary half bottle of champagne to greet guests on their arrival. Four of the bedrooms are exclusively reserved for non-smokers.

Prices include a full English or continental breakfast, and unlimited tea and coffee throughout a guest's stay.

Places of interest nearby: Beaulieu. Bucklers Hard, Exbury Gardens, Romsey and Broadlands. **Directions: M27 junction 1. A337 south for 11 miles near Lymington after the railway bridge and mini roundabout turn sharp right before Toll House Inn, head towards Hordle and hotel is on right in about 1½ miles.**

30 M 7

For hotel location, see maps on pages 223–229

MAIDSTONE (Boughton Monchelsea)

In association with MasterCard

TANYARD

WIERTON HILL, BOUGHTON MONCHELSEA, NR MAIDSTONE, KENT ME17 4JT
TEL: 01622 744705 FAX: 01622 741998

OWNER: Jan Davies

6 rms | 6 ens | SMALL HOTEL

S: £55–£75
D: £85–£115

Standing within its own ten acres of garden with gently flowing stream, Tanyard is situated in the heart of rural Kent, with far-reaching views across the Kentish Weald. The features and ambience of this medieval farmhouse have been extremely well preserved – exposed beams and inglenook fireplaces abound.

The interiors have been decorated and furnished in a style sympathetic to the age and character of the house. Antique accoutrements are combined with up-to-date facilities to ensure guests' comfort. As well as the five bedrooms, a heavily beamed suite complete with spa bath is available. Occupying the whole top floor of the house, this suite affords particularly fine views.

Dating from about 1350AD the restaurant is the oldest part of the building previously used as a tannery. An imaginative menu is offered for dinner on seven evenings a week.

Winner of the Johansens Recommended Private Country Houses Award 1993.

Places of interest nearby: Optimally located for touring the 'Garden of England', Leeds Castle and Sissinghurst. The Channel ports, tunnel and Gatwick Airport are within an hour's drive. **Directions:** From the B2163 at Boughton Monchelsea turn opposite The Cock into Park Lane, right into Wierton Road, right again for Tanyard.

Newstead Grange

NORTON-ON-DERWENT, MALTON, NORTH YORKSHIRE YO17 9PJ
TEL: 01653 692502 FAX: 01653 696951

OWNERS: Pat and Paul WIlliams

6 rms | 6 ens

S: £35–£39
D: £62–£74

Enclosed in 2½ acres of gardens and grounds, Newstead Grange is an elegant Georgian country house with wonderful views of the Wolds and Moors. Resident owners Paul and Pat Williams extend a warm welcome to their guests, who are assured of personal attention.

The Grange maintains the quality and style of a country house restored. It has antique furniture and original features including working shutters and fine fireplaces. Open fires are lit in the lounges. Bedrooms, all individual in character,have period furniture, paintings and prints. The Celebration Room contains an antique mahogany half-tester bed. The Grange prides itself on the quality of its cuisine recognised by the AA rosette award. Menus use fresh quality meat, local trout and organic seasonal fruit and vegetables from the kitchen gardens. Wines are selected to complement the food. Special diets are catered for.

Newstead Grange is an entirely non-smoking house. ETB Highly Commended. Closed mid-November to end February. Special break rates available.

Places of interest nearby: The ancient market town of Malton, York, the North York Moors National Park and the East Coast. Stately homes, abbeys, scenic walks and drives too. **Directions: Follow signs out of Malton and Norton-on-Derwent to Beverley. Newstead Grange is on the left, ½ mile beyond the last houses and at the junction with the Settrington Road**

40 M | 10

PERITON PARK HOTEL

MIDDLECOMBE, NR MINEHEAD, SOMERSET TA24 8SW
TEL: 01643 706885 FAX: 01643 706885

OWNERS: Richard and Angela Hunt

8 rms | 8 ens | SMALL HOTEL

S: £65
D: £90

As you climb the winding drive through the woods, rhododendrons and azaleas to this Victorian country house hotel on the edge of the Exmoor National Park, it is not hard to see why Periton Park is described as a place "where time stands still". Richard and Angela Hunt run the hotel in an efficient and friendly way ensuring that while their guests are staying with them, they will be carefully looked after. All the rooms are spacious and well proportioned, enlivened with warm autumn colours to create a restful atmosphere.

The wood panelled restaurant, with its double aspect views over the grounds, is the perfect place to enjoy some of the finest food on Exmoor. Menus change with the seasons to reflect the best of West Country produce – fresh fish, local game, delicately cooked vegetables, local cheeses and Somerset wine.

Exmoor is for country lovers with miles of varied, unspoilt, breathtaking landscape. A perfect retreat from the trials of everyday life. Riding is available from the adjoining stables. Shooting is also available in season and clay shooting throughout the year.

Places of interest nearby: Dunster Castle and Gardens, Knightshayes, Rosemoor, Selworthy, Arlington Court and Exmoor. **Directions: Exit M5 junction 24. Take the A39 towards Minehead. Follow signs to Porlock and Lynmouth. Hotel is on the left hand side.**

24 M | 12

For hotel location, see maps on pages 223–229

Millers House Hotel

MIDDLEHAM, WENSLEYDALE, NORTH YORKSHIRE DL8 4NR
TEL: 01969 622630 FAX: 01969 623570

OWNERS: Judith and Crossley Sunderland

7 rms | 6 ens | SMALL HOTEL

S: £35–£47
D: £79–£85

The peaceful village of Middleham nestles in the heart of the Yorkshire Dales and the Millers House Hotel is a perfect base from which to explore James Herriot country. This elegant Georgian house has been decorated in period style, including a magnificent, fully canopied four-poster bedroom. A recent addition is an attractive conservatory. Voted Hotel of the Year runner up in the Yorkshire and Humberside Tourist Board White Rose Awards.

The restaurant has won an AA Red Rosette for the last few years. Extensive use is made of fresh local produce, complemented by a fine selection of sensibly priced wines. Especially popular are the gourmet wine-tasting weekends.

Close by is Middleham Castle, once the seat of Richard III. The village is now better known as a racehorse training centre and guests can combine enjoyment of the glorious views across Wensleydale and Coverdale with watching racehorses exercising on the moorland gallops. Racing Breaks with a day at the races and a visit to a training yard are also popular. Millers House is open for Christmas and New Year breaks and is available for house parties.

Places of interest nearby: Bolton and Richmond Castles, Jervaulx Abbey, Aysgarth Falls, York, Harrogate and several golf courses. **Directions: Take the A684 to Bedale and Leyburn; the left turning immediately before Leyburn takes you to Middleham. Millers House Hotel is in the centre of the village.**

In association with MasterCard

Burleigh Court

MINCHINHAMPTON, GLOUCESTERSHIRE GL5 2PF
TEL: 01453 883804 FAX: 01453 886870

OWNERS: Ian and Fiona Hall

17 rms | 17 ens | SMALL HOTEL

S: £60–£80
D: £80–£130

Burleigh Court is a handsome 18th century Cotswold stone manor house, situated in 3½ acres of immaculate gardens on a steep hillside which affords grand views across the Golden Valley.

The emphasis at Burleigh Court is placed firmly on comfort and style, with the attractive furnishings of the lounge areas and their real log fires crackling in the hearth during the winter months, the elegant dining room and the charming and spacious bedrooms, all of which are individually furnished and where bowls of homemade pot-pourri provide a welcoming personal touch.

Sumptuous food is cooked with skill and imagination, reworking classical dishes into individual creations influenced by the hotel's well-stocked herb and vegetable gardens. The extensive menu is complemented by a cellar of specially recommended wines.

Places of interest nearby: Located on the fringe of Minchinhampton Common where you may play golf and go riding. Within a reasonable radius, Berkeley Castle, Westonbirt Arboretum, and the wild fowl trust at Slimbridge. **Directions: Leave Stroud on the A419, heading towards Cirencester. 2½ miles outside Stroud take a right turn, signposted Burleigh and Minchinhampton, about 500 yards along this road there is a sharpe left turn signposted Burleigh Court, the house will be found on your right after a further 400 yards.**

14 M

For hotel location, see maps on pages 223–229

WIGHAM

MORCHARD BISHOP, NR CREDITON, DEVON EX17 6RJ
TEL: 01363 877350 FAX: 01363 877350

OWNERS: Stephen and Dawn Chilcott

5 rms | 5 ens

S: £45–£65
D: £88–£110
(including dinner)

A picturesque, 16th century, thatched Devon longhouse, Wigham adjoins its own 30-acre organic farm which supplies the kitchen with fresh lamb, beef and pork, eggs and dairy produce, as well as fresh fruit and vegetables. Good honest home cooking, complemented by an excellent wine list, are hallmarks of this delightful country house.

After dinner, guests may take coffee in the lounge. Please note that Wigham is a totally no-smoking house.

Proprietors Stephen and Dawn Chilcott have created a warm and welcoming atmosphere at this charming retreat. The interiors are characterised by low ceilings, exposed beams, massive fireplaces and original wall panelling. The bedrooms are appropriately furnished in cottage style and have pretty, co-ordinated fabrics. In the honeymoon suite there is a rustic four-poster bed. All bedrooms are en suite and have a TV and video. There is also a self-contained cottage which sleeps six – details available on request. For further entertainment there is a snooker lounge with a 7-foot table, a heated outdoor swimming pool and a well-equipped 'honour' bar.

Places of interest nearby: Exmoor and Dartmoor, Exeter, Tiverton and Barnstaple. **Directions: From Morchard Bishop, take the road marked Chawleigh–Chulmleigh, fork right after ¾ mile, and ¾ mile further on, on the right, is a small private road marked Wigham.**

For hotel location, see maps on pages 223–229

EASTWREY BARTON HOTEL

LUSTLEIGH, NEWTON ABBOT, DEVON TQ13 9SN
TEL: 01647 277338

OWNERS: Victor and Susan Carn

6 rms | 6 ens

S: £42–£63
D: £84–£126

Built in the 17th century as a farmhouse, Eastwrey Barton Hotel is set in its own grounds and offers splendid views along the Wray Valley and across Lustleigh Cleave.

Each of the six bedrooms is individually designed and features a full range of modern comforts, including en suite bathroom, colour TV and tea/coffee facilities.Four of these rooms are spacious with a glorious outlook.

The proprietors prides themselves on providing good food, complemented by a friendly and personal service. Emphasis is on traditional English cooking using seasonal, fresh local produce. Susan is a trained chef. The hotel has its own supply of natural spring water. A small selection of wines is available from the cellar and there is a cosy bar where guests may enjoy an apéritif or a leisurely after dinner drink.

The hotel, perfect for guests seeking a peaceful environment, is situated within Dartmoor National Park and is a particularly good base for keen walkers and birdwatchers. It is closed for Christmas.

Places of interest nearby: Numerous outstanding beauty spots are all within easy reach, along with the National Trust properties of Castle Drogo, Cotehele, Compton Castle, Lydford Gorge and Killerton House. **Directions: From Exeter join the A38 and after approximately 11 miles turn right onto the A382. Eastwrey is six miles along on the right, one mile north of the sign to Lustleigh village.**

For hotel location, see maps on pages 223–229

ROMNEY BAY HOUSE

COAST ROAD, LITTLESTONE, NEW ROMNEY, KENT TN28 8QY
TEL: 01797 364747 FAX: 01797 367156

OWNERS: Jennifer and Helmut Gorlich

7 rms 7 ens

S: from £35
D: from £55

This spectacular house was built in the late 1920s for the American actress and journalist, Hedda Hopper, by the distinguished architect, Sir Clough Williams-Ellis.

The gracious drawing room overlooks the English Channel, panoramically surveyed through the telescope in the first floor library. From the house there is access to the beach, a tennis court, croquet lawn and golf course.

The owners have completed an impressive refurbishing programme. Upstairs, designated non-smoking, the charming en suite bedrooms, furnished with antiques, have television and a tea/coffee tray.

Lunch is not available, but wonderful cream teas are produced, particularly enjoyable on the terrace. in the sun-lit sea air. A traditional four-course dinner is served. The hotel is fully licensed and guests will strongly approve of the short but excellent wine list.

Places of interest nearby: There is so much history in Romney Marsh, renowned years ago for its smuggling. Caesar landed here in 55BC at Port Lympne and the famous Cinque Ports stretch along the coast. Canterbury Cathedral is a reasonable drive inland. Littlestone Golf Course is close to the hotel and wind-surfing is popular.
Directions: From New Romney head for the coast by Station Road leading to Littlestone Road – pass the miniture railway station – at the sea, turn left and follow signs for Romney Bay House for about a mile.

20 M

BEECHWOOD HOTEL

CROMER ROAD, NORTH WALSHAM, NORFOLK NR28 0HD
TEL: 01692 403231 FAX: 01692 407284

OWNERS: Don Birch and Lindsay Spalding
CHEF: Steven Norgate

9 rms | 9 ens | SMALL HOTEL

S: £33
D: £52

This is one of those special hotels to which guests return frequently and try to keep a secret. It is in the small market town of North Walsham, where Lord Nelson was educated. The Beechwood Hotel is an attractive creeper-clad Georgian house, which the new owners have recently renovated, cleverly combining style with a relaxing atmosphere, the elegant Drawing Room being well supplied with books, guides and newspapers.

The bar is frequented by the town people as well as visitors. The restaurant, which overlooks the garden, serves dinner between 7-9pm, the menu ranging from home cooking to the chef's gourmet specialities. The carefully chosen wine list is often increased by selections from the proprietors own cellar.

The bedrooms are spacious and traditionally furnished. There is a residents' lounge overlooking the grounds, with the rose walk, fish pond and sunken garden. Canvas chairs are available from the summer house.

Places of interest nearby: Sandringham, Bickling Hall and Holkham Hall. Bird watchers head for Cley Marshes and the Hickling Broad Nature Reserves while other guests enjoy the Norfolk Broads or explore Norwich cathedral.

Directions: Leave Norwich on the B1150, driving 13 miles to North Walsham. Pass under the railway bridge, turn left at the first traffic lights and right at the second set. The hotel is 150m along on the left.

30 M | 10

The Beeches Hotel and Victorian Gardens

4-6 EARLHAM ROAD, NORWICH, NORFOLK NR2 3DB
TEL: 01603 621167 FAX: 01603 620151

OWNERS: Keith and Elisabeth Hill

27 rms | 27 ens | SMALL HOTEL

S: £43–£49.50
D: £54.50–£69

With three acres of English Heritage Victorian Gardens, this hotel offers discerning guests a warm welcome and exceptionally high standards of comfort in a relaxed, informal atmosphere. Two separate Grade II listed Victorian mansions which have been beautifully restored, extended and attractively decorated and are collectively known as the Beeches. (Plantation House pictured).

When the houses were built in the mid-1800s, an idyllic Italianate garden was created in the deep hollow it overlooks. In 1980, this 'secret' garden now known as The Plantation Garden was rediscovered. It is now being restored to its former glory and guests are free to wander through this enchanting and extraodinary reminder of our Victorian heritage with its ornate Gothic fountain and amazing terraces.

All bedrooms feature charming individual decor and seperate modern facilities. 'No smoking' rooms available on request.

A varied selection of tempting dishes is cooked to order and served in the Bistro Restaurant which overlooks a delightful patio garden. The hotel is closed at Christmas.

Places of interest nearby: The city of Norwich, with its castle containing a famous collection of the Norwich school of painting and its fine cathedral, the Norfolk coast and Broads.

Directions: From the A11 take the ring road west and turn onto the B1108 (Earlham Road) to the city centre. The hotel is next to the Roman Catholic cathedral.

30 M

CATTON OLD HALL

LODGE LANE, CATTON, NORWICH, NORFOLK NR6 7HG
TEL: 01603 419379 FAX: 01603 400339

OWNERS: Roger and Anthea Cawdron

4 rms | 4 ens

S: £31.50–£45
D: £58.50–£75

Catton Old Hall was built in 1632 and has been sympathetically restored to its former glory. It lies just 2½ miles north east of Norwich city centre and within easy reach of the airport. The Hall, once a farmhouse, retains a wealth of oak beams and one of the largest inglenooks in Norwich. Now the family home of Roger and Anthea Cawdron, it provides luxurious accommodation for its guests. The en suite bedrooms are spacious, tastefully decorated and furnished to the highest standards. The dining room and lounge have a homely atmosphere and are ideal places in which to enjoy quiet comfort.

Full English breakfast is served at the Hall and evening meals are available if booked in advance. A typical evening meal might be a choice between breast of Barbary duck, cooked in blackberry and blueberry sauce laced with Crème de Mûre, or fillet of beef Wellington, a steak with a mushroom and onion farce wrapped in crisp pastry served with a rich port and thyme jus.

A full range of office facilities is available and arrangements can be made to visit local sporting events.

Places of interest nearby: The ancient cathedral city of Norwich, with its 12th century castle, fine museums and many other historic buildings. Also the Norfolk Broads and the long sandy beaches on the Norfolk coastline.

Directions: 2½ miles north east of Norwich centre. Lodge Lane is just off Spixworth Road.

10 M

For hotel location, see maps on pages 223–229

THE STOWER GRANGE

SCHOOL ROAD, DRAYTON, NORFOLK NR8 6EF
TEL: 01603 860210 FAX: 01603 860464

OWNERS: Paul and Sarah McCoy

7 rms | 7 ens | SMALL HOTEL

S: £45
D: £55
Four-poster: £75

Built of mellow old Norwich bricks, this former rectory dates back to the 17th century. The Stower Grange is set in delightful lawned gardens with mature trees and offers its guests a peaceful retreat from the busy world. Its atmosphere is friendly and informal – open fires in the reception rooms are particularly welcoming in the cooler months.

There are a variety of bedrooms to choose from, all well proportioned and prettily decorated. The pine four-poster bedroom will appeal especially to those in a romantic mood. An abundance of flowers adds a colourful personal touch to the unpretentious comfortable surroundings.

Overlooking the garden is the dining room, offering a renowned à la carte menu and imaginative four-course dinner menus. Steak and salads are served in the lounge bar on Sunday evenings.

Places of interest nearby: Norwich, Norfolk Broads, Holkham Hall, Houghton Hall, Blickling Hall, Sandringham and the Norfolk Coast. **Directions: From A11 left on to inner ring road proceed to ASDA junction with A1067 Norwich–Fakenham Road. Approximately two miles to Drayton turn right at Red Lion public house. After 80 yards bear left. The Stower Grange is on the right.**

80 M

DOWN HOUSE

DOWN STREET, NUTLEY, EAST SUSSEX TN22 3LG
TEL: 01825 712328

OWNERS: Micky and Gilly Hudson

2 rms | 2 ens

S: from £38
D: from £56

The pleasure of staying at this delightful Georgian cottage, with spectacular views of the South Downs, is like that of visiting a private home.

There are just two bedrooms with adjacent private bathrooms. Guests may have exclusive use of the drawing room or may join up with the family.

Evening meals should be arranged the day before, usually a four-course meal served in the kitchen, en famille, unless preferred otherwise. Lighter meals or special requests can always be discussed. Picnic hampers can be prepared for Glyndebourne.

There is no drinks licence but appropriate purchases may be made in the village and brought in to the house. There are also excellent inns and restaurants in the neighbourhood.

Places of interest nearby: It is extremely convenient for Glyndebourne. National Trust and famous gardens abound, including Wakehurst Place and Sheffield Park, and there is the beautiful Ashdown Forest to explore. There is racing at Lingfield, Goodwood and Plumpton. Brighton is not far away, with its Royal Pavilion, shops, theatre and beach. Riding, superb golf, clay pigeon shooting and fishing are all nearby. Railway enthusiasts have the Bluebell and Lavender Lines. **Directions: A22 to Nutley Village. Down Street is signposted opposite the Post Office and the entrance is on the right after exactly one mile.**

en famille | 9

For hotel location, see maps on pages 223–229

PEN-Y-DYFFRYN COUNTRY HOTEL

RHYDYCROESAU, NR OSWESTRY, SHROPSHIRE SY10 7DT
TEL: 01691 653700 FAX: 01691 653700

OWNERS: Miles and Audrey Hunter

8 rms | 8 ens | SMALL HOTEL

S: £35–£42
D: £56–£62

Pen-y-Dyffryn Country Hotel is a haven of peace and quiet, set in five acres of grounds in the unspoilt Shropshire hills, midway between Shrewsbury and Chester. And while civilisation is close at hand, buzzards, peregrine falcons, badgers and foxes regularly delight the guests with their unscheduled appearances. The stream in front of the hotel marks the border with neighbouring Wales.

All the bedrooms have modern amenities and overlook the attractively terraced hotel gardens. In the cooler months, log fires burning in the two homely lounges help to create a cosy and informal atmosphere in which to relax and forget the pressures of everyday life.

The best of British cuisine is served in the hall's locally renowned restaurant. Adventurous menus offer dishes using the finest fresh ingredients and traditional English puddings are a speciality of the house.

Although Pen-y-Dyffryn Country Hotel provides the perfect setting for total relaxation, for more active guests there are facilities for hill walking and riding on the doorstep and six 18-hole golf courses within 15 miles. There is also a private trout pool just yards from the hotel. **Places of interest nearby:** Four major National Trust propeties; Powys and Chirk Castles, Erddig and Attingham. Historic towns of Shrewsbury and Chester. Excursions to Snowdonia. **Directions: From Oswestry town centre take B4580 Llansilin road for three miles.**

In association with MasterCard

FALLOWFIELDS

KINGSTON BAGPUIZE WITH SOUTHMOOR, OXON OX13 5BH
TEL: 01865 820416 FAX: 01865 821275

OWNERS: Peta and Anthony Lloyd

5 rms 5 ens

S: £55–£76
D: £64–£85

Fallowfields, once the home of Begum Aga Khan, dates back more than 300 years. It has been updated and extended over past decades and today boasts a lovely early Victorian Gothic southern aspect. The house is set in two acres of gardens, surrounded by 10 acres of grassland.

The guests' bedrooms, which offer a choice of four poster or coroneted beds, are large and well appointed and offer every modern amenity to ensure maximum comfort and convenience. The house is centrally heated throughout and during the winter months there are welcoming log fires in the elegant main reception rooms.

Home cooked cuisine is imaginative in style and presentation and there is a good choice of menu available. The walled kitchen garden provides most of the vegetables and salads for the table and locally grown organic produce is otherwise used wherever possible. Weekend house parties are ever popular and additional accommodation can be arranged.

Places of interest nearby: Fallowfields is an ideal base from which to tour the surrounding countryside. It is close to Stratford, the Cotswolds, Stonehenge, Bath and Bristol to the west, Oxford, Henley on Thames, the Chilterns and Windsor to the east. Heathrow airport is less than an hour away. **Directions: Travelling on the A420 from Oxford to Swindon, take the Kingston Bagpuize exit. The entrance to Fallowfields is at the west end of Southmoor.**

12 10

For hotel location, see maps on pages 223–229

Tye Rock Hotel

LOE BAR ROAD, PORTHLEVEN, SOUTH CORNWALL TR13 9EW
TEL: 01326 572695

OWNERS: Michael and Sandra Barker

7 rms | 7 ens | SMALL HOTEL

S: £35
D: £52–£58

Whether you choose self-catering or hotel accommodation, you can be sure that Tye Rock's superb elevated position, with views extending from The Lizard to Land's End, will be hard to surpass. Set in 3½ acres surrounded by National Trust land, Tye Rock has an air of seclusion, yet the fishing village of Porthleven is only a short walk away.

The hotel's seven en suite bedrooms all have sea views. Relax and enjoy a traditional, home-cooked meal served in the dining room, which offers magnificent views of Mounts Bay. In the hotel grounds there are also eight apartments which offer guests the independence of their own front door.

In a sheltered sun-trap at the bottom of the garden is the large, outdoor heated swimming pool. Open from May to September, the pool is built into the cliff top and is unusually large for a small hotel. Evening barbecues by the pool are a great attraction. Thanks to the mild Cornish climate, spring starts early here and the warm days last well into the autumn. Closed January and February.

Places of interest nearby: St Michael's Mount, Land's End, Goonhilly Earth Satellite Station and many Cornish gardens. **Directions: From Helston take the Porthleven road, then follow signs for Loe Bar; after second Loe Bar sign take next right turn; go to T-junction and turn left – Tye Rock is on the headland.**

For hotel location, see maps on pages 223–229

CHEQUERS HOTEL

CHURCH PLACE, PULBOROUGH, WEST SUSSEX RH20 1AD
TEL: 01798 872486 FAX: 01798 872715

OWNERS: John and Ann Searancke
CHEF: Gavin Swonnell

11 rms | 10 ens | SMALL HOTEL

S: £49.50–£54.50
D: £75–£85

A warm welcome awaits visitors to this historic hotel built during the reign of Queen Anne. Situated on a sandstone ridge, Chequers has enviable views across the beautiful Arun Valley to the South Downs beyond.

Mindful of the needs of today's traveller, owners John and Ann Searancke have ensured that modern amenities have been carefully blended with old world charm and comforts. The hotel has recently enjoyed a programme of refurbishment further to enhance its appeal. All 11 bedrooms have private facilities, 10 of which are en suite. There are 4 bedrooms on the ground floor and three family rooms. Public rooms are comfortably furnished, with a log fire in the lounge on winter evenings.

In warmer weather, guests may linger over an apéritif on the patio or in the secluded garden, before dining in the restaurant, where the traditional English menu changes daily. The hotel is set in the heart of the local conservation area and its nine acre adjacent meadow is an ideal spot for walking your dog.
Places of interest nearby: Chequers Hotel is conveniently placed for the Roman city of Chichester, Arundel Castle and the Sussex coast. Packed lunches can be provided. ETB 4 Crowns Highly Commended, 2 RAC Merit Awards and an AA Rosette. **Directions: At the top of the hill, at the northern end of the village, the hotel is opposite the church.**

For hotel location, see maps on pages 223–229

THE OLD RECTORY

IPSLEY LANE, IPSLEY, REDDITCH, WORCESTERSHIRE B98 0AP
TEL: 01527 523000 FAX: 01527 517003

OWNERS: David Moore and Family

10 rms | 8 ens | SMALL HOTEL

S: £55–£65
D: £75–£85

The Old Rectory at Redditch dates back to the 15th century, although well before that the Romans built Icknield Street which forms one boundary of the grounds. The house was substantially modernised in 1812 by the great grandson of Sir Christopher Wren, who lived here for 40 years.

In this historic setting secluded by trees, guests find the atmosphere restful and the comfortable accommodation is complemented by the desire of the owners to look after their guests.

The bedrooms are of different shapes and sizes: some with exposed beams, one with a barrel ceiling, and are all tastefully decorated. In the 17th century connecting stable block is the working mechanism of the 100 year old clock.

Meals are served in the Conservatory. The surroundings are delightful in the early morning sun whilst you enjoy fresh fruit juices, cereals and your light or full English breakfast. The three-course evening meal (which should be ordered by 1pm), followed by coffee in the lounge, will have been specially prepared for you that day in the large farmhouse kitchen.

Places of interest nearby: Stratford-upon-Avon, Warwick, Leamington Spa, the Cotswolds, Oxford, Worcester, the NEC and Birmingham. **Directions:** Arriving in Redditch, follow signs for 'All Other Redditch Districts' to Ipsley. Ipsley Lane is off Icknield Street Drive.

30 M

In association with MasterCard

GLEWSTONE COURT

NR ROSS-ON-WYE, HEREFORDSHIRE HR9 6AW
TEL: 01989 770367 FAX: 01989 770282

OWNERS: Bill and Christine Reeve-Tucker

7 rms | 7 ens | SMALL HOTEL

S: £40–£60
D: £60–£90

Glewstone Court is set in three acres of orchards, lawns and flowerbeds. Although secluded, it is only three miles from Ross-on-Wye. Furnishings and décor reflect the hospitable personality of the owners and the variety of prints, antiques and bric-à-brac always excites curiosity.

Most country pursuits can be arranged, including canoeing, hot-air ballooning, fishing and riding. This is marvellous country for walking – or just lazing around, too!

Christine's food is always pleasing and both the restaurant and extensive bar menus feature local recipes using only the freshest of ingredients. Dishes are both traditional and unusual and are always prepared and served with care and attention to detail. Wine appreciation evenings are held monthly, while festivals are often celebrated with a themed culinary extravaganza. A traditional roast is served at lunchtime on Sundays. The restaurant and the drawing room bar feature log fires and, like the rest if the hotel, are furnished for comfort.

The bedrooms are large and comfortable too. Each has en suite facilities, a hospitality tray and many extras. Closed Christmas Day and Boxing Day.

Places of interest nearby: Ross-on-Wye, Hay-on-Wye, the Welsh Marches and Hereford. **Directions: From M50 junction 4 follow A40 signposted Monmouth. One mile past Wilton roundabout turn right to Glewstone; the Court is 1/2 mile on left.**

25 M

For hotel location, see maps on pages 223–229

Orchard House

ASTON INGHAM ROAD, KILCOT, NR NEWENT, GLOUCESTERSHIRE GL18 1NP
TEL: 01989 720417

OWNERS: Basil and Anne Thompson

4 rms | 2 ens

S: £30
D: £45–£59

Orchard House is situated in a peaceful, rural position on the borders of Gloucestershire and Herefordshire. Set in five acres of beautiful grounds this is a spacious property which dates back in parts to the 18th century. It has been extended in Tudor style, with many of the original beams intact.

The welcome provided by Sophie, the Golden Labrador, reflects that of the owners, Anne and Basil Thompson. They have created accommodation of the highest standard and offer the use of their home to discerning guests. A friendly atmosphere pervades the house and immaculately manicured grounds. The four bedrooms, two en suite and two with private facilities, are very well appointed and extremely peaceful, enjoying views over gardens and countryside.

Anne's delicious home cooking is one of the main attractions here. With wines from Basil's cellar, dinner is round the Regency dining table. English and Continental breakfasts are unhurried next morning.

After dining, guests may relax in the beamed colour TV lounge, beside a log fire in winter, or in the conservatory overlooking the fountain, courtyard and lawns. More active guests can go walking in the nearby Forest of Dean, an area of outstanding natural beauty.

Places of interest nearby: Chepstow, Monmouth, Tewkesbury, Bath, the Cotswolds and the Malverns.

Directions: At Kilcot, take the Aston Ingham road to Mitcheldean. Orchard House is 400 yards on the right.

en famille | 12 M | 12

Peterstow Country House

PETERSTOW, ROSS-ON-WYE, HEREFORDSHIRE HR9 6LB
TEL: 01989 562826 FAX: 01989 567264

OWNERS: Mike and Jeanne Denne

9 rms | 9 ens | SMALL HOTEL

S: £38.50–£69
D: £50–£90

In 1987, Jeanne and Mike Denne fell in love with a dilapidated rectory built long ago by the side of the church of St Peter and surrounded by 28 acres of woodland and pasture. With careful determination they set about restoring the house into a delightful family home. By late 1989 they opened Peterstow Country House to share its beauty with guests from all over the world.

Upon entering the spacious hall, with its flagstone floor and grand winding staircase, every visitor senses immediately the relaxed atmosphere. The nine bedrooms are Georgian or Victorian in style, ranging from half-tester suites to double and twin-bedded rooms.

Peterstow's centrepiece is its award winning restaurant where a team of enthusiastic and creative chefs marry home and local produce with the wide range available in today's European market place. There is an extensive world wide wine list. There is a variety of specialist weekends, two and three day breaks and Christmas and New Year three day house parties. Clay pigeon shooting and trout lake fishing are in the grounds. Accolades include two AA Rosettes, ETB 4 Crowns Highly Commended and AA Care and Courtesy Award 1993. **Places of interest nearby:** Good walking country, the Welsh Marches and the Wye Valley. **Directions: On the A49, three miles north of Ross-on-Wye.**

50 M | 7

For hotel location, see maps on pages 223–229

Rocks Place

YATTON, ROSS-ON-WYE, HEREFORDSHIRE HR9 7RD
TEL: 01531 660218 FAX: 01531 660460

OWNERS: Peter and Mollie Cotton

7 rms | 7 ens | SMALL HOTEL

S: from £35
D: from £50

The Wye Valley is full of romance. It was at Tintern Abbey that William Wordsworth wrote the poem describing the impact of his first glimpse of this spectacular scenery. Every visit to the glorious Wye Valley is a refreshing experience for any traveller.

Midway between Ross-on-Wye and Ledbury lies Yatton, and in Yatton is Rocks Place, a converted 16th century barn which has become a delightful country hotel and restaurant.

The seven no-smoking bedrooms are all en suite with TV and tea-making facilities and each has a view over the countryside. The atmosphere is comfortable and easy-going.

The restaurant is neat and unpretentious and the cuisine is of superb quality and excellent value..

Places of interest nearby: Hereford, Worcester and Gloucester (and their cathedrals) and, of course, the Wye Valley and Malvern Hills. Golf, racing and theatres not very far away, nor is Hay-on-Wye, the famous centre of the second-hand book trade. **Directions: Off the A449. Leave M50 at Exit 4. Take A449 to Ledbury and Worcester, then 4th turn to left signed Yatton.**

20 M

For hotel location, see maps on pages 223–229

THE COUNTRYMAN AT TRINK HOTEL AND RESTAURANT

OLD COACH ROAD, ST IVES, CORNWALL TR26 3JQ
TEL: 01736 797571

OWNERS: Howard and Cathy Massey

6 rms | 6 ens | SMALL HOTEL

S: £35
D: £50–£60

Five minutes drive from the quaint town of St Ives is the Countryman Hotel and Restaurant at Trink. St Ives has become a mecca for artists and one of the latest attractions is the new Tate Gallery with its collection of modern paintings and contemporary exhibits. Cornwall has a wealth of interesting things to see not least its dramatic coastline ideal for lovers of nature and walkers.

The Countryman dates from the 17th century. Today the small hotel has been renovated to meet the needs of the modern visitor, all rooms have en suite shower and toilet, colour T.V. and tea making facilities.

The atmosphere of the hotel is friendly and inviting, the emphasis being on hospitality and good value for money. In the restaurant, Howard Massey, the chef-patron, likes cooking to order from his varied and interesting menu supported by a sensibly priced wine-list. St Ives has always had a gastronomic tradition. A former mayor, the legendary John Knill, bequeathed £10 for an annual banquet. Prices may have altered a little but the high quality of the local cooking has not changed.

Places of interest nearby: Tate Gallery, Lands End. Barbara Hepworth's house, St Michael's Mount. Golf, riding and the sea. **Directions: A30, A3074 to St Ives, then B3311 for about two miles.**

For hotel location, see maps on pages 223–229

THE PHEASANT HOTEL

SEAVINGTON ST MARY, NR ILMINSTER, SOMERSET TA19 0HQ
TEL: 01460 240502 FAX: 01460 242388

OWNERS: Edmondo and Jacqueline Paoloni
CHEF: Edmondo Paoloni

8 rms | 8 ens | SMALL HOTEL

S: from £60
D: from £80

Visitors to The Pheasant are immediately captivated by the distinctive charm and character of this sumptuously furnished old-world style hotel and restaurant. Set in the heart of Somerset and surrounded by landscaped lawns and splendid gardens, it exudes a restful warmth and welcome. The charming bedrooms are individually styled and very comfortably furnished.

Sympathetic décor and furnishings complement the traditional character of the bar and highly acclaimed restaurant, with their oak-beamed ceilings and large inglenook fireplaces. The cooking is recommended by many of the other hotel and food guides. An extensive menu of imaginatively prepared dishes includes a good choice for vegetarians, while delicious home-made desserts are crammed on to the sweet trolley.

Places of interest nearby: Being situated near the Somerset border close to both Dorset and Devon. There are many attractions to suit all age groups, including Montacute House, the abbey town of Sherborne, the Fleet Air Museum at Yeovilton and Cricket St Thomas, where the BBC TV series *To The Manor Born* was filmed. **Directions: Leave the A303 at South Petherton roundabout by Ilminster bypass. Take the left spur, (Crewkerne–Seavington St Michael), followed by Seavington exit at the next roundabout. Left by the Volunteer Inn and The Pheasant is 200 yards further on the right.**

For hotel location, see maps on pages 223–229

The Eastbury Hotel

LONG STREET, SHERBORNE, DORSET DT9 3BY
TEL: 01935 813131 FAX: 01935 817296

OWNERS: Tom and Alison Pickford

15 rms | 15 ens | SMALL HOTEL

S: from £45
D: from £65

The Eastbury Hotel is a traditional town house which was built in 1740 during the reign of George II. During its refurbishment great care was taken to preserve its 18th century character. In fine weather guests can enjoy the seclusion of the hotel's walled garden, which encompasses an acre of shrubs and formal plants and a listed walnut tree.

Bedrooms are individually named after English garden flowers and each is equipped with a full range of modern comforts and conveniences. The Eastbury is ideal for parents visiting sons or daughters at the Sherborne schools.

Traditional English cooking is a feature of the Eastbury restaurant and the dishes are complemented by an extensive list of the world's fine wines.

Places of interest nearby: Sherborne is rich in history and has a 15th century abbey and two castles, in one of which Sir Walter Raleigh founded the national smoking habit. At Compton is a silk farm and a collection of butterflies. Beyond Yeovil is Montacute House (N.T.) and at Yeovilton is the Fleet Air Arm Museum. **Directions: Long Street is in the town centre, south of and parallel to the A30. Parking is at the rear of the hotel.**

40 M

For hotel location, see maps on pages 223–229

SIMONSBATH HOUSE HOTEL

SIMONSBATH, EXMOOR, SOMERSET TA24 7SH
TEL: 01643 831259 FAX: 01643 831577

OWNERS: Mike and Sue Burns

7 rms | 7 ens | SMALL HOTEL

S: £44–£60
D: £78–£90

Simonsbath House was built by James Boevey, Warden of the Forest of Exmoor, in 1654, on rising ground facing due south across the beautiful valley of the River Barle. You are welcomed with log fires in the oak-panelled lounge, and with mineral water, fresh fruit and flowers in the bedrooms. A relaxing atmosphere pervades throughout the house, which is still essentially a home, with welcoming owners and caring staff to pamper you with old-fashioned hospitality.

The bedroom windows overlook beech forests of everchanging hue, a crystal river bubbling through the valley and fold after fold of heather-clad hills. Guests can saddle up and gallop off to Exmoor's highest point – Dunkery Beacon – or set out on foot. The surrounding forests are ideal for strollers; hikers will enjoy the challenge of the high moorlands. Sue Burns is the chef and she uses only fresh local produce. Vegetarian meals by arrangement. Closed during December and January. **Places of interest nearby:** The cathedral cities of Exeter and Wells; Glastonbury, Bath and Devon's beautiful coast. **Directions: Simonsbath is on the B3223, situated within the village, nine miles south of Lynton.**

Marsh Hall Country House Hotel

SOUTH MOLTON, NORTH DEVON EX36 3HQ
TEL: 01769 572666 FAX: 01769 574230

OWNERS: Tony and Judy Griffiths

7 rms | 7 ens | SMALL HOTEL

S: £38–£53
D: £65–£85

Marsh Hall is the perfect place for a refreshing and relaxing holiday and is also ideal for business travellers who require a special overnight stay.

Tony and Judy Griffiths took over ownership of the hotel in 1993 and have created a friendly and informal atmosphere that has guests returning time after time.

The hotel is set in three acres of attractive gardens, and was reputedly built by the local squire for his mistress. Here guests can relax in either the elegant chandelier-lit lounge or the friendly bar, both of which have log fires burning during winter. The large hall and stairway lights the gallery which leads to the seven en suite bedrooms, all of which are individually furnished and have country views.

The highlight at Marsh hall is the food. In the delightful award winning restaurant great attention is paid to the quality of the cuisine with the four course table d'hôte menu changing daily. The finest fresh local produce is used together with vegetables, herbs and fruit from the hotel's kitchen gardens. Special diets are catered for.

Places of interest nearby: Exmoor National Park, beaches and cliffs of North Devon, many houses and gardens open to the public. **Directions: Leave the M5 at junction 27 and take the A361 to North Devon, continue for 25 miles then turn right at junction signposted North Molton, after ½ mile turn right then sharp right into hotel drive.**

For hotel location, see maps on pages 223–229

THE PRIORY

CHURCH ROAD, KETTON, STAMFORD, LINCOLNSHIRE PE9 3RD
TEL: 01780 720215 FAX: 01780 721881

OWNERS: John and Moya Acton
CHEF: Liz Stevenson

3 rms | 3 ens

S: £34–£37
D: £48–£55

The Priory is an oasis off the A1, a listed country house which has the ambience of a family home offering rooms for guests. The manor house dates back to the 16th century and has been meticulously restored. The magnificent gardens include a terrace by the River Chater, formal rosebeds and a croquet lawn.

The graceful reception rooms are well proportioned. An attractive conservatory has been added where a full English breakfast and dinner may be served as an alternative to eating in the dining room. The evening menu, changing daily, has a choice of meat, fish and vegetarian dishes.

Most of the beautifully decorated and spacious guest rooms overlook the gardens and all have colour TV, telephone and tea and coffee making facilities.
Places of interest nearby: Rutland Water offers sailing and fishing with cycling and walking around a 25 mile perimeter. Burghley House and Belvoir Castle are close by. Cambridge is only 45 minutes drive away. House Party Weekends can be arranged filling The Priory with ones friends. Theme weekends such as Murder are also featured. **Directions: Leave the A1 at Stamford. Take the A6121 to Ketton. Follow the sign Ketton Station, Collyweston. The entrance to The Priory is opposite the Churchyard, down some steps. There is a large car-park for guests' use.**

14 M

For hotel location, see maps on pages 223–229

KINGSTON HOUSE

STAVERTON, TOTNES, DEVON TQ9 6AR
TEL: 01803 762 235 FAX: 01803 762 444

OWNERS: Michael, Elizabeth and Piers Corfield

3 rms | 2 ens

S: £60–£67.50
D: £90
Suite: £95–£105

The Kingston Estate nestles amongst the rolling hills and valleys of the South Hams region of Devon, bounded by Dartmoor and the sea, with the focal point, Kingston House, commanding sweeping views of the moor.

The Mansion, together with the superb self-catering cottages, have been sympathetically restored by the Corfield family to their former glory, and now offer some of the highest standard accommodation to be found in the South West. The House boasts three period suites, (reached by way of the finest example of a marquetry staircase in England), which are hung with authentic wall papers and fabrics, and include a 1735 Angel tester bed, and an 1830 four-poster.

Dinner guests dine by candlelight in the elegant dining room at tables set with sparkling crystal, shining silver and starched linen. In winter, log fires crackle in the hearths, whilst in the summer pre-dinner drinks may be taken on the terrace overlooking the formal 18th century gardens. For every visitor to Kingston, hospitality and comfort are assured in this magnificent historic setting.

Places of interest nearby: Dartington Hall, Dartmouth, Totnes, Dartmoor & Devon's famous coastline.

Directions: Take A38 from Exeter or Plymouth, at Buckfastleigh take A384 Totnes road for two miles. Turn left to Staverton. At Sea Trout Inn, take left fork to Kingston and follow signs.

42 M

For hotel location, see maps on pages 223–229

MIDDLE LYPIATT HOUSE

MIDDLE LYPIATT, STROUD, GLOUCESTERSHIRE GL6 7LW
TEL: 01453 882151 FAX: 01453 886300

OWNER: Gillian Graham

3 rms | 1 ens

S: £30–£45
D: £50–£70

Those seeking somewhere secluded and not too large and those who appreciate beautiful surroundings will be delighted with this 16th century manor house high on the Cotswold Scarp with magnificent views across the valley. The estate stretches over 34 acres, with the enchanting formal gardens and lawns reflecting loving planning and care.

Gillian Graham, proprietress and chef, welcomes guests into her charming home, the residents' lounge filled with big armchairs and superb antiques. There is one master suite, the dressing room having a single bed, on the first floor and the two double rooms on the second floor are linked to a shared bathroom.

With few diners, dinner is naturally served at a pre-arranged time and the delicious three-course menu is limited. Wine and food should be discussed beforehand.

Guests enjoy the hard tennis court and outdoor pool, with its own poolhouse, or a stroll in the gardens. Polo, ballooning and gliding are local sporting activities.

Places of interest nearby: The Rococco Gardens and topiary churchyard at Painswick, while Cheltenham, Gloucester, Bath and Stratford are within striking distance. Bisley Village, two miles away, has excellent pubs. **Directions: Leaving Stroud on the Bisley road, after one mile turn right to Middle Lypiatt.**

12 M

In association with MasterCard

FARTHINGS HOTEL AND RESTAURANT

HATCH BEAUCHAMP, TAUNTON, SOMERSET TA3 6SG
TEL: 01823 480664 FAX: 01823 481118

OWNERS: David and Marie Barker
CHEF: Neil McKellar

8 rms | 8 ens | SMALL HOTEL

S: £50–£65
D: £65–£75

Farthings offers peace and quiet in the Somerset countryside yet is under ten minutes from the M5 or A303.

The new owners' criteria are good food, excellent wine, immaculate service, giving value for money and offering the ideal ambience for a few days away.

The hotel is set is three acres of landscaped gardens in a quiet village only five miles from Taunton. There are all the communication facilities for businessmen, yet all the peace needed by those escaping from a hectic city life.

The restaurant has an extensive ever-changing dinner menu and there are bar lunches midday and wonderful afternoon teas. Many of the wines are new world in addition to traditional favourites.

The décor throughout the extremely comfortable reception rooms and the eight en suite bedrooms is elegant to match the Georgian era of the original house. **Places of interest nearby:** The cathedral cities of Wells, Bath and Exeter are all in easy reach, as are Exmoor and the many stately homes and gardens. Golf, country walks, riding and visits to Somerset County Cricket Ground can be arranged. **Directions: Leave the M5 at exit 25, taking the A358. Hatch Beauchamp is signposted three miles along on the left.**

For hotel location, see maps on pages 223–229

UPPER COURT

KEMERTON, NR TEWKESBURY, GLOUCESTERSHIRE GL20 7HY
TEL: 01386 725351 FAX: 01386 725472

OWNERS: Bill and Diana Herford

4 rms | 4 ens

S: from £50
D: from £75

A fine Grade II listed Georgian manor house, Upper Court is the home of antique dealers Bill and Diana Herford and their family. They are happy to welcome all guests, whether visiting on holiday or for business. Antiques, open fires and dried flowers abound. The beautiful four-poster and twin-bedded rooms all have en suite bathrooms, TV and tea trays.

The main feature of the National Garden Scheme garden is the lake: it is perfect for boating, fly-fishing or romantic picnics. In the walled garden there is a heated pool or enjoy a game of croquet or tennis. Riding stables, golf and clay-pigeon shooting are all nearby. Dinner is served in the candle-lit dining room. The coach house and stables have been converted into self-catering cottages from £230 per week for two people in low season. Kemerton is a beautiful village on Bredon Hill, surrounded by footpaths and riding tracks which offer wonderful views.

Places of interest nearby: Stratford, Sudeley and Warwick Castles, Hidcote, Snowshill Manor, Oxford, Bath, Cheltenham and Broadway. **Directions: From Cheltenham north on A435/B4079. One mile after A438 crossroads sign to Kemerton on the right. Turn off main road at War Memorial. House behind church. From M5 junction 9, go east on A438 to the B4079 crossroads, then left and one mile as above.**

BROOM HALL

RICHMOND ROAD, SAHAM TONEY, THETFORD, NORFOLK
TEL: 01953 882125

OWNERS: Nigel and Angela Rowling

8 rms | 8 ens | SMALL HOTEL

S: £25–£35
D: £50

Broom Hall is a charming Victorian country house set in 15 acres of parkland. It is situated in the friendly Norfolk village of Saham Toney, with its 15th century church, 13 acre mere and 18-hole golf course.

Airy and spacious bedrooms, mostly offering lovely views, provide guests with both comfort and a range of modern amenities.

A home cooked three course meal is available in the dining room overlooking the garden and there is a large lounge with an open fire in which to relax.

Places of interest nearby: The cultural and historic centres of Norwich, Cambridge, Bury St Edmunds and Kings Lynn are all within easy reach. The area is the site of many country houses and gardens, including Sandringham and Blickling Hall, also Wayland Wood, the legendary location of 'The Babes in the Wood'. On the North Norfolk coast there are a number of nature reserves and bird sanctuaries. In between lie the Norfolk Broads. **Directions: One mile north of Watton on the B1077 towards Swaffham.**

20 M

For hotel location, see maps on pages 223–229

In association with MasterCard

TREBREA LODGE

TRENALE, TINTAGEL, CORNWALL PL34 0HR
TEL: 01840 770410 FAX: 01840 770092

OWNERS: John Charlick and Sean Devlin

7 rms | 7 ens | SMALL HOTEL

S: £47.50–£52.50
D: £60–£80

Trebrea Lodge overlooks the beauty and grandeur of the North Cornish coast and is set in 4½ acres of wooded hillside. This Grade II listed house was built on land granted to the Bray family by the Black Prince in the 14th century and has been lived in and improved by successive generations of the Brays for almost 600 years.

All the bedrooms are individually decorated with traditional and antique furniture and they offer uninterrupted views across open fields to the Atlantic Ocean. The elegant first-floor drawing room also boasts spectacular views, while there is a comfortable smoking room downstairs with an open log fire.

A full English breakfast and four-course dinner are served in the oak-panelled dining room and the menu changes daily. The meals use the finest local ingredients, including sea trout and wild salmon from the River Tamar, and have been awarded an AA Rosette.

Places of interest nearby: Tintagel Island and Boscastle. Bodmin Moor, Lanhydrock House and gardens, Pencarrow House and extensive coastal walks.

Directions: From Launceston take Wadebridge–Camelford road. At A39 follow Tintagel sign – turn left for Trenale ½ mile before reaching Tintagel.

For hotel location, see maps on pages 223-229

HOOKE HALL

HIGH STREET, UCKFIELD, EAST SUSSEX TN22 1EN
TEL: 01825 761578 FAX: 01825 768025

OWNERS: Alister and Juliet Percy

9 rms | 9 ens

S: from £40
D: from £65

Uckfield lies on the borders of Ashdown Forest, near the South Downs and resorts of Brighton and Eastbourne and 40 minutes from Gatwick Airport. Hooke Hall is an elegant Queen Anne town house, the home of its owners, Juliet and Alister Percy, who have carried out extensive renovations.

The rooms are individually decorated to a high standard with private facilities. In the panelled study guests can relax by the open fire before having dinner at 'La Scaletta' known for its high quality North Italian Regional cuisine. Private lunch and dinner parties are arranged in other rooms and looked after by Juliet, herself a Cordon Bleu cook.

Places of interest nearby: Within easy reach are Leeds, Hever and Bodiam Castles, Penshurst Place and Battle Abbey. The gardens of Sissinghurst, Nymans, Great Dixter, Sheffield Park, Wakehurst Place and Leonardslee are no distance nor is Batemans, Rudyard Kipling's home. Glyndebourne Opera is only 15 minutes by car. There are several English vineyards nearby to be visited. Closed for Christmas. **Directions: From M25 take the exit for East Grinstead and continue South on the A22 to Uckfield. Hooke Hall is at the northern end of the High Street.**

20 M · 10

For hotel location, see maps on pages 223–229

KEMPS COUNTRY HOUSE HOTEL AND RESTAURANT

EAST STOKE, WAREHAM, DORSET BH20 6AL
TEL: 01929 462563 FAX: 01929 405287

OWNERS: Jill and Paul Warren

15 rms | 14 ens

S: £48–£68
D: £58–£108

This small and welcoming country house hotel, surrounded by unspoilt Dorset countryside, overlooks the Frome Valley and offers lovely views of the Purbeck Hills. The house was originally a Victorian Rectory and its tasteful extension was undertaken with great care to preserve Victorian atmosphere.

There are five bedrooms in the main house, while the Old Coach House has been converted to include four en suite rooms. More recently, six spacious new bedrooms have been added in an annexe, all facing the Purbecks. Decorated and furnished to equally high standards, one of these rooms has a traditional four-poster bed and a whirlpool bath.

Before dinner guests are invited to enjoy a drink in the lounge and bar whilst ordering their meal. The bar features the ornate wallpaper and heavy hangings of the Victorian period. The comfortable dining room extends into the conservatory, from which there are picturesque views of the hills as dusk falls. Kemps restaurant, which has been awarded an AA Rosette, enjoys an excellent local reputation for first-rate cuisine. The table d'hôte menu changes daily and there is also an à la carte menu. Food is prepared to order, everything possible is home-made, and the service is second to none.

Places of interest nearby: Lulworth and Corfe Castles, Athelhampton House and gardens. **Directions: On the A352 main road between Wareham and Wool.**

50 M

BERYL

WELLS, SOMERSET BA5 3JP
TEL: 01749 678738 FAX: 01749 670508

OWNERS: Eddie and Holly Nowell

6 rms | 6 ens

S: £45
D: £65–£75

This nineteenth century Gothic mansion is a gardener's paradise. It also offers hospitality of the highest order.

The host is a famous antique dealer, with a long established shop in Wells, his gardening talents are reflected in the 13 acres of parkland which he has restored with great skill.

His wife is a charming and talented hostess, evident in the attention paid to detail, and an excellent cook. Dinner is served by arrangement, a set menu with fine wines appropriate to the elegant dining room. House wines and other drinks are available. It is possible to have small conferences (maximum 12) or private celebrations.

The six en suite bedrooms have wonderful views, with all the requisites for modern comfort.

Places of interest nearby: One mile from Wells Cathedral, among other fascinating places to visit are the Roman Baths at Bath, Longleat House and the Tropical Bird Gardens. For active guests there is marvellous golf, fishing, riding and excellent walking. **Directions: Leave Wells on Radstock Road B3139. Opposite B.P. garage turn left into Hawkers Lane, Beryl is signed at top with a leafy 500yd drive to the main gate.**

en famille | 12 M

Glencot House

GLENCOT LANE, WOOKEY HOLE, NR WELLS, SOMERSET BA5 1BH
TEL: 01749 677160 FAX: 01749 670210

OWNER: Jenny Attia

12 rms | 12 ens | SMALL HOTEL

S: £48–£52
D: £72.50–£85

Glencot House, a Grade II Jacobean style mansion, is a Victorian piece of architecture, sensitively renovated in recent years, and beautifully sited in 18 acres of tranquil gardens and parkland with river frontage. The building derives its unique character from its mullioned windows, carved ceilings, massive fireplaces, antiques and sumptuous chandeliers, making it a truly magnificent place to stay.

All bedrooms are individually decorated and furnished for total comfort, with central heating and fine views. The four honeymoon suites have four-poster beds; all rooms have tea and coffee-making facilities.

This is all complemented by an honest, friendly service and homely atmosphere. A constantly changing menu presents diverse and delicious fare, painstakingly prepared by chef Danny Cannon from fresh local produce. Guests can enjoy a three-course dinner with coffee from £19.50 before retiring to the panelled drawing room to relax and/or socialise, or stroll to the river for a little exercise.

Places of interest nearby: the cathedral town of Wells, the Mendip Hills, the caves at Wookey Hole, Cheddar Gorge, Stourhead House and garden, and Bath. **Directions: Exit M5 junction 22, following signs for Cheddar then Wookey Hole. Pass through village of Easton and over crossroads, a mile on, to Haybridge. Take next left, signposted Wookey Hole, over bridge and, as the roads bends right, turn left into Glencot Lane. The second gate is Glencot House.**

40 M

For hotel location, see maps on pages 223–229

DUNSLEY HALL

DUNSLEY, WHITBY, NORTH YORKSHIRE YO21 3TL
TEL: 01947 893437 FAX: 01947 893505

OWNERS: William and Carol Ward
CHEF: Billy Chambers

11 rms | 11 ens | SMALL HOTEL

S: £37–£45
D: £73–£85

Set in the North York Moors National Park, Dunsley Hall's own 4 acres of landscaped gardens include a tennis court, putting green and croquet lawn. Those dedicated to exercise can also enjoy the facilities of the fitness room and indoor heated swimming pool. A game of snooker may suit those seeking a more gentle form of relaxation, and this can be enjoyed in the oak-panelled billiard room, with its full-size, matchplay standard table, stained glass windows and carved fireplace, or why not languish in the 4-6 person sauna.

Each of the eleven bedrooms is individually furnished and there are two rooms with four-poster beds. Each evening a four-course table d'hôte dinner is served from a menu that changes nightly and is based on the abundant supply of fresh local produce. Special price spring and winter breaks are available.

Places of interest nearby: The birthplace of Captain Cook at Great Ayton, North York Moors, Castle Howard, Pickering Steam Railway and the city of York. Reduced green fees are available at Whitby Golf Course.

Directions: From the A171 Whitby–Teeside road, turn right at signpost for Newholme, three miles north of Whitby. Dunsley is the first turning on the left. Dunsley Hall is one mile further on the right.

15 M

For hotel location, see maps on pages 223–229

BEECHLEAS

17 POOLE ROAD, WIMBORNE MINSTER, DORSET BH21 1QA
TEL: 01202 841684 FAX: 01202 849344

OWNER: Josephine McQuillan

9 rms | 9 ens | SMALL HOTEL

S: £53–£73
D: £63–£83

Beechleas is a delightful Georgian Grade II listed town house hotel. It has been carefully restored and offers guests comfortable accommodation in beautifully furnished quality en suite bedrooms.

The hotel's own charming restaurant, which overlooks a pretty walled garden, is bright and airy in the summer and warmed by cosy log fires in the winter. The carefully prepared menu is changed daily and offers dishes using natural produce wherever possible along with the finest fresh ingredients available from the local market.

Sailing trips are available from Poole Harbour, where guests may choose to go fishing. They can play golf on one of the many local courses. It takes just five minutes to walk into the centre of Wimborne, a historic market town with an interesting twintower church built on the site of its old Saxon Abbey during the 12th and 13th centuries.

The hotel, which is closed from 24 December to the end of January, has been awarded two red Stars by the AA and two Rosettes for its restaurant.

Places of interest nearby: There are many National Trust properties within easy reach, including Kingston Lacy House, Badbury Rings and Corfe Castle. Bournemouth is a 20 minute drive away. **Directions: From London take M3, M27, A31 and then B3073 to Wimborne.**

12 M

THE COUNTRY HOUSE AT WINCHELSEA

HASTINGS ROAD, WINCHELSEA, EAST SUSSEX TN36 4AD
TEL: 01797 226669

OWNER: Mary Carmichael

3 rms 3 ens

S: from £46
D: from £60

With spectacular views toward the ancient hill town of Winchelsea and completely surrounded by National Trust countryside, this traditional Sussex farmhouse commands a unique position. A listed building of great character and charm standing in its own two acres of lovely walled garden.

The individually styled bedrooms offer guests a wonderful garden and country views with en suite facilities, colour T.V., direct-dial telephone and complimentary beverage trays.

Apéritifs and cocktails can be enjoyed in the lounge bar whilst anticipating your 'dining experience'. Mary Carmichael's enthusiasm for cooking is reflected in the quality and variety of the courses she prepares for her guests. After dinner you can relax with your coffee and liqueurs in the cosy sitting room or, weather permitting, on the terrace with those lovely views. Nothing is too much trouble for your caring hostess at this delightful house, to ensure a most relaxing and memorable stay. **Places of interest nearby:** The medieval towns of Rye and Winchelsea, National Trust properties and gardens, coastal or Romney Marsh walks. **Directions: Set back from the A259 on the Hastings side of Winchelsea and approximately seven minutes from Rye by car.**

For hotel location, see maps on pages 223–229

In association with MasterCard

FAYRER GARDEN HOUSE HOTEL

LYTH VALLEY ROAD, BOWNESS-ON-WINDERMERE, CUMBRIA LA23 3JP
TEL: 015394 88195 FAX: 015394 45986

OWNERS: Iain and Jackie Garside

12 rms | 12 ens | SMALL HOTEL

S: £40–£65
D: £75–£125
(including dinner)

Overlooking Lake Windermere, this lovely Victorian house, completely refurbished in 1991, is a comfortable hotel where guests enjoy the spectacular view over the water, a real welcome, friendly service and marvellous value for money! The delightful drawing room and sitting room, looking out over the lake and countryside, are warmed by roaring fires in the winter. Some of the attractive bedrooms have four-posters, others whirlpool baths, all face the lake or beautiful five-acre gardens, and are equipped with television and hair-dryers. A few are on the ground floor with easy access for disabled visitors.

The restaurant overlooks Lake Windermere. There is an excellent table d'hôte menu, changing daily, using local produce – especially fish – whenever possible and an exciting à la carte choice. The wine list is superb. A full English breakfast prepares walkers for their day. The nearby Parklands Leisure Complex has an indoor pool, sauna, steam room, badminton, snooker and squash. Membership is complimentary for hotel residents. Special breaks available.

Places of interest nearby: Boating from Bowness Pier and golf at Windermere Golf Club. Fell scenery at Kirkstone Pass via A592. **Directions: Junction 36 off the M6, A590 past Kendal. Take B5284 at the next roundabout, turn left at the end and the hotel is 350 yards on the right.**

In association with MasterCard

THE OLD VICARAGE COUNTRY HOUSE HOTEL

CHURCH ROAD, WITHERSLACK, NR GRANGE-OVER- SANDS, CUMBRIA LA11 6RS
TEL: 015395 52381 FAX: 015395 52373

OWNERS: Roger and Jill Burrington-Brown and Stan and Irene Reeve

14 rms | 14 ens | SMALL HOTEL

S: £75–£90
D: £110–£155
(including dinner)

The traditional values of an English vicarage where comfort and refuge were sought and a warm welcome was always given are well preserved at the family-run Old Vicarage. The tranquil, timeless atmosphere reflects the calm and beauty of the surrounding countryside, in this surprisingly quiet and little-known corner of the Lake District National Park.

The delightful, mature garden is stocked with many interesting plants and part of it is left natural for wild flowers, unusual orchids, butterflies, dragonflies and birds.

In the old house, each of the comfortable en suite bedrooms has its own particular character yet all the modern facilities.

Orchard House close by set beside an ancient damson orchard has particularly well-equipped, spacious rooms each with its own woodland terrace.

With top culinary awards and recommendations, the well-planned menus are supported by fresh local ingredients of which there is a tempting abundance. Any diets can, of course, easily be catered for.

Places of interest nearby: Lake Winderemere, Wordsworth and Beatrix Potter Heritage, Levens Hall with world famous topiary gardens and Sizergh Castle (National Trust). **Directions: From M6 junction 36, follow A590 to Barrow. After 6 miles turn right into Witherslack, then first left after the telephone box.**

For hotel location, see maps on pages 223–229

OTLEY HOUSE

OTLEY, IPSWICH, SUFFOLK IP6 9NR
TEL: 01473 890253 FAX: 01473 890009

OWNERS: Thomas and Colette Hoepli

4 rms | 4 ens

S: £42–£52
D: £58–£72

A beautiful 17th century listed manor house standing in peaceful mature grounds with ponds and wildfowl, on the edge of the village of Otley, just west of Woodbridge and seven miles from Ipswich, is the home of Colette and Thomas Hoepli and their daughter Lara.

The house offers a high standard of accommodation with four luxuriously furnished bedrooms, individually designed and with en suite bathrooms. The wide lawn and the charming summerhouse invite outdoor activities and relaxation. Colette is Swiss with a French family background which is, together with Leith's School of Food and Wine training, reflected in her cooking.

Guests dine at a large table in the candle-lit dining room. There is a good selection of wines available. Other spacious public rooms with open fireplaces include the hall, an elegant drawing room and a billiard room with comfortable leather chairs. Overall a delightful and stimulating atmosphere of a splendid country house. **Places of interest nearby:** Framlingham Castle, Orford Castle, Snape Maltings, the coast at Dunwich Heath, Southwold and Aldeburgh. Golf: The proprietors will be pleased to arrange tee-off times at many of the nearby links or courses. Open from March to November. **Directions: From Woodbridge take the B1079 through Grundisburgh to Otley. Pass the Post Office on your right. The house is 250 yards on your right.**

12

4 SOUTH PARADE

4 SOUTH PARADE, YORK, NORTH YORKSHIRE YO2 2BA
TEL: 01904 628229 FAX: 01904 628229

OWNERS: Robin and Anne McClure

3 rms | 3 ens

S: £60–£80
D: £70–£90

This attractive Regency terraced town house stands in the centre of York and is an excellent base for exploring the historic city or for touring the Yorkshire Moors and Dales. The house has been carefully restored by the friendly owners, Anne and Robin McClure, who have created a beautiful home with many interesting antiques. The bedrooms are decorated with fine fabrics and comfortably equipped to high standards with welcoming touches like bowls of pot-pourri, fresh flowers and fruit.

The day begins with early-morning tea and newspapers, followed by an appetising traditional breakfast.

Afternoon tea is served on bone china in the elegant drawing room. A freshly prepared, candle-lit supper is available by prior arrangement and guests may bring their own wine.

York Minster, theatres and many sports facilities are within walking distance and Anne and Robin are only too happy to share their local knowledge with guests. Special breaks are available. Guests are advised that a no-smoking policy applies to the whole house.

Places of interest nearby: The National Railway, Yorkshire and Castle Museums, Fairfax House, Jorvic Viking Centre, Castle Howard, Rievaulx and Fountains Abbey. **Directions: Take the A1036 into York, past the racecourse on the right and the Odeon cinema on the left. Directly opposite is South Parade, a small, cobbled street.**

en famille | 8 M

For hotel location, see maps on pages 223–229

The Parsonage Country House Hotel

ESCRICK, YORK, NORTH YORKSHIRE YO4 6LF
TEL: 01904 728111 FAX: 01904 728151

MANAGER: John Pettifer

13 rms | 13 ens | SMALL HOTEL

S: £62.50–£88
D: £95–£110

Surrounded by wide expanses of lawn, formal gardens and wild woodland, The Parsonage Country House Hotel provides an oasis of comfort and tranquillity. In the nearby breathtakingly beautiful hills and valleys are hidden ancient hamlets and villages still immersed in the old way of life.

The Parsonage has been passed down through various noble families and baronies from Count Alan of Brittany in the early 11th century, to the de Lascelles, the Knyvetts, Thompsons, Lawleys and finally the Forbes Adams retaining all of its charm and many original features.

Each bedroom has been furnished with comfort and luxury in mind and features a full range of modern facilities. Two of the larger rooms contain magnificent four poster beds the ultimate in nostalgic indulgence! At the end of the day, the comfortable lounge bar is the perfect place to be seduced by an atmosphere of total relaxation.

A highly appetising selection of Anglo-French dishes is created by the chef, who uses only the freshest, high quality local ingredients. A varied and carefully selected wine list is available to complement any meal.

Places of interest nearby: The Parsonage is a perfect base from which to visit York and Harrogate, the estates of Castle Howard, the three Cistercian Abbeys, the Yorkshire coastline or the Yorkshire Dales. **Directions: Escrick is on the A19 a few miles south of York.**

150 M

For hotel location, see maps on pages 223–229

EVENTIVE

SPECIALISTS IN PROVIDING A FULLY MOBILE RANGE OF ACTIVITIES FOR CORPORATE PARTICIPATION EVENTS AND FUNCTIONS
TEL: 01252 24885 CONTACT: RODNEY STONE

To complement your event at one of Johansens recommended hotels and business meetings venues, Eventive offer a full range of indoor and outdoor activities suitable for post conference and promotional events, team building, staff incentives, social functions and client entertainment days. Our activities and events are staffed by erudite and smartly attired professional instructors and managers, all of whom provide consistently high standards in event instruction and organisation and, have the ability to communicate with people at all levels. Having organised corporate events at many of the UK's top hotels and conference venues, we have put together a large database of information regarding suitable locations for our activities, and offer a free advisory service to both clients and venue staff. As a member of the Corporate Hospitality and Event Association (CHA) we adhere to a strict code of practice, and are continually surpassing industry guidelines, to ensure our clients receive the highest degree of quality, safety and service excellence. Whatever your requirements, be they single activities for a small group, country pursuits, off road driving, or large multi-activity days, we can advise on budget and content, and help you plan the best event for your guests.

Please telephone for a copy of our brochure, and to discuss your corporate entertainment.

AMERICAN EXPRESS

- CLAY SHOOTING
- ARCHERY
- FALCONRY
- CROQUET
- FLY FISHING
- LASER CLAY SHOOTING
- RIFLE SHOOTING
- PILOT BUGGIES
- QUAD BIKES
- 8X8 ARGOCATS
- TRIALS AND RALLY CARS
- HOVERCRAFT
- THEME EVENTS
- MURDER MYSTERIES
- TEAM BUILDING
- ASSAULT COURSE
- SURVIVAL TRAINING
- CASINOS
- SCALEXTRIC
- SKITTLES
- MODEL CAR RACING
- TREASURE HUNTS
- FAMILY DAYS
- MULTI-ACTIVITY DAYS
- YACHTING

CHA

Johansens Recommended Country Houses in Wales

*M**agnificent** scenery, a rich variety of natural, cultural and modern leisure attractions, and the very best accommodation await the Johansens visitor to Wales.*

Each year, millions of visitors head for Wales to discover or rediscover all that the country has to offer. An exceptionally high proportion come back year after year – a sure sign of satisfaction.

Wales has some of the most fabulous scenery imaginable, with much to see and do, and boasts three national parks covering nearly 1,600 square miles, as well as five areas designated as being of Outstanding Natural Beauty.

There are numerous large country parks, nature reserves, sites of special scientific interest and more than 700 miles of breathtakingly beautiful coastline to discover, plus delightful off shore islands, home to colonies of seals and rare birds.

But quite apart from the country's unspoilt natural beauty and endless scenic variety, the principality has a wealth of interesting and unusual attractions to enjoy.

There are a whole host of fascinating places to visit, many of them unique like the Centre for Alternative Technology, the green village of the future at Machynlleth in Mid Wales or Portmeirion, the dreamlike Italianate village in North Wales.

Visitors can take a ride on a narrow gauge steam railway, take a trip on a horse drawn canal boat, go to the summit of the Great Orme in the only cable hauled tramway in Britain, travel across Aberaeron harbour by the Aeron Express Aerial ferry or journey to the summit of Aberystwyth's Constitution Hill by cliff railway, one of the most spectacular in Britain.

In Wales there are working farms open to the public with rare breeds, and also fascinating factory workshops where visitors can watch glass being blown, carpets woven, candles being made and at several potteries visitors can enjoy a real hands-on experience by throwing a pot on a wheel.

The Industrial heritage of the past now provides fascinating visitor attractions like Big Pit in Blaenafon where ex-miners act as underground guides or the ever expanding Rhondda Heritage Park. In North Wales there are vast slate caverns and copper mines to explore, several narrow gauge steam railways to enjoy while in Mid Wales, visitors can tour a real goldmine, try their hand at panning and mining for gold – and keep anything they find!

Apart from these unique attractions, there are old working mills, art and craft centres, mountain and sea zoos, a hawking centre, sea aquariums, bird gardens, butterfly houses and wildlife parks.

There are exceptional museums like the 100 acre Welsh Folk Museum near Cardiff where buildings from all over Wales have been carefully reerected, and museums covering the maritime, motoring, industrial and aviation history of Wales, as well as those dedicated to the memory of famous personalities like Lloyd George and Dylan Thomas.

Wales also has her share of magnificent stately homes with priceless art treasures and antiques, world class gardens like Bodnant or Dyffryn, exciting new attractions like the haunted Llancaiach Fawr Manor in Rhymney Valley – a living history museum with guides dressed in costume, as well as vast medieval fortresses, castles and cromlechs.

There are also excellent leisure centres and sporting facilities throughout the country, in fact, Wales could have been tailormade for activity holidays and visitors can undertake virtually all types of outdoor activities and go abseiling or angling, ballooning or gliding, rafting or riding, climbing, canoeing or caving – to mention a few!

With family fun parks like Oakwood Park in West Wales, Starcoast World on the Llyn peninsula and Ocean Beach Amusement Park in Rhyl, famed for its whiteknuckle rides, Wales truly has something for everyone.

Centre for Alternative Technology
Machynlleth
Powys SY20 9AZ
Tel: 01654 702400

Great Little Trains of Wales
c/o The Station
Llanfair Caereinion
Powys SY21 OSF
Tel: 01938 810441

Big Pit
Blaenafon
Gwent NP4 9XP
Tel: 01495 790311

Rhondda Heritage Park
Lewis Merthyr
Coed Cae Road
Trehafod
Mid Glamorgan CF37 7NP
Tel: 01443 682036

Welsh Folk Museum
St Fagans
Cardiff CF5 6XB
Tel: 01222 569441

Bodnant Gardens
Tal y Cafn
Colwyn Bay
Clwyd LL28 5RE
Tel: 01492 650460

Dyffryn Gardens
St Nicholas
Nr Cardiff
South Glamorgan CF5 6SU
Tel: 01222 593328

Llancaiach Fawr Manor
Gelligaer Road
Nelson
Mid Glamorgan CF46 6ER
Tel: 01443 412248

For more information about Wales, please contact:-

Wales Tourist Board
Brunel House
2 Fitzalan Road
Cardiff CF2 1UY
Tel: 01222 499909

GLANGRWYNEY COURT

GLANGRWYNEY, NR ABERGAVENNY, POWYS
TEL: 01873 811288 FAX: 01873 810317

OWNERS: Warwick and Christina Jackson

4 rms | 2 ens

S: £35
D: £60

This graceful Georgian mansion is set in four acres of secluded mature gardens on the Monmouthshire–Powys borders. It has been refurbished to accommodate guests in great style and comfort, and babies and children are welcome.

The house is furnished with antiques, fine porcelain and paintings. The delightful drawing room and elegant dining room are exclusive to guests. The music room has a grand piano and other instruments which guests may be invited to play. Log fires blaze in winter, books and journals abound.

Hospitality offered includes a traditional breakfast and, by prior discussion, a delicious four-course dinner based on the seasonal fresh produce available.

Two of the four charming bedrooms are en suite, the other two have adjacent private bathrooms. All have television and tea-making facilities.

Places of interest nearby: In summer, guests play croquet, tennis and boules or relax in the garden. If agreed beforehand, dogs are welcome. Golf, pony trekking, and fishing are nearby, also the Brecon Beacons National Park for walkers. Hereford Cathedral and the market towns of Abergavenny and Crickhowell are close by, as are the spectacular Talybont and Gwryne Fawr Reservoirs.

Directions: The Court is signed from Crickhowell on the A40 between Brecon and Abergavenny.

For hotel location, see maps on pages 223–229

LLANWENARTH HOUSE

GOVILON, ABERGAVENNY, GWENT NP7 9SF
TEL: 01873 830289 FAX: 01873 832199

OWNERS: Bruce and Amanda Weatherill

4 rms | 4 ens

S: £50–£62
D: £64–£75

Llanwenarth House overlooks the Vale of Usk and stands in its own beautiful grounds within the Brecon Beacons National Park. It was built from local rose-grey limestone in the 16th century by the Morgan family, ancestors of Sir Henry Morgan, privateer and Lieutenant Governor of Jamaica. Careful restoration has ensured that the house has retained all of its character, while bringing it up to the highest level of comfort.

Guests are personally looked after by the family, who offer comfortable accommodation in period furnished rooms. Many of the elegant spacious bedrooms offer lovely views of the grounds and surrounding countryside.

Fine cuisine is prepared by Amanda, a Cordon Bleu cook who makes full use of local game, fish, home-produced meat, poultry and organically grown garden vegetables. Dinner is served by candlelight in the beautiful Georgian dining room.

Sporting opportunities in the vicinity include trout and salmon fishing on the River Usk, walking, pony trekking, climbing, rough shooting and golf.

Places of interest nearby: Chepstow and Raglan Castles, and Tintern Abbey. **Directions: From the roundabout one mile east of Abergavenny follow the A465 towards Merthyr Tydfil for three miles to the next roundabout. Take first exit to Govilon and the ½ mile driveway is 150 yards along on the righthand side.**

10

For hotel location, see maps on pages 223–229

PENYCLAWDD COURT

LLANFIHANGEL CRUCORNEY, ABERGAVENNY, GWENT NP7 7LB
TEL: 01873 890719 FAX: 01873 890848

OWNERS: Julia Horton Evans and Ken Peacock
CHEF: Julia Horton Evans

3 rms 3 ens

S: £45
D: £60

Penyclawdd Court is a Grade II Star Listed Tudor Manor House, situated at the foot of Bryn Arw mountain in the Brecon Beacons National Park. The authentic restoration of the house has been recognised by an award from H.R.H. the Prince of Wales. In the grounds is to be found a Norman motte and bailey – a scheduled ancient monument. There is also a traditional herb garden and a walled knot garden. The Court has its own free-range hens and a flock of prize-winning pedigree Jacob sheep.

Featured regularly in magazines and on T.V. and Radio, the house is furnished with antiques and there are huge stone fireplaces, flagstone floors and exposed beams. Because of its age, there are many steps, stairs and sloping floors to negotiate, which sadly means that the house is not best suited to everybody.

Four-course dinners can be provided by prior arrangement using home produced or local ingredients. Groups can enjoy researched 15th to 17th Century feasts. **Places of interest nearby:** Situated as it is in a National Park, the surrounding area offers some wonderful walks. Pony-trekking and golf are available locally. **Directions: Penyclawdd Court is ½ mile off A465 Abergavenny –Hereford road signposted Pantygelli.**

12 12

For hotel location, see maps on pages 223–229

Plas Bach

GLANDWR, NR BARMOUTH, GWYNEDD LL42 1TG
TEL: 01341 281234

OWNERS: Hazel and Barrie Michael

4 rms | 4 ens

S: £28.50–£40
D: £55–£60

This pretty Georgian house situated in 4 acres of natural gardens on the sunnyside of the Mawddach estuary must be almost unrivalled for its spectacular views – from mountain peaks to shoreline. Here the mountains of Snowdonia really do come down to the sea!

This is a recommendation for guests who prefer an informal atmosphere. Hazel and Barrie are friendly and welcoming hosts who create a relaxed and happy ambience for their guests.

The spotlessly clean comfortable bedrooms, with pretty patchwork quilts, are equipped with hospitality trays and television. The en suite bath/shower rooms have big fluffy towels and hairdryers.

Breakfast is described as a feast! Evening meals, home cooking using the best of local produce, are by arrangement, but they can be ordered for most evenings except Wednesday. The house is licensed and is a non-smoking establishment. **Places of interest nearby:** Guests can go fishing from Barmouth, play golf at Aberdovey, Royal St David's or tackle Snowdonia. Alternatives are marvellous bird-watching from the saltflats, strolling through the back gate on to the miles of walkway along the magnificent coastline, enjoying the superb local beaches or going inland exploring castles. Off road tours (available next season). Excellent Christmas package available. **Directions: Plas Bach is about two miles from Barmouth and 400 yards off the A496.**

For hotel location, see maps on pages 223–229

In association with MasterCard

TAN-Y-FOEL

CAPEL GARMON, NR BETWS-Y-COED, GWYNEDD LL26 0RE
TEL: 01690 710507 FAX: 01690 710681

OWNERS: Peter and Janet Pitman

7 rms | 7 ens

S: £69.50–£75
D: £99–£110

The name of this beautiful country retreat means 'the house under the hillside'. Set in eight acres under the slopes of Moel Trefriw it commands spectacular views of the Conwy Valley and the rugged peaks of Snowdonia.

Peter and Janet provide accommodation for just a few visiting couples. There is a variety of bedrooms from which to choose: twins, king-size and even super king-size beds. Furnishings are carefully chosen, colours and fabrics finely blended and fresh flowers are to be seen everywhere.

Within this little gem of a country house you will have the opportunity to sample plenty of superb cordon bleu style cuisine, from a small and carefully prepared menu, fish straight from the sea, local Welsh lamb, home-made bread, all reserved exclusively for residents.

This whole area is rich in historic sites and structures, with mines, museums and mills adding interest.

Tan-Y-Foel is a totally no-smoking establishment. Children over the age of seven are welcome. Special two day breaks available.

Places of interest nearby: Great Little Trains of Wales, Bodnant Gardens, Conwy Castle and Snowdonia.

Directions: From Chester take the A55 to Llandudno. Then A470 towards Betws-y-Coed. Two miles outside of Llanwrst fork left towards Capel Garmon–Nebo. Tan-y-Foel is just over a mile up the hill on the left-hand side.

For hotel location, see maps on pages 223–229

OLD GWERNYFED COUNTRY MANOR

FELINDRE, THREE COCKS, BRECON, POWYS LD3 0SU
TEL: 01497 847376

OWNERS: Roger and Dawn Beetham

10 rms | 10 ens

S: £39–£43
D: £60–£88

Old Gwernyfed is a historian's delight – its passage through the ages has been carefully documented and its antiquated features well preserved. Set in 13 acres in the foothills of the Black Mountains, it was built circa 1600 as a manor house of great importance in its day.

Over the years, Roger and Dawn Beetham have lavished much attention on the building to restore it to its former glory. They have made no attempt to disguise the age of the building, preferring to enhance its original characteristics.

One of the lounges, which is oak panelled from floor to ceiling, is overlooked by the splendid balustraded minstrels gallery. Most of the bedrooms enjoy outstanding views and there is a good choice of four-poster, half-tester and canopied beds. Traffic noise is non-existent.

The dining room is dominated by its cavernous 12 foot fireplace, only rediscovered in recent years. A small table d'hôte menu is changed daily and all dishes are cooked freshly using produce from the garden or local suppliers. Closed mid-December to mid-March.

Places of interest nearby: Hay-on-Wye and the market town of Brecon. Local activities include canoeing, sailing, pony-trekking and gliding. **Directions: From Brecon turn off A438 after the Three Cocks Hotel. Take every turning to right for 1¾ miles. Go through Felindre and Old Gwernyfed is 200 yards on right.**

For hotel location, see maps on pages 223–229

TY'N RHOS COUNTRY HOUSE

LLANDDEINIOLEN, CAERNARFON, GWYNEDD LL55 3AE
TEL: 01248 670489 FAX: 01248 670079

OWNERS: Lynda and Nigel Kettle

10 rms | 10 ens | SMALL HOTEL

S: £40–£45
D: £56–£80

Ty'n Rhos is not the typical country house hotel. This immaculate small hotel of 10 bedrooms is based on a farmhouse which has been extended and improved to provide the highest standards of accommodation and food. Guests enjoy the peaceful surroundings of green fields with wonderful open views across to nearby Caernarfon, the Menai Strait and Anglesey.

Award-winning Ty'n Rhos is the creation of Lynda and Nigel Kettle. They originally intended to run Ty'n Rhos as a full-time farm. Although a 72 acre farm still, the emphasis is firmly on looking after their guests. Ty'n Rhos's appeal is now based on a unique blend of personal service, the highest professional standards and exceptional value for money.

The beautifully appointed bedrooms, all fully en suite, have all the comforts of a stylish hotel. But perhaps the most important single element in Ty'n Rhos's success is the food. Lynda is an accomplished chef, one of the best known in Wales, whose dishes – many with a 'Taste of Wales' Theme – are based on the finest fresh ingredients. It's a refreshing change to stay at this small hotel with a big reputation for its food, quality and value for money, superbly located between Snowdonia and the sea within easy touring distance of all of North Wales. **Directions: Situated in the hamlet on Seion off the B4366 and B4547. Reached from the East by A5 or A55.**

Berthlwyd Hall Hotel

LLECHWEDD, NR CONWY, GWYNEDD LL32 8DQ
TEL: 01492 592409 FAX: 01492 572290

OWNERS: Brian and Joanna Griffin

9 rms | 9 ens | SMALL HOTEL

VISA

S: £49
D: from £70

One mile from historic Conwy and in sight of its famous castle, is Berthlwyd Hall Hotel, a charming Victorian manor surrounded by the country byways and woodlands of the picturesque Conwy Valley. Many of the Victorian characteristics have been preserved, such as the splendid oak panelling in the entrance hall, a wide staircase sweeping up to an impressive galleried landing, elaborately carved fireplaces and stained-glass windows. Each of the bedrooms has been individually styled and comfortably appointed.

Resident proprietors Brian and Joanna Griffin spent some years in the Périgord region of south-west France, renowned for its gastronomic heritage and the inspiration for their award-winning restaurant, 'Truffles'. The 140-year-old wine press, brought back from Bordeaux, evokes a Gallic atmosphere appropriate for the imaginative menu of French dishes and a wine list of good clarets and regional vintages. 4 crown highly commended.

Places of interest nearby: From Berthlwyd Hall the majestic peaks of Snowdonia, the Welsh coast and Anglesey can be explored, while Bodnant Gardens are nearby.

Directions: The hall is approached through a small private chalet park. Proceed off the A55 into Conwy town, round the one way system turning left after Lancaster square into the Sychant Pass Road, after one mile look for hotel sign on the left. Turn left and continue for half a mile.

30 M

THE OLD RECTORY

LLANRWST ROAD, LLANSANFFRAID GLAN CONWY, NR CONWY, GWYNEDD LL28 5LF
TEL: 01492 580611 FAX: 01492 584555

OWNERS: Michael and Wendy Vaughan

6 rms 6 ens

S: £62–£72
D: £74–£114

Dramatic Snowdonian vistas, breathtaking sunsets and views of floodlit Conwy Castle are enjoyed from this idyllically situated Welsh country house set in large gardens. Awarded Red Stars status by the AA for providing oustanding levels of hospitality, service, food and comfort.

Wendy Vaughan's cooking features in Egon Ronay and all other good food guides. Her gourmet four-course dinners combine a lightness of touch and delicacy of flavour with artistic presentation. Welsh mountain lamb, locally reared Welsh black beef and fish landed at Conwy feature on her menu. An award-winning wine list complements her fine cuisine. Most diets are catered for.

Antiques and Victorian watercolours decorate the interiors. The luxury en suite bedrooms have draped beds, bathrobes, ironing centres, fresh fruit and flowers.

Michael Vaughan is happy to share his knowledge of Welsh history, language and culture and always has time to assist in planning touring routes. Relax in the garden and watch the River Conwy ebb and flow and you will see why this elegant Georgian home is a 'beautiful haven of peace'.

Places of interest nearby: Bodnant Gardens, Conwy Castle, Snowdonia and the elegant spa of Llandudno.

Directions: The Old Rectory is situated on the A470, 1/2 mile south of its junction with the A55, three miles from Llandudno Junction Station. London Euston is 3 1/2 hours away, Manchester Airport is 1 1/4 hours.

For hotel location, see maps on pages 223–229

Tyddyn Llan Country House Hotel

LLANDRILLO, NR CORWEN, CLWYD LL21 0ST
TEL: 01490 440264 FAX: 01490 440414

OWNERS: Peter and Bridget Kindred

10 rms 10 ens

S: £66–£86
D: £126–£147
(including dinner)

Tyddyn Llan is an elegant Georgian country house situated amid breathtaking scenery in the Vale of Edeyrnion. Owned and run by Peter and Bridget Kindred, the hotel is a quiet oasis in an area of outstanding natural beauty at the foot of the Berwyn Mountains.

There are 10 bedrooms, all individual in style and elegantly furnished with antiques and period furniture. Each enjoys views of the gardens and the mountains beyond and has a bathroom en suite.

The hotel is proud of the reputation it has established for the quality of the food served in the restaurant. Inventive and frequently changing menus feature dishes using fresh local ingredients and herbs from the kitchen garden. A carefully selected wine list complements the cuisine. In the gardens, guests may enjoy a game of croquet and tea is served on fine days.

Places of interest nearby: The hotel has rights to 4 miles of fly-fishing on the River Dee. Keen walkers can trace the ancient Roman road, Ffordd Gam Elin, which traverses the Berwyn Mountains. Here naturalists will find many different species of birds and wild flowers. Tyddyn Llan is well placed for exploring nearby Snowdonia, and the Roman city of Chester is only 35 miles away.

Directions: Llandrillo is midway between Corwen and Bala on the B4401, 4 miles from the A5 at Corwen.

35 M

MYNYDD EDNYFED COUNTRY HOUSE HOTEL

CAERNARFON ROAD, CRICCIETH, GWYNEDD LL52 OP11
TEL: 01766 523269

OWNERS: Ian and Maureen Edwards

9 rms | 9 ens | SMALL HOTEL

S: £35
D: £56–£64

Mynydd Ednyfed offers guests a chance to stay at a 400 year old Welsh country house which is extremely comfortable and well appointed, set in seven acres of garden, woods and paddocks overlooking Tremadog Bay and Criccieth Castle. The house itself has been refurbished to a high standard with bedrooms ensuite and four poster beds available. Television, radio, direct-dial telephone and tea/coffee making facilities are standard in all rooms.

The Coach House and Tack Room have recently been converted into a well-equipped gymnasium and solarium. There is an excellent choice of home cooking using all local produce, fish and game. There is also a comfortable bar lounge to relax in before dinner.

The hotel is owned and run by Ian and Maureen Edwards. Ian was a Welsh International footballer and Maureen graduated from Birmingham College of Food as a Home Economist. They, along with their two small boys, ensure a friendly family atmosphere in this delightfully situated, WTB 4 Crowns Highly Commended country house hotel with lots to do in the area.

Places of interest nearby: Portmeirion (Italianate village), Llanystumdwy Lloyd George Museum, Ffestiniog Steam Railway, Harlech Castle, Caernarfon Castle, Starcoast Holiday World (Splashpool), Rabbit Farm Llanystumdwy, Porthmadog Pottery. **Directions: Just north of Criccieth (1½ miles) on the B4411 Caernarfon road.**

60 M

For hotel location, see maps on pages 223–229

DOLMELYNLLYN HALL

GANLLWYD, DOLGELLAU, GWYNEDD LL40 2HP
TEL: 01341 440273 FAX: 01341 440273

OWNERS: Jon Barkwith and Joanna Reddicliffe
CHEF: Joanna Reddicliffe

10 rms | 10 ens | SMALL HOTEL

S: £42.50–£55
D: £80–£110

The approach to Dolmelynllyn Hall, which is entirely non-smoking, leads through the amazing scenery of south Snowdonia, leads to a winding, beech-lined drive that brings guests to the doorway. A house has stood on the site since the 1500s, extended in the 18th and 19th centuries. Bedrooms are individually decorated and comfortably furnished. Joanna Reddicliffe, the daughter of the house, prepares a daily changing four-course menu with choices in each course including vegetarian dishes.

There is a conservatory bar, a library/writing room and a large sitting room with full-length windows overlooking the valley. Dogs are allowed in three of the bedrooms only.

The hotel is surrounded by three acres of formal gardens, bounded by a swiftly running stream which flows into a small lake. Guests can take advantage of the hotel's free fishing on 10 miles of river and three local lakes. **Places of interest nearby:** Adjoining the grounds are 1,200 acres of mountains, meadow and forest, where it is possible to walk all day without seeing a car or crossing a road. Castles, slate caverns, waterfalls and a gold mine can all be visitied nearby, but the theme here is relaxation amid wonderful surroundings, comfort and only the gentlest of activities. **Directions: Dolmelynllyn Hall is off the main A470 Dolgellau– Llandudno road, just north of Dolgellau. Dinner, bed and breakfast, combined rates and short breaks are available.**

30 M | 10

For hotel location, see maps on pages 223–229

Plâs-Glyn-y-Mêl

LOWER TOWN, FISHGUARD, PEMBROKESHIRE SA65 9LY
TEL: 01348 872296

OWNERS: Mike and Jenny Moore

5 rms | 5 ens

S: £42
D: £72

Plâs-Glyn-y-Mêl is an imposing Georgian country house situated in a glorious position just minutes from the old harbour of Lower Fishguard and nestling in the sheltered valley of the River Gwaun. It stands in 20 acres and enjoys beautiful views over garden meadows and the river. In its refurbishment, great attention was paid to ensure that the house's unique character remained unchanged.

All modern comforts are provided in harmony with the surroundings to preserve the atmosphere of the building's past. Suites offer the visitor extra space and flexibility – each suite comprises two bedrooms – one double, one twin – plus a lounge with colour TV, a kitchen/diner with all modern conveniences, and a bathroom. Breakfast is served although dinner is catered for at nearby restaurants. One within walking distance is Good Food Guide recommended (five Good Food Guide establishments are within 10 miles). The hotel can provide transport.

The splendid swimming pool is situated on the site of an old conservatory (and still covered by one) the pool offers visitors opportunites for healthy relaxation – whatever the weather.

Places of interest nearby: St David's Cathedral, Nevern Church, Preseli Mountains and the 186-mile unbroken coastal path around Pembrokeshire. **Directions: Take the A487 towards Lower Fishguard harbour, following the signpostes to Plâs-Glyn-y-Mêl.**

For hotel location, see maps on pages 223–229

STONE HALL HOTEL AND RESTAURANT

WELSH HOOK, HAVERFORDWEST, PEMBROKESHIRE, DYFED SA62 5NS
TEL: 01348 840212 FAX: 01348 840815

OWNERS: Alan and Martine Watson

4 rms | 4 ens

S: £48
D: £63

Near the lovely hamlet of Welsh Hook stands Stone Hall. The original old Pembrokshire manor house, which is over 600 years old, is characterised by slate-flagged floors and rough-hewn oak beams. The house was extended in the 17th century and notable relics from this era include wood panelling and decorative ceilings.

The building was converted into a country hotel in 1984 and great care has been taken to preserve the features and atmosphere of the various periods in its long history. Three double and two single bedrooms offer spotless and homely accommodation, with delightful views of the gardens.

The bar and restaurant are set in the oldest part of the building and, in addition, there are a comfortable residents' lounge and private dining room. Genuine French cuisine is one of the joys to be experienced at Stone Hall. Extensive à la carte and table d'hôte menus offer a generous choice of dishes accompanied by a comprehensive list of wines.

Stone Hall is set in 10 acres of sheltered gardens with lawns, shrubberies and woods. The area has plenty to interest historians, sporting enthusiasts and naturalists. Golf, fishing, sailing and riding are available nearby. Open all year.

Places of interest nearby: Wolf's Castle, the Pembrokeshire Coastal Path and St Bride's Bay. **Directions: Stone Hall is signposted off the A40. Haverfordwest–Fishguard road, approximately six miles from Fishguard.**

20 M

For hotel location, see maps on pages 223–229

BODFACH HALL COUNTRY HOUSE HOTEL

LLANFYLLIN, POWYS SY22 5HS
TEL: 01691 648272 FAX: 01691 648272

OWNERS: Ian and Ann Gray

9 rms | 9 ens | SMALL HOTEL

S: £30–£34
D: £65–£70

There has been a house on the site of Bodfach Hall since the 12th century. The earliest date on the present building is 1661 and over the past 300 years there have been alterations and additions which yet maintain the dignity and charm of the old Jacobean mansion.

The oak-panelled dining room and some fine ornamental ceilings have been preserved during the conversion into a small, traditional country house hotel, offering excellent value for money.

The setting is ideal in four acres of enchanting gardens with magnificent rhododendrums and azalias, rare shrubs and a wealth of birdlife. It is indeed a haven of peace in today's strident world.

The nine well appointed bedrooms are all on the first floor. A charming lounge is set aside for residents and there is a spacious bar with adjoining sun room and terrace.

Dinner, with classic set menus or an à la carte choice, which remembers vegetarians, is served in the Oak Room and breakfast in the east facing morning room.

Places of interest nearby: The green hills of Montgomeryshire and the craggy mountains further north provide some of the most beautifully varied scenery to explore by car or on foot. There are several golf courses nearby. Pony-trekking and fishing are also available.

Directions: Bodfach Hall is signposted off the Oswestry–Lake Vyrnwy road at the end of A490.

For hotel location, see maps on pages 223–229

Tower

OFF NERCWYS ROAD, MOLD, CLWYD CH7 4ED
TEL: 01352 700220

OWNERS: Charles and Wendy Wynne-Eyton

3 rms | 1 ens

S: £40
D: £60

The 15th century poet Hywel Cilcan referred to Tower as 'the fair Tower...a fortress twenty fathoms high'. This gives some idea of the romance and mystery surrounding this Grade I listed house, which is still owned by the original family. Robed in history, Tower stands in its own parkland beside its own lake.

The medieval dining hall, which forms the ground floor ot the tower, has a stone, barrel-vaulted ceiling in which an iron staple marks the spot from where the Mayor of Chester was hanged in 1465. With its lurid past, this is a place with plenty of character and it makes a facinating venue for lunch, dinner, special interest tours and memorable functions.

All the guest rooms have antique furnishings, paintings and porcelain which impart a sense of the past. As Tower is a family home, Charles and Wendy Wynne-Eyton are able to offer their overnight visitors a personal country house welcome.

Places of interest nearby: Chester, which is just 10 miles away, Llangollen, home of the international Eisteddford, and Conwy Castle with its walled town. The town of Mold itself is a mile away and Tower is only 45 minutes' drive from Manchester Airport. **Directions: From traffic lights in centre of Mold on A494, turn into Wrexham Street (B5444). Go ¾ mile; fork right to Nercwys; on for ½ mile. Entrance on right, through black gates.**

12 M

WATERWYNCH HOUSE HOTEL

WATERWYNCH BAY, TENBY, PEMBROKESHIRE, DYFED SA70 8TJ
TEL: 01834 842464 FAX: 01834 845076

OWNERS: Bette and Geoff Hampton

17 rms | 17 ens

S: £32–£40
D: £48–£88

With its beautiful views of the Pembrokeshire Coast National Park, Waterwynch House Hotel is a clean, homely, secluded establishment in a superlative location: built in a cove on Carmarthen Bay (also known as 'Paradise Valley'). Dating from 1820, when it was constructed as a family home by Tenby-based artist Charles Norris, Waterwynch is a quiet, intimate hotel which has cultivated a reputation for hospitality and service.

The 17 individually designed bedrooms (some with sea views, others overlooking the 27 acres of gardens) offer tea- and coffee-making facilities, colour TV and direct-dial telephone. There is also a honeymoon suite. The comfort is complemented by a sincere welcome from proprietors Bette and Geoff Hampton.

In the cosy Dining Room, an ample selection of table d'hôte and à la carte menus caters for the most discerning connoisseur. Apart from the less common specialities diners can choose from a selection of expertly crafted fish dishes accompanied by a wine from the well-chosen list. Guests may retire to the non-smoker-friendly lounge or sun lounge for post-prandial relaxation.

Places of interest nearby: superb walking along the adjacent Pembrokeshire coastal path, bird-watching, painting, fishing, golf and croquet, bowls and putting. **Directions: Off the A478 Kilgetty to Tenby road. Signposted on the left half a mile after the New Hedges roundabout.**

For hotel location, see maps on pages 223–229

PARVA FARMHOUSE AND RESTAURANT

TINTERN, CHEPSTOW, GWENT NP6 6SQ
TEL: 01291 689411 FAX: 01291 689557

OWNERS: Dereck and Vickie Stubbs

9 rms 9 ens

S: £42–£59
D: £59–£68

Standing on the peaceful northern fringe of the picturesque village of Tintern is Parva Farmhouse, a stone building built around the mid-17th century and completely refurbished in recent years. It is surrounded by wooded hillsides and provides an idyllic haven away from the pressures of the world.

The bedrooms are well furnished and offer all modern comforts as well as pretty views across the River Wye. A large, beamed lounge provides a selection of reading material and as there is no television this is an ideal place to relax away from the cares of the world – perhaps after a busy day sightseeing. There is an 'Honesty Bar' where guests may help themselves to drinks if they wish.

With its one AA Rosette, the crowning glory is the food, all home-cooked by chef-patron Dereck Stubbs. In the Inglenook Restaurant, with its intimate atmosphere, a four-course menu is served which offers something for both the adventurous diner and those with a more conservative palate.

Places of interest nearby: Offa's Dyke and Wye Valley walks are on the doorstep, while the area's rich heritage is marked by castles, old ruins and ancient monuments. Bath, Cardiff, Bristol, the Brecon Beacons and Hay-on-Wye are within an hour's drive. **Directions: Just off the A466, on the River Wye, a mile north of Tintern Abbey, on the north edge of Tintern Village.**

Drummond Castle, Perthshire

Johansens Recommended Country Houses in Scotland

*S**cotland** offers the Johansens visitor a fine choice of recommendations amid breathtaking scenery. An abundance of outdoor pursuits will challenge the adventurous, blended with the warmth and charm of traditional hospitality.*

The Scottish Borders is one of the finest introductions to the nature and character of a country. The open space of green hills and rich farming plains with their network of well established fishing rivers indicate a land blessed with good agriculture and unpolluted water.

The picturesque ruins of several abbeys bear witness to the turbulence of centuries of Border wars and religious strife focusing attention on a tapestry of history, heritage, culture and recreation.

Small towns like Kelso and Peebles unspoiled in their rural setting unveil to the visitor the timeless appeal of Scotland - breathing space, charming locations, and people friendly, spirited and generous. All this is evident at the colourful festivals of the Border Ridings hosted in many towns.

Turn north to Scotland's capital, Edinburgh, a stunningly beautiful city. Here nature's gift of volcanic rock as a site for a castle and medieval town enhanced by enlightened municipal planning of magnificent gardens and Georgian architecture has created visual splendour which has escaped the ravages of time. There is no finer stage for the world's biggest festival of arts and music. Take time for a walk in the Royal Botanic Garden renowned for its plant collection, rock garden and with a Chinese garden in the making. There are gardens of all varieties throughout Scotland.

Edinburgh is beside the River Forth close to small towns and villages which hug the coastline to the North Sea. Seaside means golf courses, all challenging and most open to visitors at reasonable cost.

St Andrews, across the Forth, has several courses to test the enthusiast. The Home of Golf it is attractive and is home also to Scotland's oldest medieval university. The Fife coast has a ribbon of former fishing villages (the East Neuk) which are delightful and charming places to relax.

The pastoral landscape is marked in the neighbouring Perthshire which gives a first glimpse of the Highlands. Through Angus to the north east and Royal Deeside and the private home of the Queen and the Royal Family at Balmoral Castle with the gardens open to the public in summer. Nearby, at the eastern end of the Cairngorm Mountains, the village of Braemar, venue for the Braemar Gathering, the best known of the Highland Games.

Sixty miles along Deeside to Aberdeen, award winning Britain in Bloom city endowed with public gardens and parks, granite architecture and wedding its ancient culture of fishing and farming to the modern oil industry. From the overnight trip to the Shetland Isles is an ideal introduction to Scotland's network of passenger and vehicle ferries, most of which operate on the west coast. They reveal a unique world of mystical, timeless experience in the Western Isles. Lewis, Harris, Uist, Skye and Mull are but a few of these magical islands.

Aberdeen is also a base to embark on the adventure of the Malt Whisky Trail in the glens of the Livet and the Spey and their many famous distilleries where a dram awaits. Excellent fishing country, too.

Leave Speyside for Aviemore, premier winter sport resort, one of five in Scotland, and then to Inverness, the Highland capital. To the north the moors and hills of Ross-shire and Sutherland, to the west, Loch Ness with its famous inhabitant. Continue down the Caledonian Canal to Fort William and Britain's highest mountain, Ben Nevis.

The tour circle includes the Pass of Glencoe en route to Glasgow. Glencoe is a climbing and ski centre and notorious in clan history for the massacre of the Macdonalds.

Glasgow has impressive art galleries and museums and a vibrant music and theatre lifestyle. Fashion is a major keynote in its extensive shopping facilities.

Head for the Borders again through Ayrshire, home of the national poet Robert Burns who died in 1796. Many will respect his Immortal Memory on the bicentenary commemoration at his mausoleum in St Michael's Kirkyard, Dumfries.

Palace of Holyroodhouse
Canongate
Edinburgh EH8 8DX
Tel: 0131 556 7371

Inveraray Jail Visitor Centre
Church Square
Inveraray PA32 8TX
Tel: 01499 302 381

Balnain House Heritage Centre
40 Hunty Street
Inverness IV3 5HR
Tel: 01463 715 757

Drummond Castle Gardens
Muthill
Crieff PH7 4HZ
Tel: 01764 681 321

New Lanark Visitor Centre
New Lanark Mills
Lanark ML11 9DB
Tel: 01555 661 345

Discovery Point
Discovery Quay
Dundee DD1 4XA
Tel: 01382 201 245

Burns House
Burns Street
Dumfries DG1 2PS
Tel: 01387 255 297

Malt Whisky Trail
Grampian Highlands and Aberdeen
Migvie House
North Silver Street
Aberdeen AB1 1RJ
Tel: 01224 632727

For more information about Scotland, please contact:-

Scottish Tourist Board
23 Ravelston Terrace
Edinburgh EH4 3EU
Tel: 0131 332 2433

Conchra House

ARDELVE, KYLE OF LOCHALSH, ROSS-SHIRE IV40 8DZ
TEL: 01599 555233 FAX: 01599 555433

OWNERS: Colin and Mary Deans

6 rms | 5 ens

S: £25–£35
D: £40–£60

Conchra, the old Gaelic word for the Fold or Haven, stands in its own grounds at the foot of Ben Conchra, looking out across Loch Long towards the village of Dornie and the famous Eilean Donan castle. The house was built in the 1760s and was once the seat and ancestral home of the Macraes of Conchra (and Eilean Donan) who extended it for use as a hunting lodge. More recently, the present proprietors have sympathetically updated and refurbished the house to convert it into a luxurious country house hotel.

The house is furnished in appropriately comfortable style and decorated, with the original pine woodwork exposed, to reflect its traditional character. Guests have their own entrance hall, a large inviting lounge, dining room and bedrooms with either en suite facilities or private bathrooms nearby.

The hospitality and management of the hotel are geared to provide a warm and friendly atmosphere. Appetising menus offer dishes cooked using fresh and locally produced meat, fish, fruit and vegetables. "Taste of Scotland" recommended.

The close proximity of the Cuillins of Skye and the Five Sisters of Kintail make the surrounding area ideal for touring, hill walking, natural history and bird watching. **Places of interest nearby:** Eilean Donan Castle and Plockton. **Directions: Off A87, eight miles from Kyle of Lochalsh near the village of Ardelve and Dornie.**

20 M

CORROUR HOUSE HOTEL

INVERDRUIE, AVIEMORE, INVERNESS-SHIRE PH22 1QH
TEL: 01479 810220 FAX: 01479 811500

OWNERS: David and Sheana Catto

8 rms | 8 ens

S: £35
D: £70

Standing in 4 acres of secluded garden and woodland, where roe deer and red squirrels are regular visitors and birdlife abounds, Corrour House is a family-run hotel built in the 19th century. Hosts David and Sheana Catto offer their guests – some who return year after year – personal service and true Highland hospitality. The hotel looks out over Rothiemurchus Forest and enjoys views of the Lairig Ghru Pass and the Cairngorms. Tastefully decorated and furnished throughout, Corrour House combines the elegance of the past with the modern comforts expected by today's visitor. The 8 bedrooms all have private facilities.

The drawing room has a cosy log fire, ample reading material and a selection of games. There is a cocktail lounge with a small bar where guests may enjoy a drink while they peruse the menu before dinner. In the dining room, the table d'hôte menu changes daily with the emphasis at all times on fresh produce, including prime Scottish beef, local game and venison, salmon and trout.

Away from the madding crowd, Corrour House is the perfect base for a Scottish holiday.

Places of interest nearby: Cairngorm Mountain chairlift; Strathspey Steam Railway; Loch Garten – home to Ospreys; Blair and Ballindalloch Castles; the Whisky Trail. **Directions: Before entering Aviemore from Kingussie, turn right to Coylumbridge (B970), hotel is then 500 yards on right.**

20 M

For hotel location, see maps on pages 223–229

BALGONIE COUNTRY HOUSE

BRAEMAR PLACE, BALLATER, ROYAL DEESIDE, ABERDEENSHIRE AB35 5RQ
TEL: 013397 55482 FAX: 013397 55482

OWNERS: John and Priscilla Finnie

9 rms | 9 ens

S: £55
D: £86–£96

In the heart of one of Scotland's most unspoilt areas, on the outskirts of the village of Ballater, lies Balgonie House. This Edwardian-style building is set within four acres of mature gardens and commands wonderful views over the local golf course towards the hills of Glen Muick beyond.

Balgonie's nine bedrooms are each named after a fishing pool on the River Dee. They are individually decorated and furnished and most offer lovely outlooks from their windows. Amenities include private bathrooms, colour television and direct-dial telephones.

At the heart of the hotel is the dining room, offering superb Scottish menus. Fresh salmon from the Dee, succulent local game, high quality Aberdeen Angus beef and seafood from the coastal fishing ports can be savoured alongside a vintage wine chosen from an excellent list. Balgonie has won the coveted Taste of Scotland Prestige Award for its cuisine.

Places of interest nearby: The village of Ballater, a five minute walk away, is a thriving community. As suppliers to the Queen, many of its shops sport Royal Warrant shields. This is an ideal centre for golf, hillwalking, sightseeing and touring. Balmoral Castle is within easy reach, as are both the Malt Whisky Trail and Castle Trail.

Directions: Upon entering Ballater from Braemar on the A93, Balgonie House is signposted on the right.

40 M

For hotel location, see maps on pages 223–229

Altamount House Hotel

COUPAR ANGUS ROAD, BLAIRGOWRIE, PERTHSHIRE PH10 6JN
TEL: 01250 873512 FAX: 01250 876200

OWNERS: Ritchie and Sue Russell

7 rms | 7 ens | SMALL HOTEL

S: £39–£50
D: £75

Altamount House is an elegant Georgian manor, built originally as a private residence in 1806. Ritchie and Sue Russell took over the premises in 1980 and converted it into a hotel that will delight the discerning traveller. The atmosphere throughout is comfortable and relaxed. Attractively furnished and decorated, the house has many fine features, including Adam fireplaces, corniced ceilings and pinewood doors and panelling. All seven bedrooms have private facilities and all the little extras one would normally find in a first-class hotel.

The hotel has established an enviable reputation for its fine Scottish cooking. The menu changes daily and all meals are based on fresh local produce. A carefully chosen wine list offers something to complement every meal. the tables are laid with silver cutlery and the finest crystal glass. The recently built Terrace Room is ideal for private dinner parties or small family celebrations. Set in six acres of lovely grounds, including extensive lawns, rose gardens and mature woodland, Altamount is the perfect setting for weddings and parties. Special early and late season rates are available. Closed from 7 January to 14 February. **Places of interest nearby:** Perth and Dundee are within easy reach by car. The River Tay for fishing, Butterstone Loch, Loch of Lowes Nature Reserve and Glamis Castle are all close by. **Directions: Altamount House is on the A92 Coupar–Angus–Blairgowrie road.**

100 M

POLMAILY HOUSE HOTEL

DRUMNADROCHIT, LOCH NESS, INVERNESS-SHIRE IV3 6XT
TEL: 01456 450343 FAX: 01456 450813

OWNERS: John and Sonia Whittington-Davies

11 rms | 11 ens | SMALL HOTEL

S: £45
D: £90–£105

The mysterious Loch Ness lies just below this stylish Edwardian house from which there are views of the slopes of Glen Urquhart and the peaks of Glen Afric. Soaring eagles, deer, wild cat and salmon abound and guests enjoy the 18 acres of garden, woodland and trout pond

A family run hotel making other families especially welcome and the safe facilities for youngsters help parents relax and appreciate their surroundings. With an indoor and outdoor play area and seperate childrens dinner, Polmaily House is unique in country house facilities for families.

The new owners are proud of their kitchen, and guests can start the day with a full Highland breakfast. Dinner, served in the spacious and elegant dining room, reflects the local game, beef, fish and garden produce stocking the larder. Carefully chosen wines are reasonably priced.

The delightful bedrooms are all en suite, with one ground floor room ideal for elderly and disabled guests. The family rooms have videos!

Places of interest nearby: On the estate there are ponies, hard tennis court and a croquet lawn. Nearby there is superb golf, skiing, fishing with tuition available, and stalking. **Directions: By car fromInverness, follow the A82 signposted to Fort William, after 16 miles at Drumnadrochit turn onto the A831 signposted to Glen Affric and the hotel is on this road after two miles.**

20 M

For hotel location, see maps on pages 223–229

ARDFILLAYNE HOUSE AND RESTAURANT

WEST BAY, DUNOON, ARGYLL PA23 7QJ
TEL: 01369 702267 FAX: 01369 702501

OWNERS: Bill and Beverley McCaffrey

7 rms | 7 ens

S: £30–£50
D: £60–£100

There is a special quality at Ardfillayne, a compact, comfortable country house set in 16 acres of natural woodland garden overlooking the Firth of Clyde. Built in 1835, Ardfillayne was originally the author's retreat of Robert Buchanan, a Glasgow University professor, better known as A. D. Fillan, writer of romantic novels about the Jacobite Rebellions of 1715 and 1745.

First-time visitors are captivated by the period charm, relaxed informal elegance and eminently Victorian style of the interiors. Fine furnishings and *objets d'art* embellish the drawing rooms, while the bedrooms are beautifully decorated with guests' comfort in mind.

The *fin de siècle* ambience of Beverley's Restaurant makes a romantic and sumptuous setting for dinner. Exceptional food, friendly service and fine wines combine to ensure that dining here is a memorable occasion. Fresh game and prime local beef feature prominently on the menu, with fish a true speciality: depending on the daily catch you might be offered a choice of halibut steak, Loch Fyne scallops, baby squid, wild salmon, lobster, sole and prawns.

Places of interest nearby: The marvellous countryside, including Argyll Forest Park, and coastline offer limitless scope to those who enjoy exploring – whether on foot, by ferry or by car. **Directions: Take the M8 to the port at Gourock; catch the ferry to Dunoon. Ardfillayne is one mile from the ferry terminal on Innellan Road.**

CULCREUCH CASTLE HOTEL

FINTRY, STIRLINGSHIRE G63 0LW
TEL: 01360 860228; FAX: 01360 860555

OWNER: Andrew Haslam

8 rms | 8 ens

S: £45–£59
D: £70–£99

Less than 20 miles from the bustle of Glasgow, Culcreuch Castle stands among the moors, lochs, glens and pinewooded wilds of Stirlingshire, close to Loch Lomond. Built in 1296, this grand ancestral seat of the once-feared Galbraith clan today overlooks 1,600 acres of superb parkland between the Campsie Fells and the Fintry Hills.

The owners, the Haslams, have renovated Culcreuch as a first-class country hotel while preserving its august past in antiques, oil paintings and old, worn steps. All eight bedrooms are en suite, some with four-poster beds. Their names – The Barons' Suite, The Keep Room, or The Speirs' Room – help piece together the Castle's history.

Stay a night in the Chinese Bird Room, with its 18th century hand-painted wallpaper. After dark the Phantom Piper sometimes roams and plays. Dinner prepared by chef James Walker is served by candlelight in the panelled dining room; a three-course meal prepared from fresh, local produce costs £20, and there is a cellar of fine wines. Self-catering accommodation is also available.

Places of interest nearby: Fishing, walking in the Endrick Valley, visiting Loch Lomond, the village of Fintry, and Stirling, to the east. Glasgow and Edinburgh airports are a 55 minute drive. **Directions: Exit M9 junction 10. A84 east towards Stirling. First right, first right and then join A811. Go 10 miles west to junction with B822 at Kippen. Turn left, go via Kippen to Fintry.**

25 16

For hotel location, see maps on pages 223–229

KNOCKOMIE HOTEL

GRANTOWN ROAD, FORRES, MORAY IV36 0SG
TEL: 01309 673146 FAX: 01309 673290

OWNERS: The Ellis Family

14 rms | 14 ens | SMALL HOTEL

S: £45–£59
D: £70–£99
Suite: £160

Secluded in pretty gardens at the end of a quiet drive, Knockomie is a listed building, part of which dates back 150 years and part from the Arts and Crafts period. The house is run by Gavin Ellis, an enthusiastic host who always aims to provide the best for his guests, whether their stay is for business or relaxation. The restaurant specialises in good Scottish cooking using innovative menus making excellent use of the abundant supply of seafood and game: choices might include roast langoustines with chives, poached angler fish with a sauce of fresh mussels, or fried lamb steak in a fresh herb sauce. In addition to the extensive wine list, over 70 malt whiskies are kept behind the bar.

The en suite bedrooms are individually furnished and decorated. Some bedrooms are on the ground floor. Private and business functions are well provided for, with three rooms for conferences, meetings and dinner parties.

Guests can play croquet or boules on the lawn. Shooting, stalking, fishing, riding, falconry and golf can be arranged and, if desired, incorporated in advance into a special holiday package.

Places of interest nearby: Cawdor Castle, Fort George, Pluscarden Abbey, Brodie Castle and the Whisky Trail.

Directions: One mile south of Forres on the A940.

40 M

CULDEARN HOUSE

WOODLANDS TERRACE, GRANTOWN-ON-SPEY, MORAY PH26 3JU
TEL: 01479 872106 FAX: 01479 873641

OWNERS: Alasdair and Isobel Little

9 rms | 9 ens

S: £49.50
D: £99
(including dinner)

Scottish proprietors Alasdair and Isobel Little delight in maintaining a distinctive Scottish atmosphere at Culdearn House, a family house built over 100 years ago by an admirer of granite stone, wood panelling and fine moulded ceilings. The guest rooms have been sympathetically modernised and decorated to offer every comfort, while the dining room and lounge have fine marble fireplaces which burn logs and peat when appropriate.

Freshly prepared food, using local produce whenever possible, is a feature of the house. The fare includes soups, pâtés, venison, beef, lamb, salmon and trout – all complemented by a modestly priced wine list.

Culdearn House is Highly Acclaimed by the RAC and is one of only ten in Scotland to be Premier Selected by the AA. The Scottish Tourist Board has awarded Culdearn the top rating of de luxe whilst the quality of food is recognised in the Taste of Scotland guide.

Three and seven day breaks are available and all rates include dinner. The hotel is closed from 1 November to 28 February.

Places of interest nearby: A wealth of castles and historic sites including Cawdor and Brodie Castles, Culloden and the famous Osprey reserve. Golf and salmon fishing can be arranged. **Directions: The house stands some 50 yards from the A95 road at the south west entrance to Grantown-on-Spey.**

For hotel location, see maps on pages 223–229

Culduthel Lodge

14 CULDUTHEL ROAD, INVERNESS, INVERNESS-SHIRE IV2 4AG
TEL: 01463 240089

OWNERS: David and Marion Bonsor

12 rms | 12 ens | SMALL HOTEL

S: £42
D: £70–£74

This beautifully appointed hotel, just a few minutes walk from the town centre, is a Grade II Georgian residence set in its own grounds and offering splendid views of the River Ness and surrounding countryside. Great emphasis is placed on providing good food, comfort and a quiet, friendly atmosphere.

On arrival in their rooms, guests are greeted with fresh fruit, flowers and a small decanter of sherry. Each bedroom is individually decorated and furnished to a high standard of comfort and provides every modern amenity including a CD/cassette player.

Delicious, freshly prepared food is offered by a table d'hôte menu which offers choices at each course, including Scottish fare and local produce. A carefully selected range of wines is available to complement the cuisine.

Places of interest nearby: Inverness is a good base for guests wishing to tour the Highlands and the north and west coasts. The Isle of Skye, Royal Deeside and the splendours of the Spey Valley are within a day's travel.

Directions: Take the B851 out of Inverness. Culduthel Road is a continuation of Castle Street and the Lodge is less than half a mile from the city centre on the right.

For hotel location, see maps on pages 223–229

ARDVOURLIE CASTLE

AIRD AMHULAIDH, ISLE OF HARRIS, WESTERN ISLES HS3 3AB
TEL: 01859 502307

OWNER: Derek Martin

4 rms

S: £65–£70
D: £130–£140
(including dinner)

Despite its name, this was a hunting lodge built in 1863 by the Earl of Dunmore now restored recently to its full glory. Some rooms have gas and oil lamps, and fire-grates from the original period: mahogany-panelled baths with brass fittings add to the luxurious setting. With just four guest rooms, visitors are guaranteed a warm welcome and personal service from brother and sister team Pamela and Derek Martin. Each room has a private bathroom.

The castle stands on the shores of Loch Seaforth: further on are the sandy beaches of the west coast and the rocky wilderness of South Harris. Otters and seals frequent the bay and golden eagles can be seen over the hills.

The menu at Ardvourlie is based upon local produce wherever possible, including salmon, trout, island lamb, Scottish cheeses and Stornaway oatcakes. Vegetarian meals are available by arrangement. The food is Taste of Scotland Michelin and *Ackerman Guide* recommended. Ardvourlie Castle has a residents' licence and a self-service bar.

Places of interest nearby: Hill-walking (it is advisable to bring suitable clothing), Isle of Skye, Lewis, Barra and North and South Uist. Salmon and trout fishing on Harris. **Directions: The castle stands on the shores of Loch Seaforth 24 miles from Stornaway and 10 miles from Tarbert.**

For hotel location, see maps on pages 223–229

KILLIECHRONAN

KILLIECHRONAN, ISLE OF MULL, ARGYLL PA72 6JU
TEL: 01680 300403 FAX: 01680 300463

OWNERS: Mr and Mrs J. Leroy
MANAGERS: Margaret and Patrick Freytag

6 rms 6 ens

S: £70–£85
D: £54–£65

An original Highland lodge, built in 1846, now a superb country house hotel, ideally located at the head of Loch na Keal. The owners already have an established reputation in Scotland with The Manor House Hotel at Oban and The Lake Hotel at Port of Menteith.

This, their third hotel, is their own family home and contains a magnificent collection of antiques and pictures. Most of the rooms face South, overlooking the sheltered grounds, part of the 5,000 acre estate.

Bringing the chef from the Manor House has ensured those high standards in the restaurant that one associates with the Leroy family and there is a fine wine list to complement the menu.

There are just six bedrooms, all en suite, with telephone and other modern comforts.

The area is renowned for its outstanding beauty. Visit Fingal's Cave, the white beach at Calgary, Duart Castle, the herring village of Tobermory and Torosay set in Italianate gardens. There is fishing, sailing, golf, pony treking and a fairly easy walk to the summit of Ben More.

Directions: Mull is reached by the ferry from Oban or Lochalin. Then go via Salen.

In association with MasterCard

HARLOSH HOUSE

BY DUNVEGAN, ISLE OF SKYE IV55 8ZG
TEL: 01470 521367 FAX: 01470 521367

OWNERS: Peter and Lindsey Elford

6 rms | 5 ens

S: £44–£65
D: £68–£90

Harlosh House, once known as Balmore House, stands on a small peninsula of land jutting out into Loch Bracadale and is one of north west Skye's oldest buildings. It was built in 1750, probably as a tackman's house, and became a hotel in the early 1970s.

The hotel's bedrooms vary in size, but all are newly and tastefully decorated and provide every modern comfort. Most enjoy lovely views of the loch and surrounding countryside.

In the restaurant, which has been awarded two AA Rosettes, the dishes served make full use of good Scottish produce, with an emphasis on local fish and shellfish. Meticulous attention is paid to detail and the breads, soups, desserts and chocolates are all homemade.

With its stunning views of the Cuillin Hills, this hotel is a perfect setting for guests seeking peace. Aided by the lounge telescope, a patient guest may be lucky enough to observe otters, eagles, seals and other fascinating wildlife. Riding, fishing, boat trips and an inexhaustible supply of wonderful scenic walks are all in the locality.

The house is closed from mid October until Easter.

Places of interest nearby: Harlosh is within reach of many historic sites, craft shops, galleries and museums. **Directions: A few miles south of Dunvegan on the A863, between Roag and Caroy, Harlosh is signposted via a minor road. Follow this road for about two miles.**

For hotel location, see maps on pages 223–229

THE KILLIECRANKIE HOTEL

KILLIECRANKIE, BY PITLOCHRY, PERTHSHIRE PH16 5LG
TEL: 01796 473220 FAX: 01796 472451

OWNERS: Colin and Carole Anderson

10 rms | 10 ens

S: £46–£50
D: £92–£100

The Killiecrankie Hotel is peacefully situated in four acres of landscaped gardens overlooking the Pass of Killiecrankie and River Garry. It was here, in 1689, that the Jacobites clashed with William of Orange's army in a battle to gain supremacy over the crowns of England and Scotland – an event which illustrates the area's rich heritage.

Guests will find a friendly welcome and a relaxed, informal atmosphere. There are 10 charming bedrooms, including one suite, all comfortably furnished and decorated to a high standard. There is a residents' sitting room on the first floor.

With two AA Rosettes for food, the restaurant has a very good reputation. Fresh ingredients indigenous to Scotland are used wherever possible and are presented with panache. Menus offer a good, balanced choice: start perhaps with a slice of Arbroath smokie mousse & smoked trout terrine, before going to a main course such as steamed silver bream with straw vegetables and citrus segments or braised pigeon filled with venison and rosemary forcemeat in white wine sauce. In the bar and sun-lounge a superb range of bar meals is served. Closed 3 January to early March. Excellent value Spring/Autumn breaks available.

Places of interest nearby: Blair Castle, Pitlochry Festival Theatre and numerous opportunities for golfing, fishing, shooting and hill-walking. **Directions: Turn off the main A9 Perth to Inverness at sign for Killiecrankie.**

WELL VIEW HOTEL

BALLPLAY ROAD, MOFFAT, DUMFRIESSHIRE DG10 9JU
TEL: 01683 220184

OWNERS: John and Janet Schuckardt

6 rms | 6 ens

S: £35–£44
D: £52–£78

This delightful Victorian house on the edge of Moffat has been in excellent hands for the last ten years – the host being elected to the Academy of Wine Service and the hostess a member of the Craft Guild of Chefs, giving master classes on special occasions.

Guests enjoy an apéritif and canapé in the elegant lounge while studying the menu, or, after dinner, relax with homemade sweets accompanying the coffee – and, may be, an excellent malt whisky. Dinner, in the charming, non-smoking, dining room, is five courses – including a sorbet – cooked with great flair and beautifully presented. Vegetarian dishes are available by prior request. The Cellar holds many fine wines from all parts of the world.

The bedrooms are all en suite and extremely comfortable, reflecting the high standards of hospitality throughout the hotel.

Places of interest nearby: Moffat is surrounded by mountains: Glasgow is reached over Beattock Summit, Edinburgh over the Devil's Beef Tub. St Mary's Loch and the Border Abbeys are also within driving distance.

Directions: Moffat is three miles from the M74/A74 trunk road between Carlisle and Glasgow. Pass the centre of the town on A708 (Selkirk) and turn left at crossroads into Ballplay Road. The hotel is a short distance on the right.

THE MANOR HOUSE HOTEL

GALLANACH ROAD, OBAN, ARGYLL PA34 4LS
TEL: 01631 562087 FAX: 01631 563053

OWNERS: Mr and Mrs J.L. Leroy

11 rms | 11 ens

S: £45–£79
D: £87–£155
(including dinner)

Late Georgian in style, The Manor House was built in 1780 as the principal residence of the Duke of Argyll's Oban estate and later became a dower house. Today it is a hotel where great consideration has been taken to preserve the elegance of its bygone days. The Manor House Hotel occupies a prime position overlooking Oban Bay, the adjacent islands and the mountains of Movern and Mull.

In the dining room guests can enjoy a fine blend of Scottish and French cooking, with an emphasis on local seafood and game in season. The table d'hôte menus take pride of place and are changed daily to offer a choice of starters, intermediate fish course or soup, home-made sorbet, choice of main courses, choice of puddings, and to round off, coffee and mints. The restaurant menu is partnered by a cellar of wines and selection of malt whiskies.

The bedrooms have twin or double beds, all with en suite bathrooms, TV and tea-making facilities. The Manor House Hotel is quietly located on the outskirts of Oban, yet within easy walking distance of the town. Special mini-breaks are available for stays of two nights or more. Closed in January.

Places of interest nearby: Oban is Scotland's main ferry port for trips to the Western Isles and the many day tours are a splendid way of discovering this beautiful area.

Directions: The Manor House Hotel is situated on the western outskirts of Oban beyond the ferry boat pier.

For hotel location, see maps on pages 223–229

Dupplin Castle

DUPPLIN ESTATE, BY PERTH, PERTHSHIRE PH2 OPY
TEL: 01738 623224 FAX: 01738 444140

OWNERS: Derek and Angela Straker

4 rms | 4 ens

S:£60
D: ££90

Dupplin, a rare mid-20th century Scottish Mansion, stands in 30 acres of private parkland, with sweeping lawns and mature woodlands. The original ediface was razed by fire and its 19th century successor was replaced by the current building, completed in 1969, to the design of one of Scotland's leading architects, Schomber Scott. The Castle has now been upgraded to the comfort and luxury expected of today's discerning guests.

The original castle's balustraded terrace and rose garden remain and the impressive landscaping, of some antiquity, offers panoramic views south over the lovely River Earn valley to the hills beyond.

The luxurious bedrooms are individually appointed, with en suite facilities, and the gracious reception rooms are elegantly furnished with fine antiques, paintings and books, creating an atmosphere of a bygone era of tranquillity and elegance.

Dinner is served house-party style, with all guests seated round the dining room table. Scottish country house cuisine is complemented by informal but highly efficient and friendly service.

Shooting, Roe-stalking, fishing and golf are all within easy reach and available by prior arrangement.

Places of interest nearby: Scone Palace, Perth, the ancient capital of Scotland. Both Edinburgh and Glasgow are just an hour's drive away. **Directions: Please contact the Castle.**

en famille | 20 M | 12

CRAIGMHOR LODGE

27 WEST MOULIN ROAD, PITLOCHRY, PERTHSHIRE PH16 5EF
TEL: 01796 472123 FAX: 01796 472123

OWNER: Sandra Wallace Hutton

9 rms | 9 ens | SMALL HOTEL

S: £50–£65
D: £80–£115
(including dinner)

Reaching this charming Victorian lodge over a small bridge crossing the Moulin Burn, adjacent to a pond with ducks and herons, prepares guests for the delights of this small hotel with its two acres of private grounds overlooking the Tummel Valley.

The reception rooms include an elegant lounge with an Adam fireplace, a mahogany panelled bar stocking over 60 malt whiskies and the stylish restaurant, with its splendid views of the hills, presided over by the talented chef, who creates the finest of cuisine with flair and imagination from only the freshest of Scottish produce which is accompanied by fine wines.

The attractive bedrooms of individual character, some in the garden cottage, are all en suite with bath and shower, centrally heated, and equipped with tea/coffee trays and colour TV. Accommodation for disabled guests is available, with easy access to the public rooms and ground floor bedrooms. Throughout their stay, guests will value the professional service offered by the young and well trained staff ensuring Highland hospitality at its best

Places of interest nearby: Pitlochry has its own theatre. Golf, fishing, riding and water sports can be arranged. Within reasonable distance are Blair Castle, Balmoral, Aviemore, Speyside Whisky Trail and St Andrews.

Directions: A9 to Pitlochry, take A924 towards Moulin and Braemar. Hotel is 800 yards uphill on left.

30 M

For hotel location, see maps on pages 223–229

DUNFALLANDY HOUSE

LOGIERAIT ROAD, PITLOCHRY, PERTHSHIRE PH16 5NA
TEL: 01796 472648 FAX: 01796 472017

OWNERS: Michael and Jane Bardsley

8 rms | 8 ens

S: £37–£42
D: £50–£60

Dunfallandy House is a secluded Georgian Mansion House built in 1790 and now lovingly restored and converted into a fine small Country House Hotel.

In an elevated position, in three and a half acres of grounds, within the Dunfallandy Estate, surrounded by the splendour of the Tummel Valley it stands above the highland town of Pitlochry. The House retains many historic features, yet it has all been sympathetically modernised to provide year round comfort including central heating.

The bedrooms are designed and furnished to a high standard. All double/twin rooms have en-suite shower/bath, toilet and washbasin. Some have four-poster beds. All are equipped with colour televisions, clock radios, tea and coffee making facilities, hairdryers and trouser presses.

Full Scottish or light continental breakfasts are served in the Georgian dining room, where guests can later enjoy a delicious dinner – vegetarian dishes available. Relax in front of the open fire in the Green Room, where you may select a good book and enjoy a fine malt whisky from the oak-panelled bar.

Places of interest nearby: Golf, fishing, shooting and riding. Pitochry Theatre and the famous salmon ladder.

Directions: From Pitlochry take road signposted Pitlochry Festival Theatre, cross river, turn left on road signposted Dunfallandy, hotel is 500 yards on the right.

16

For hotel location, see maps on pages 223–229

The Lake Hotel

PORT OF MENTEITH, PERTHSHIRE FK8 3RA
TEL: 01877 385258 FAX: 01877 385671

OWNERS: Mr and Mrs Leroy

12 rms | 12 ens | SMALL HOTEL

S: £55–£85
D: £88–£165
(including dinner)

The Lake Hotel is set in a splendid sheltered position on the banks of the Lake of Menteith in the Trossachs. Its lawn runs down to the edge of the lake, which in winter months often freezes over. When this happens, it is not unusual for locals to bring out their skates for a skim over the ice.

Guests are assured of all the amenities of an STB 4 Crown hotel when they visit. A thorough programme of refurbishment has recently been completed, so the interiors have fresh decoration and new furnishings. All of the bedrooms have en suite facilities, and all the small details that will make your stay much more comfortable. There is an elegant lounge and a large conservatory from which the vista of lake and mountains is stunning.

The à la carte and table d'hôte menus present a varied choice of imaginatively prepared dishes. The table d'hôte menus are particularly good value: start with Stilton and leek quiche, followed by sorbet, then, after a main course of stuffed breast of guinea fowl with onion marmalade, red wine and shallot sauce, enjoy a crème brûlée before your coffee and home-made petits fours. Special rates are available for mini-breaks of two nights or more.

Places of interest nearby: Inchmahome Priory – haven for both Mary, Queen of Scots and Robert the Bruce – Loch Lomond and Stirling Castle. **Directions: Situated on the A81 road, south of Callander and east of Aberfoyle, on the northern banks of the Lake of Menteith.**

30 M

SCIBERSCROSS LODGE

STRATH BRORA, ROGART, SUTHERLAND IV28 3YQ
TEL: 01408 641246 FAX: 01408 641465

OWNERS: Peter and Kate Hammond

7 rms | 5 ens

S: £85
D: £170
(fully inclusive)

This classic Victorian Highland Sporting Lodge, built in 1876 for the Duke of Sutherland, is an ideal base for anyone keen on fishing, stalking, shooting or walking through the magnificent countryside of heathered hills. Period furniture, family portraits and a warm welcome make for a convivial atmosphere. Guests will find their bedrooms comfortably furnished, with thoughtful extras. Sciberscross is owned and personally run by Peter and Kate Hammond.

Indulge yourself with a hearty Scottish breakfast before setting out for your day. The five-course dinner, including aperitifs, accompanying wines, ports and liqueurs, makes the most of local produce including smoked salmon, the finest Rogart lamb and a selection of delicious local cheeses.

Sciberscross has its own boats on salmon and sea trout lochs and on hill lochs for wild brown trout; local rivers also offer good salmon fishing. There are riding facilities locally. Shooting and stalking are available on nearby estates. Three golf courses including Royal Dornoch are close by. Dogs accommodated by arrangement. Closed December and January. Taste of Scotland Recommended.

Places of interest nearby: Dunrobin Castle, woollen mills and distilleries. **Directions: Take the A9 over Dornoch Firth Bridge. After ten miles, at Mound, turn left onto A839. After four miles you arrive in Rogart: turn right opposite war memorial on to the Balnacoil road, Sciberscross Lodge is seven miles on.**

en famille

For hotel location, see maps on pages 223–229

St Patrick's Cathedral, Dublin

Johansens Recommended Country Houses in Ireland

Celtic treasures and legends, medieval architecture, racecourses and golf courses, great art collections and a richness of literature are found amongst the green landscapes of Ireland.

Ireland today is not just the popular holiday location it has always been; it has now achieved the status of being Europe's fastest growing visitor destination and the graph continues to rise. The traditional, the cosmopolitan and the 'state-of-the-art' have been successfully combined, with nothing sacrificed to impersonal efficiency. The Irish welcome remains the same.

So much of Ireland's history is preserved in the architecture and ancient monuments of many of the towns and villages around the country that an umbrella body has been formed to assist the visitor in achieving the most comprehensive experience during a visit. Heritage Towns of Ireland has already designated 30 centres as of outstanding historic interest, and modern interpretative facilities have been provided in each to tell its story dramatically as well as entertainingly.

Dublin, the capital, is of modest size with a history spanning over a thousand years and is a centre of infinite variety and interest. The National Gallery houses Ireland's foremost collection of paintings, including works by Rembrandt, Reynolds, El Greco and Goya. The Royal Hospital Kilmainham and the Municipal Art Gallery in Dublin also have extensive collections of great quality. The Chester Beatty Library has some of the rarest oriental manuscripts in existence. The National Cathedral of St Patrick, where Jonathan Swift was once the Dean and now lies buried, maintains a choir school providing the great church's music continuously since 1492.

Arthur Guinness launched his now world-renowned black brew in Dublin in 1759. The tradition flourishes today and visitors are welcome to St James's Gate to explore the history and, of course, to sample the product. Not to be outdone, the Irish Whiskey Corner at Bow Street Distillery also welcomes visitors to learn the process and sample 'Uisge Beatha – the Water of Life'.

For the classical music lover, the National Concert Hall and the Royal Dublin Society offer a full range of recitals and concerts featuring the best of Irish and international talent.

Both Siamsa Tire – the National Folk Theatre of Ireland in Tralee, Co Kerry, and Bru Boru Heritage Centre in Cashel, Co Tipperary, are especially worth a visit for their interpretation in music, song and dance of the Irish folk tradition.

Heritage Towns of Ireland
92 Sandymount Road
Sandymount Village
Dublin 4
Tel: 00 353 1 668 9688

Irish Distillers Group Limited
Irish Whiskey Corner
Bow Street Distillery
Dublin 7
Tel: 00 353 1 872 5566

For more information about Ireland, please contact:

The Irish Tourist Board
Bord Failte
Baggot Street Bridge
Dublin 2
Tel: 00 353 1 676 5871

Northern Ireland is different. In an area which covers only one-sixth of the island of Ireland, the six counties of Ulster combine to present a wealth of unspoilt beauty, breathtaking coastlines, some of the best fishing in Ireland and a welcome that is second to none.

In addition, each county spreads its own rich tapestry of historical and scenic beauty. On uncongested roads the visitor can explore a varied landscape that changes from county to county. From the famous Giant's Causeway in Co. Antrim, to Benone Strand, the longest beach in Ireland in Co. Londonderry, and the lakeland landscape of Co. Fermanagh to 'Where the Mountains of Mourne Sweep Down to the Sea' in Co. Down.

The nature of the landscape provides the visitor with a feast of beauty and a superb environment for such activities as golf, fishing, walking, water sports, horse-riding and hire-cruising. For those whose interests lie in more leisurely pursuits, a varied cultural life is easily accessible by way of established theatres, museums, visitor and interpretative centres.

Belfast's most prestigious theatre is the Grand Opera House, a wonderful elaborate confection designed by Frank Matcham with a somewhat oriental theme celebrates its centenary in December 1995 with a year-long programme of special events planned, including two seasons of opera from Opera Northern Ireland in the spring and autumn.

Opera lovers are also well served by the annual season at Castleward. Taking place in mid-summer, this highly rated company presents its operas in the beautiful surroundings of a 700 acre National Trust country estate on the shores of Strangford Lough. Ariadne auf Naxos by Richard Strauss and Puccini's La Bohème are planned for the 1996 season.

Recent history may have obscured the essential character of Northern Ireland but nothing can eliminate the inherent friendliness of the people and the unique beauty of the surroundings.

Giant's Causeway Centre
44 Causeway Road
Bushmills BT57 8SU
Tel: 012657 31855

National Trust
Belfast Shop
86 Botanic Avenue
Belfast BT7 1JR
Tel: 01232 230018

For more information about Northern Ireland, please contact:-

Northern Ireland Tourist Board
St Anne's Court
59 North Street
Belfast BT1 1NB
Tel: 01232 246609

In association with MasterCard

KINNITTY CASTLE

BIRR, CO OFFALY, IRELAND
TEL: 0509 37318 FAX: 0509 37284

OWNER: Cornelius Ryan
MANAGING DIRECTOR: Matt Connolly
CHEF: Declan Leonard

15 rms | 15 ens

S: £80
D: £120

Kinnitty Castle is located just outside the picturesque village of Kinnitty and nestles amid the beautiful forested Slieve Bloom mountains. This neogothic style castellated mansion offers luxurious accommodation and a wonderfully peaceful environment in which to relax and unwind.

The spacious restaurant, which features period furniture and an open hearth fire, serves excellent cuisine. In addition to the restaurant there are two private dining rooms, both of which can seat up to ten persons.

The old estate encompasses 10,000 acres which are directly accessible from the Castle. Guests are invited to wander through the unspoilt woodland and lose themselves in the peace and tranquillity of their surroundings. Equestrian holidays are a speciality and activities include tuition, trekking and trailing. Walking and clay pigeon shooting are also available and fishing expeditions can be arranged by the Castle. A transfer service is organised for guests wishing to take advantage of the weekend golfing trips.

Places of interest nearby: Featured among the many attractions in the area are The Old Mill at Cadamstown, St Finbars Abbey, Kinnitty Cross, Ashbrook Open Farm, Lockes Distillery and Birr Castle Demesne, the world famous gardens of the countess of Rosse. **Directions: About 80 miles west of Dublin just off N7, halfway between Port Laoise and Limerick.**

For hotel location, see maps on pages 223–229

BEECH HILL

23 BALLYMONEY ROAD, CRAIGANTLET, NEWTOWNARDS BT23 4TG
TEL: 01232 425892 FAX: 01232 425892

OWNER: Victoria Brann

3 rms | 3 ens

S: £25–£45
D: £45–£90

This lovely Georgian style house is set in the peaceful Holywood Hills, 15 minutes from Belfast city airport, 20 minutes from the Seacat dock and 45 minutes from Aldergrove International Airport.

The bedrooms are all on the ground floor, with panoramic views over the beautiful North Down countryside. They are furnished with antique furniture, and the beds are made up with fine Irish linen. All have en suite bathrooms, colour televisions, radios, tea/coffee making facilities, hairdryers and electric blankets.

Start the day with a full Irish or continental breakfast served in the spacious conservatory overlooking the croquet lawn.

Accommodation is offered on a bed-and-breakfast basis; dinner can be provided by arrangement. Fax/phone and use of a word processor are available on request.
Places of interest nearby: Mount Stewart House and Gardens (NT), Rowllane Gardens (NT), Castle Espie Wildlife and Wetlands Centre, Holywood Priory, Bangor Marina, Somme Heritage Centre, Dundonald Motte and Greyabbey with its herb garden and antique centre. Many golf courses, equestrian centres and country walks.
Directions: Leave Belfast for Bangor on A2, bypass Holywood, 1½ miles from bridge at Ulster Folk Museum turn right up Ballymoney Road signed Craigantlet. Beech Hill is 1¾ miles on left.

For hotel location, see maps on pages 223–229

CASTLE GROVE COUNTRY HOUSE

RAMELTON ROAD, LETTERKENNY, CO DONEGAL
TEL: 074 51118 FAX: 074 51384

OWNER: Mary J. Sweeny

8 rms | 8 ens

S: IR£45
D: IR£60–IR£90

This elegant Georgian House, reached by a mile long avenue through parkland, is in a sheltered position with a spectacular view of Lough Swilly.

True Irish hospitality is offered at this family-owned country residence with its gracious reception rooms, the charming drawing room looking out on the extensive grounds. There is a separate television room.

The dining room is very popular with the people who live in the neighbourhood so reservations are necessary. The succulent dishes offered on the extensive menu reflecting the marvellous local produce – especially the fish – all served in great style accompanied by wines from a list of the highest calibre. Small corporate lunches are a speciality.

The bedrooms are spacious, all recently refurbished and equipped with modern necessities.

Donegal is famous for its white sand beaches and clean seas. The scenery is superb along the coast roads and in the mountains. Glenveagh National Park is fascinating, with its castle and famous gardens. One can meet Derek Hill at his fine Art Gallery at Churchill. Activities nearby include golf, fishing (lake, river and deep sea). Rough and walked up shoots are available throughout the season. Riding can be arranged on request. **Directions: Castle Grove is three miles from Letterkenny, off the N17 (Knock to Sligo).**

25 M 5

For hotel location, see maps on pages 223–229

BELCAMP HUTCHINSON

BALGRIFFIN, DUBLIN 17
TEL: 01 846 0843 FAX: 01 848 5703

OWNERS: Doreen Gleeson and Karl Waldburg

6 rms | 6 ens

S: IR£36
D: IR£72

Belcamp Hutchinson is a Georgian house, built primarily as a family home for its original owner, Francis Hely Hutchinson, 3rd Earl of Donoughmore. Its present owner, Count Waldburg, has taken tremendous care to preserve its simple beauty during its recent refurbishment.

Today's country mansion features many ornate characteristics, retained from a bygone era. Its generously sized rooms, with high ceilings and lovely décor, offer the most up-to-date facilities.

After a leisurely stroll in the delightful grounds of the house, guests are invited to relax in the drawing room with a pre-dinner drink. Well cooked and beautifully presented meals are served in the old family dining room. The proprietors are warm and enthusiastic hosts.

The nearby village offers visitors golf, tennis, riding and sailing. There are a variety of up-market restaurants, local inns and some fine shops.

Places of interest nearby: The fishing village of Howth, Howth Castle, Malahide Castle, Newbridge House, Newgrange, Botanic Gardens and the Casino Marino.

Directions: 20 minutes drive north of Dublin on Malahide road, 15 minutes from the airport.

en famille | 20 M

In association with MasterCard

St David's Country House and Restaurant

PUCKANE, NENAGH, CO TIPPERARY
TEL: 353 67 24145 FAX: 353 67 24388

OWNERS: Bernhard Klotz, Rätus Gassner and Coni Largiader

9 rms | 9 ens | SMALL HOTEL

S: IR£80–£100
D: IR£90–£150

St David's, a former fishing lodge, is situated in a beautiful and quiet location on the shores of Lough Derg in the heart of Ireland. Surrounded by 17 acres of parkland and overlooking the lake, it offers its guests an oasis of luxury and comfort. A warm welcome and excellent service are guaranteed. The gardens and house have recently been renovated by the owners.

There are nine prettily decorated and homely bedrooms, all of which are individually furnished to the highest standards; the views from the bedrooms are beautiful,some face the water, others face the gardens. The public rooms are graced with lovely paintings and an abundance of cut flowers.

A four-course dinner menu is prepared by a chef who can produce dishes to suit all tastes and there is a good choice of wines ranging in price from £14 to £100. Lunch is not available, but picnic hampers can be provided on request.

There is no shortage of leisurely activities in the vicinity and these include boating on the lake, fishing and walking. The house is closed for two months from January 15 to March 15.

Places of interest nearby: Nenagh Heritage Town, Roscrea Damer House, Portumna Castle. Five golf courses are within easy reach of St David's. Riding, fishing and water sports can be enjoyed nearby. **Directions: From Nenagh Town take direction Borrisokane to Puckane. St David's is signposted from there on.**

35 M

For hotel location, see maps on pages 223–229

EDENVALE HOUSE

130 PORTAFERRY ROAD, NEWTOWNARDS, NORTHERN IRELAND BT22 2AH
TEL: 01247 814881

OWNERS: Diane and Gordon Whyte

3 rms | 3 ens

S: £30–£35
D: £45–£50

This pretty Georgian house is peacefully situated on the Ards peninsula, with spectacular views across the beautiful Strangford Lough to the Mourne mountains. It is well set back from a quiet road, surrounded by seven acres of garden and paddock, with a National Trust wildfowl reserve opposite its gate.

A warm and friendly Irish welcome awaits arrivals as they enter the house, which has been thoughtfully restored and modernised without it losing its character. The en suite and well-equipped bedrooms overlook the superb countryside.

Breakfasts here will not be forgotten – as well as the traditional dishes, guests can feast on hot homemade bread, fried potato bread, hot fruit compote and cream! They return in the afternoon to tea and scones. Other meals can be arranged, or enjoyed in one of many recommended and reasonably priced restaurants in the vicinity. **Places of interest nearby:** Visitors relax playing croquet on the lawn, or trying the nine golf courses within easy driving distance. Other local activities include sailing, windsurfing, riding, sea fishing and birdwatching. Close by are the Greyabbey Cisterican Abbey, Scrabo Tower, Mount Stewart House (N.T), Ulster Folk Museum and Castle Espie Wildlife and Wetlands Centre. **Directions: Leave Belfast for Newtownards and Edenvale is two miles along the A20 Portaferry Road.**

12 M

PORTAFERRY, Co Down (Northern Ireland)

In association with MasterCard

PORTAFERRY HOTEL

THE STRAND, PORTAFERRY, CO DOWN BT22 1PE
TEL: 012477 28231 FAX: 012477 28999

OWNERS: John and Marie Herlihy

14 rms | 14 ens | SMALL HOTEL

S: £50
D: £89

The welcome that awaits guests to Portaferry Hotel is in the best traditions of Irish hospitality. The original terrace which now forms the Portaferry dates back to the mid-18th century. Recent extensions have been carried out with great care to preserve the unique character of this charming waterside hostelry.

The hotel's superbly appointed bedrooms are individually styled and many have attractive views of Strangford Lough. A good range of facilities is available to ensure maximum comfort and convenience.

Diners in the AA Rosette award-winning restaurant can enjoy an abundance of freshly caught prawns, turbot, brill, sole, scallops, lobster and mussels. The hotel enjoys an international reputation for its seafood, landed daily. Also available is the best Ulster beef, Mourne lamb and game from neighbouring estates.

Places of interest nearby: Within easy reach are the National Trust properties at Castleward and Mount Stewart; Castle Espie Wildfowl and Wetlands Centre; the Northern Ireland Aquarium; the heritage town of Downpatrick, the Mountains of Mourne and the world renowned Royal County Down golf course. **Directions: From Belfast via Newtownards, Greyabbey and Kircubbin (A20). From Newry via Castlewellan, Downpatrick and Strangford (A25).**

For hotel location, see maps on pages 223–229

Coopershill House

RIVERSTOWN, CO SLIGO
TEL: 071 65108 FAX: 071 65466 TELEX: 40301

OWNERS: Brian and Lindy O'Hara

7 rms | 6 ens

S: IR£55–IR£57.50
D: IR£90–IR£95

Coopershill is a fine example of a Georgian family mansion. Home to seven generations of the O'Hara family since 1774, it combines the spaciousness and elegance of an earlier age with modern comforts. Public rooms are furnished in period style with gilt-framed portraits, hunting trophies and antiques. Five of the bedrooms have four-poster or canopy beds and all have private bathrooms.

Dinner is served by candle-light in the elegant dining room, where good cooking is complemented by a wide choice of wines. Open log fires and personal attention from owners Brian and Lindy O'Hara help to create the warm atmosphere and hospitality that typify Coopershill. Out of season the house is open to parties of 8 to 12 people at a special rate. Tariffs are reduced if guests stay for three consecutive nights or more.

The River Arrow winds through the 500-acre estate and boating, trout and coarse fishing are available. Shooting is not permitted, leaving the abundant wildlife undisturbed. There is an excellent hard tennis court and also a croquet lawn. There are marvellous mountain and lakeside walks to enjoy in the area. From the UK phone 00 353 71 65108. Closed 1st November to mid-March.

Places of interest nearby: Sligo, megalithic tombs and Yeats country. **Directions: Leave N4 Sligo–Dublin road at Drumfin and follow signs for Coopershill. One mile further on, turn left and follow signs.**

LISS ARD LAKE LODGE

SKIBBEREEN, CO CORK
TEL: 353 28 22365 FAX: 353 28 22839

OWNERS Delwyn Klevenow and Claudia Meister

16 rms 16 ens

S: IR£75–IR£90
D: IR£80–IR£200

This recently renovated hotel set in the tranquil and beautiful West Cork countryside was originally the summer home of a wealthy Victorian landowner.

Refined and minimalistic furnishings are to be found in the excellent bedrooms, each of which is equipped with a TV, video, stereo and PC and Fax points.

A generous and balanced breakfast is available until noon, so there is no rush for late risers! The hotel's restaurant serves light, imaginative, international cuisine, with local meat, fish and vegetables carefully prepared to suit all tastes. An excellent wine list is available.

Guests are invited to stroll through the surrounding Liss Ard Gardens, a unique project which creates ten contemporary landscaped "garden-rooms" out of a 50-acre park. Sample the delights of a Woodland Walk, Wild Flower Meadow or Irish Sky Garden. Other leisure activities available close by include golf, cycling, fishing in the hotel's own lake, tennis, and fitness training.

Places of interest nearby: Cape Clear, Baltimore, Castletownsend, Mizen Head and Fastnet. **Directions: In Skibbereen, follow the one way system for 400 metres and turn left at crossroads onto L60, direction Castletownsend (Liss Ard signpost 5km). After 3½kms you will see Lake Abisdealy on your right. Turn right after lake, direction Tragumna, (Liss Ard signpost 1½km) and follow this road to the Lodge.**

For hotel location, see maps on pages 223–229

MARKREE CASTLE

COLLOONEY, COUNTY SLIGO, IRELAND
TEL: 071 67800 FAX: 071 67840

OWNER: Charles Cooper

14 rms | 14 ens

S: IR£58.50–IR£62.50
D: IR£46.50–IR£52.50
De luxe: IR£51.50–IR£57.50

Regarded as one of Ireland's major architectural masterpieces, Markree Castle is Sligo's oldest inhabited castle. It has been the home of the Cooper family since 1640, but over the years the house has undergone a number of transformations. Today, the castle retains its family atmosphere and the character of the old building, while providing every modern comfort.

The interior boasts a spectacular /oak staircase. This is overlooked by a stained glass window, purportedly tracing the Cooper family tree back to the time of King John of England. There are a variety of notable reception rooms, in addition to the interconnecting dining rooms which feature Louis-Philippe style plasterwork created by Italian craftsmen in 1845. An imaginative menu is provided

The bedrooms vary in character and style, but all offer views over the gardens or surrounding countryside.

Markree is in the heart of "Yeats Country", with magnificent scenery all around. The Rosses Point golf course and the Strandhill course are within a few miles. Trout and salmon fishing can be arranged nearby. **Places of interest nearby:** Carrowmore, which has Europe's largest and oldest collection of megalithic remains; Lissadell House; Yeats's grave at Drumcliffe; and the town of Donegal. **Directions: Nine miles from Sligo airport, 125 from Dublin via N4. Collooney is just south of Sligo town.**

15 M

In association with MasterCard

BARBERSTOWN CASTLE

STRAFFAN, CO KILDARE
TEL: 01 6288157/6288206 FAX: 01 6277027

OWNERS: Kenneth and Catherine Healy

14 rms | 14 ens | SMALL HOTEL

S: IR£71
D: IR£121

Barberstown Castle was one of the first great Irish country houses to open up its splendour to the outside world. The Castle was built in the early 13th century by Nicholas Barby, a heritage that embraces over 750 years of Irish history.

The restaurant at Barberstown is renowned for its creative food and has received the RAC Restaurant Award for 1993/94 and also two Rosettes from the AA for 1993/94. Each of the en suite bedrooms has been decorated in an individual style and dedicated to the ordinary and extraordinary people who have lived within its walls. The Castle received Hospitality and Comfort Awards from the RAC for 1993/94.

Places of interest nearby: Golf can be arranged at The Kildare Country Club and at several other courses nearby. Expert equestrian tuition as well as hunting, racing, tennis, gym, squash and clay pigeon shooting are all available in the area. Coarse, trout and salmon fishing on the River Liffey, Ghillies available. For the less active, relax in an atmosphere of pure calm and tranquillity, deep in the heart of County Kildare. **Directions: Barberstown Castle is 30 minutes drive from Dublin City centre and 40 minutes drive from the airport. It is an ideal first or last stop on your country house tour of Ireland. South on the N7 take the turn for Straffan at Kill. Travelling west on N4 take the turn for Straffan at Maynooth.**

14 M | 12

For hotel location, see maps on pages 223–229

The Old Rectory

WICKLOW TOWN, CO WICKLOW, IRELAND
TEL: 0404 67048 FAX: 0404 69181

OWNERS: Paul and Linda Saunders

5 rms | 5 ens

S: IR£69
D: IR£92

The Old Rectory is situated in secluded gardens on the edge of the harbour town of Wicklow in County Wicklow, "the Garden of Ireland". A peaceful Victorian house, personally run by Paul and Linda Saunders, it combines charming country house accommodation with an elegant gourmet restaurant. The house is freshly decorated throughout and furnished with antiques: public rooms also feature marble fireplaces and attractive plaster cornices. Individually designed bedrooms offer en suite bathrooms and lots of little extras to make you feel welcome. This special ambience made it a previous winner of the coveted AA "Inspector's Selected" award for Ireland. The restaurant is exceptional and featured on TV's *"Gourmet Ireland"* series. Set gourmet and à la carte menus use fresh sea food, local and organic produce enhanced with herbs and edible flowers. Vegetarians welcome. In May/June 10-course "floral dinners" are a highlight of the Wicklow Gardens Festival. The Old Rectory also offers a choice of breakfasts which have won the National Breakfast award for Ireland.
Places of interest nearby: Glendalough and the Wicklow Mountains, many gardens including Mount Usher, Powerscourt and Avondale; Russborough stately home, the National Gardens Centre, 12 golf courses and sandy beaches. **Directions: 30m south of Dublin on N11, then 1m south of Rathenew on R750.**

For hotel location, see maps on pages 223–229

View over St Ouen's Bay, Jersey

Johansens Recommended Country Houses in the Channel Islands

With a wealth of wonderful scenery, magnificent coastlines, historic buildings, natural and man-made attractions plus mouthwatering local produce, the Channel Islands provide a memorable destination that's distinctly different.

Throughout their history, the Channel Islands have been closely linked with France. And, being so far south, claim higher sunshine rates than even the sunniest resorts on the south coast of England.

The 1995 Readers Digest Good Beach Guide, which gives awards for cleanliness on behalf of the Marine Conservation Society, voted several of both Jersey's and Guernsey's beaches among the best in the British Isles.

Both islands offer VAT and duty-free shopping, the official language is English, passports are not required and both islands can be reached by sea from Weymouth or any one of about 30 airports in Britain and Europe.

And don't forget the other islands. Herm has dazzling beaches, Sark lives in a rural timewarp without traffic and Alderney's cobbled streets, pretty cottages and Victorian forts are another world again.

JERSEY

The largest and furthest south of the whole group of the Channel Islands, Jersey measures just nine miles by five and is only twelve miles from the French coast.

The magnificent coastline ranges from rocky cliffs, which rise above 400 feet in some parts, to wide stretches of fine golden sand. An island of immense variety and great beauty, its many historic and traditional buildings and diverse natural habitats are enjoyed by residents and tourists alike.

Jersey's sightseeing has much to offer. This small island is home to one of the world's most famous zoos, and the Jersey Museum reopened in 1992 after a £3.8 million investment, and was voted 'Britain's most outstanding new tourist attraction' by the British Guild of Travel Writers. Mont Orgueil Castle, one of Europe's finest castles, is also well worth a visit, and so is the German Underground Hospital, left over from the German Occupation. The 50th anniversary of the Liberation of the Island from the German occupying forces during World War II was celebrated in May 1995 when amongst Islandwide celebrations the Occupation Tapestry was opened to the public. The culmination of a five year project, the tapestry consists of 12 panels, one from each of the Island's parishes. The scenes depict life on the Island during the occupation and liberation.

Food is also one of Jersey's best known attractions, with more restaurants per square mile than most major cities. The annual Jersey Good Food Festival, held in June, is a must for food lovers, and in May, the Jersey International Festival takes place. This is a major arts event with theatre, dance, visual arts and music.

GUERNSEY

Guernsey, washed by the last tides of the Gulf stream, is smaller than Jersey, being around twenty-five square miles. 59,000 islanders support a successful and self-sufficient economy that mingles offshore finance with tourism and horticulture. Unemployment and taxes are low while the quality of life is high. Traditional values are respected (the pubs remain closed on Sundays) and there is little crime.

Visitors soon notice signs of Guernseys independent status; the post boxes are royal blue, the telephone kiosks yellow and you may get a £1 note in your change, but the differences don't end there. The Channel islands were the only part of the British Isles to be occupied by the Germans in World War II, and the coastline bristles with fortifications now being developed as heritage sites. There are also museums, castles, art galleries and Victor Hugo's House.

French style farmhouses in verdant little valleys speckled with cows, fishermen's cottages peeping over the sea wall at sandy beaches and rocky coves, the hillside capital, St Peter Port, commanding spectacular views across the harbour and islands of Sark and Herm. These are the impressions that visitors take away, along with memories of fresh seafood (for gourmets, the island's annual restaurant competition is held in April) and cliff top walks among the wildflowers.

Mont Orgueil Castle
Gorey
St Martin
Jersey
Tel: 01534 853292

Jersey Museum
The Weighbridge
St Helier
Jersey
Tel: 01534 30511

Jersey Zoo
Les Augres Manor
Trinity
Jersey
Tel: 01534 864666

German Underground Hospital
Meadowbank
St Lawrence
Jersey
Tel: 01534 863442

German Occupation Museum
Forest
Guernsey
Tel: 01481 38205

Victor Hugo's House
38 Hauteville
Guernsey
Tel: 01481 721911

Castle Cornet
St Peter Port
Guernsey
Tel: 01481 721657

INFORMATION SUPPLIED BY

Jersey Tourism
Liberation Square
St Helier
Jersey JE1 1BB
Tel: 01534 500700

Guernsey Tourist Board
PO Box 23
St Peter Port
Guernsey GY1 3AN
Tel: 01481 723552

LES EMBRUNS HOUSE HOTEL

ROUTE DE LA MARGION, VAZON BAY, CASTEL, GUERNSEY
TEL: 01481 64834 FAX: 01481 66024

OWNERS: Jack and Jane Kennedy

16 rms | 16 ens | SMALL HOTEL

S: £30
D: £60

Les Embruns is a cosy, family-run hotel set in its own acre of gardens on the west coast of Guernsey just minutes from the sands of magnificent Vazon Bay. Les Embruns seamlessly blends hospitality and modern facilities to offer the visitor a retreat from the pressures of urban life that is both comfortable and exceptionally good value for money.

Owners Jack and Jane Kennedy have successfully created a happy and relaxed atmosphere through attention to detail and personal requirements: each of the 16 individually decorated rooms contains colour TV, tea and coffee making facilities and direct-dial telephone. Guests can meet for drinks before or after dinner either in the lounge/bar or the non-smoking lounge, or, when the weather is sunny, outside on the patio overlooking the south-facing gardens. In the restaurant, diners' wishes have been meticulously observed by Jane to produce a menu that is simply mouth-watering: varied fare, created where possible from fresh, local produce and accompanied by wine from the carefully compiled list. Special needs (vegetarian, for instance), are gladly catered for. Residents also have access to an outdoor pool and private car park. **Places of interest nearby:** The safe, sandy stretch of Vazon Beach, Saumarez Park and good walking opportunities in the vicinity of Les Embruns. **Directions: On the main coast road at Vazon Bay on the west side of the island.**

For hotel location, see maps on pages 223–229

La Favorita Hotel

FERMAIN BAY, GUERNSEY, CHANNEL ISLANDS GY4 6SD
TEL: 01481 35666 FAX: 01481 35413

OWNERS: Simon and Helen Wood

37 rms | 37 ens | SMALL HOTEL

S: from £37
D: from £64

Once a fine country house, La Favorita retains all the charm and character of those former days. The hotel is comfortable and fully licensed. Set in its own grounds, just a few minutes walk from Guernsey's famous Fermain Bay, it enjoys spectacular views over the sea towards Jersey.

The bedrooms are comfortable and offer every modern amenity, including colour TV, radio, and refreshment tray. Guernsey's mild climate means that it has much to offer out of season and the hotel also offers a full range of facilities to satisfy the extra needs of spring, autumn and winter guests, including the indoor pool.

La Favorita has an excellent reputation for traditional English cooking and Island seafood specialities. The restaurant is strictly no smoking. A coffee shop offers a wide range of lunch dishes and bar suppers for those who enjoy a more informal meal.

St Peter Port is within easy walking distance, whether taking the woodland walk which follows the coastline or the more direct route past Victor Hugo's house.

Places of interest nearby: The coast of Guernsey and all the island's attractions. **Directions: Fermain Bay is 10 minutes from the airport and five minutes from St Peter Port on the east coast of Guernsey.**

60 M

In association with MasterCard

ALMORAH HOTEL

ONE ALMORAH CRESENT, LOWER KINGS CLIFF, ST HELIER, JERSEY JE2 3GU
TEL: 01534 21648 FAX: 01534 68600

OWNERS: Bill and Rita Mills

16 rms | 16 ens

S: £40.50–£49.50
D: £63–£79

Overlooking the town of St Helier and its harbour the Almorah is a small family run hotel which frequently hosts visitors from all over Europe. The rooms are elegant and comfortable, including a very cosy bar in which to contemplate the six-course dinner about to be served in the Breton-style dining room.

Dinner could typically be; melon with satsumas, fresh cream of Normandie leek soup, orange sorbet, navarin of lamb à la parisienne, hot black cherries with vodka, followed by the cheese-board. Rita and Bill also pride themselves on a good selection of fine wines.

Some of the bedrooms have their own balcony and can happily accommodate a family. A small walled garden adds to the feeling of privacy despite the location close to Jersey's main town centre.

Renowned for the hosts' warmth and hospitality, the Almorah staff will gladly advise on local facilities; car or bicycle hire, boat trips and entertainment.

Places of interest nearby: Elizabeth Castle, Port of St Helier, Jersey Museum, the central fish and vegetable markets. **Directions: Take any road to the town of St Helier and enter Rouge Bouillon ring road. At the roundabout go up Queens Road and take the first right turn, Lower Kings Cliff.**

en famille

For hotel location, see maps on pages 223–229

MINI LISTINGS: JOHANSENS INNS WITH RESTAURANTS

Here in brief are the entries that appear in full in Johansens 1996 Guide to Inns with Restaurants.
To order any of these guides see pages 235–240.

Adderbury (Banbury)
The Red Lion Inn
The Green
Adderbury
Nr Banbury
Oxfordshire OX17 3JU
01295 810269

Alcester
Arrow Mill
Arrow
Nr Alcester
Warwickshire B49 5NL
01789 762419

Amberley (Nr Arundel)
The Boathouse Brasserie
Houghton Bridge
Amberley
Nr Arundel
West Sussex BN18 9LR
01798 831059

Ambleside (Great Langdale)
The New Dungeon Ghyll Hotel
Great Langdale
Ambleside
Cumbria LA22 9JY
015394 37213

Appleby-In-Westmorland
The Royal Oak Inn
Bongate
Appleby-In-Westmorland
Cumbria CA16 6UN
017683 51463

Ashbourne (Waterhouses)
The Old Beams Restaurant with Rooms
Waterhouses
Staffordshire ST10 3TW
01538 308254

Askrigg (Wensleydale)
The Kings Arms Hotel And Restaurant
Market Place,
Askrigg Wensleydale,
North Yorkshire DL8 3HQ
01969 650258

Badby (near Daventry)
The Windmill Inn Hotel
Main Street
Badby,
Nr Daventry,
Northants NN11 6AN
01327 702363

Barnard Castle (Greta Bridge)
The Morritt Arms Hotel
Greta Bridge
Nr Barnard Castle
Durham DL12 9SE
01833 627232

Basingstoke (Odiham)
The George Hotel
Basingstoke
High Street
Basingstoke
Hampshire RG25 1LP
01256 702081

Beckington (Nr Bath)
The Woolpack Inn
Beckington
Nr Bath
Somerset BA3 6SP
01373 831244

Belbroughton
Freshmans Restaurant
Church Hill
Belbroughton
Near Stourbridge
Worcestershire DY9 0DT
01562 730467

Belford
Blue Bell Hotel
Belford Market Place
Belford
Northumberland NE70 7NE
01668 213543

Bourton-on-the-Water
The Old Manse Hotel
Victoria Street
Bourton-on-the-Water
Gloucestershire GL54 2BX
01451 820082

Bridport
Manor Hotel
West Bexington
Dorset DT2 9DF
01308 897616

Brimfield
Poppies at the Roebuck
Brimfield
Ludlow
Shropshire SY8 4NE
01584 711230

Burford
Cotswold Gateway Hotel and Restaurant
Cheltenham Road
Burford
Oxfordshire OX18 4HX
01993 822695

Burford
The Lamb Inn
Sheep Street
Burford
Oxon OX18 4LR
01993 823155

Burnham Market
The Hoste Arms
The Green
Burnham Market
Norfolk PE31 8HD
01328 738257

Burton upon Trent (Branston)
The Old Vicarage
Main Street
Branston
Burton upon Trent
Staffordshire DE14 3EX
01283 533222

Burton upon Trent (Sudbury)
Boar's Head Hotel
Lichfield Road
Sudbury
Derbyshire DE6 5GX
01283 820344

Calver, Nr Bakewell
The Chequers Inn
Froggatt Edge
Nr Calver
Derbyshire S30 1ZB
01433 630231

Camborne
Tyacks Hotel
27 Commercial Street
Camborne
Cornwall TR14 8LD
01209 612424

Cambridge
Panos Hotel and Restaurant
154-156 Hills Road
Cambridge
Cambridgeshire CB2 2PB
01223 212958

Cambridge (Quy)
Quy Mill Hotel
Newmarket Road
Stow-cum-Quy
Cambridge CB5 9AY
01223 293383

Castle Ashby (Northampton)
The Falcon Hotel and Restaurant
Castle Ashby
Northampton
Northamptonshire NN7 1LF
01604 696200

Castle Carey
The George Hotel
Market Place
Castle Carey
Somerset BA7 7AH
01963 350761

Castle Combe
The Castle Inn
Castle Combe
Nr Chippenham
Wiltshire SN14 7HN
01249 783030

Castleton
Ye Olde Nags Head
Cross Street
Castleton
Derbyshire S30 2WH
01433 620248

Cheltenham (Birdlip)
Kingshead House Restaurant
Birdlip
Gloucestershire GL4 8JH
01452 862299

Chester (Higher Burwardsley)
The Pheasant
Higher Burwardsley
Tattenhall
Chester
Cheshire CH2 9PF
01829 770434

Chipping Campden
The Noel Arms
Chipping Campden
Gloucestershire GL55 6AT
01386 840317

Cirencester (Coln St Aldwyns)
The New Inn
Coln St Aldwyns
Cirencester
Gloucestershire GL7 5AN
01285 750651

Clavering (Stansted)
The Cricketers
Clavering
Nr Saffron Walden
Essex CV11 4QT
01799 550042

Cleobury Mortimer
The Crown At Hopton
Hopton Waters
Cleobury Mortimer
Nr Kidderminster
Worcestershire DY14 0NB
01299 270372

Cleobury Mortimer
The Redfern Hotel
Cleobury Mortimer
Shropshire DY14 8AA
01299 270395

Doddiscombleigh
The Nobody Inn
Doddiscombleigh
Nr Exeter
Devon EX6 7PS
01647 52394

Dorchester-on-Thames
The George Hotel
High Street
Dorchester-on-Thames
OX9 8HH
01865 340404

Dronfield (Sheffield)
Manor House Hotel & Restaurant
Dronfield
High Street
Old Dronfield
Derbyshire S18 6PY
01246 413971

Dulverton (Exebridge)
The Anchor Inn
Exebridge
Nr Dulverton
Somerset TA22 9AZ
01398 23433

Easington (Long Crendon)
The Mole and Chicken
The Terrace
Long Crendon
Aylesbury
Buckinghamshire HP18 9EY
01844 208387

East Witton
The Blue Lion
East Witton
Nr Leyburn
North Yorkshire DL8 4SN
01969 624273

Egton
The Wheatsheaf Inn
Egton
Nr Whitby
North Yorkshire YO21 1TZ
01947 85271

Ely (Sutton)
The Anchor Inn
Sutton Gault
Sutton
Nr Ely
Cambridge CB6 2BD
01353 778537

Eton/Windsor
The Christopher Hotel
High Street
Eton
Windsor
Berkshire SL4 6AN
01753 852359

Evershot
The Acorn Inn Hotel
Fore Street
Evershot
Dorset DT2 0JW
01935 83228

Evesham (Offenham)
Riverside Restaurant and Hotel
The Parks
Offenham Road
Nr Evesham
Worcestershire WR11 5JP
01386 446200

Exeter (Trusham)
The Cridford Inn
Trusham
Nr Newton Abbot
Devon TQ13 0NR
01626 853694

Exlade Street
The Highwayman
Checkingdon
Berkshire IG8 0UA
01491 682020

Exmoor
The Royal Oak Inn
Winsford
Exmoor National Park
Somerset TA24 7JE
01643 851455

Fakenham (Sculthrpe)
Sculthorpe Mill
Sculthorpe
Nr Fakenham
Norfolk NR21 9QG
01328 856161/86275

Falmouth (Constantine)
Trengilly Wartha Country Inn
Nancenoy
Constantine
Falmouth
Cornwall TR11 5RP
01326 40332

Ford (Nr Bath)
The White Hart
Ford
Chippenham
Wiltshire SN14 8LP
01249 782213

Fordingbridge (New Forest)
The Woodfalls Inn
The Ridge
Woodfalls
Fordingbridge
Hampshire SP5 2LN
01725 513222

Fulbeck (Lincoln)
Hare and Hounds
The Green
Fulbeck
Lincolnshire HG32 3JJ
01400 272090

Glaston (Uppingham)
The Monckton Arms Hotel
Glaston
Nr Uppingham
Rutland
Leicestershire LE15 9BP
01572 822326

Goathland
Mallyan Spout Hotel
Goathland
Whitby
North Yorkshire YO22 5AN
01947 864866

Goldaming
The Inn On The Lake
Ockford Road
Godalming
Surrey GU7 1RH
01483 415575

Goring-On-Thames
Leatherne Bottel Riverside Inn
And The Bridleway
Goring On Thames
Berkshire RG8 0HS
01491 872667

Great Dunmow
The Starr
Market Place
Great Dunmow
Essex CM16 1AX
01371 874321

Grimsthorpe (Bourne)
The Black Horse Inn
Grimsthorpe
Bourne
Lincolnshire PE10 0LY
01778 591247

Grindleford
Maynard Arms Hotel
Main Road
Grindleford
Derbyshire S30 1HP
01433 630321

Halifax (Holywell Green)
The Rock Inn Hotel
Holywell Green
Halifax
West Yorkshire HX4 9BS
01422 379721

Handcross
The Chequers At Slaugham
Slaugham
Nr Handcross
West Sussex RH17 6AQ
01444 400239

Hatherleigh
The George Hotel
Market Street
Hatherleigh
Devon
01837 810454

Hawkshead
The Red Lion Inn
The Square
Hawkshead
Nr Ambleside
Cumbria LA22 0NS
015394 36213

Haworth
Old White Lion Hotel
Haworth
Keighley
West Yorkshire BD22 8DU
01535 642313

Hay-On-Wye
Rhydspence Inn
Rhydspence
Whitney-On-Wye
Nr Hay-On-Wye
Hereford & Worcester HR3 6EU
01497 831262

Hayfield (Birch Vale)
The Waltzing Weasel
New Mills Road
Birch Vale
Derbyshire SK12 5BT
01663 743402

Helmsley
The Feversham Arms Hotel
Helmsley
North Yorkshire YO6 5AG
01439 770766

Henley (Ibstone)
The Fox Country Hotel
Ibstone
Nr High Wycombe
Buckinghamshire HP14 3GG
01491 638289

Hinkley (Nr Leicester)
Barnacles Restaurant
Watlins Street
Nr Hinkley
Leicestershire LE10 3JA
01455 633220

Honiton (Wilmington)
Home Farm Hotel
Wilmington
Nr Honiton
Devon EX14 9JQ
01404 831278

Kingsbury (Nr Sutton Coldfield)
Marston Farm Hotel
Bodymoor Heath
Sutton Coldfield
Warwickshire B76 9JD
01827 872133

Kirkby Lonsdale (Casterton)
The Pheasant Inn
Casterton
Kirkby Lonsdale
Cumbria LA6 2RX
015242 71230

Kirkby Lonsdale
The Snooty Fox
Main Street
Kirkby Lonsdale
Cumbria LA6 2AH
015242 71308

Kirkby Lonsdale
Whoop Hall Inn
Burrow With Burrow
Kirkby Lonsdale
Carnforth
Lancashire LA6 2HP
015242 71284

Kirkbymoorside
The George & Dragon
Kirkbymoorside
Market Place
Kirkbymoorside
North Yorkshire YO6 6AA
01751 433334

Knutsford
Longview Hotel and Restaurant
51-55 Manchester Road
Knutsford
Cheshire WA16 0LX
01565 632119

Ledbury
The Feathers Hotel
Ledbury High Street
Ledbury
Hereford & Worcester HR8 1DS
01531 635266

Leek (Blackshore Moor)
The Three Horseshoes Inn
Buxton Road
Blackshore Moor
Nr Leek
Staffordshire ST13 8TW
01538 300296

Leominster (Stoke Prior)
Wheelbarrow Castle
Stoke Prior
Leominster
Herefordshire HR6 0NB
01568 612219

Long Melford
The Countrymen
The Green
Long Melford
Suffolk CO10 9DN
01787 312356

Lutterworth
The Greyhound
Market Street
Lutterworth
Leicestershire LE17 4EJ
01455 553307

Lynmouth
The Rising Sun Hotel
Harbourside
Lynmouth
Devon EX38 6EQ
01598 753223

Maidenhead
Boulters Lock Hotel
Boulters Island
Maidenhead
Berkshire SL6 8PE
01628 21291

Maidstone (Warren Street)
The Harrow At Warren Street
Warren Street
New Lenham
Kent ME17 2ED
01622 858727

Maidstone (Ringlestone)
Ringlestone Inn
'Twixt'
Harrietsham and Wormshill
Nr Maidstone
Kent ME17 1NX
01622 859900

Malmesbury
The Horse & Groom Inn
Charlton
Nr Malmesbury
Wiltshire SN16 9DL
01666 823904

Malton
The Green Man
Market Street
Malton
North Yorkshire YO17 0LY
01653 600370

Meysey Hampton
The Masons Arms
Meysey Hampton
Nr Cirencester
Gloucestershire GL7 5JT
01285 850461

Minchinhampton (Hyde)
The Ragged Cot
Hyde
Minchinhampton
Gloucestershire GL6 8PE
01453 884643/731333

Montacute
The Kings Arms Inn Hotel
Montacute
Somerset TA15 6UU
01935 822513

Newby Bridge
The Swan Hotel
Newby Bridge
Newby Bridge
Nr Ulverston
Cumbria LA12 8MB
015395 31681

Norwich (Rackheath)
The Garden House Hotel
Salhouse Road
Rackheath
Norwich
Norfolk NR13 6AA
01603 720007

Nottingham
Hotel Des Clos
Old Lenton Lane
Nottingham
Nottinghamshire NG7 2SA
01159 866566

Okehampton (South Zeal)
The Oxenham Arms
South Zeal
Nr Okehampton
Devon EX20 2JT
01837 840244/577

Onneley
The Wheatsheaf Inn At Onneley
Barhill Road
Onneley
Staffordshire CW3 9QF
01782 751581

Oxford (Banbury)
The Holcombe Hotel
High Street
Dedington
Oxfordshire OX5 4SL
01869 338274

Oxford (Middleton Stoney)
The Jersey Arms
Middleton Stoney
Oxfordshire OX6 8SE
01869 343234

Oxford (Minster Lovell)
The Mill and Old Swan
Minster Lovell
Burford
Oxfordshire OX8 5RN
01993 774441

Oxford (Stanton-St-John)
The Talkhouse
Wheatley Road
Stanton-St-John
Oxfordshire OX33 1EX
01865 351648

Padstow
The Old Custom House Inn
South Quay
Padstow
Cornwall PL28 8ED
01841 532359

Pelynt (Nr Looe)
Jubilee Inn
Pelynt
Nr Looe
Cornwall PL13 2JZ
01503 220312

Petworth (Sutton)
The White Horse Inn
Sutton
Nr Pulborough
West Sussex RH20 1PS
01798 869221

Pickering
The White Swan
The Market Place
Pickering
North Yorkshire YO18 7AA
01751 472288

Port Gaverne
Port Gaverne Hotel
Port Gaverne
Nr Port Isaac
North Cornwall PL29 3SQ
01208 880244

Porthleven, Nr Helston
The Harbour Inn
Commercial Road
Porthleven
Nr Helston
Cornwall TR13 9JD
01326 573876

Preston (Goosnargh)
Ye Horns Inn
Goosnargh
Nr Preston
Lancashire PR3 2ZY
01772 865230

Quorn
Quorn Grange
Wood Lane
Quorn
Leics LE12 8DB
01509 412167

Rosedale Abbey
The Milburn Arms Hotel
Rosedale Abbey
Pickering
North Yorkshire
YO18 8RA
01751 417312

Rugby (Easenhall)
The Golden Lion Inn of Easenhall
Easenhall
Nr Rugby
Warwickshire CV23 0JA
01797 223065

Rye
The Mermaid Inn
Mermaid Street
Rye
East Sussex TN31 7NU
01797 223065

St Austell
The White Hart Hotel
Church Street
St Austell
Cornwall PL25 4AT
01726 72100

St Mawes
The Rising Sun
The Square
St Mawes
Cornwall TR2 5DJ
01326 270233

Saddleworth (Delph)
The Old Bell Inn Hotel
Huddersfield Road
Delph
Saddleworth
Lancashire OL3 5E6
01457 870130

Salisbury
The Milford Hall Hotel
206 Castle Street
Salisbury
Wiltshire SP1 3TE
01722 417411

Scarborough (East Ayton)
East Ayton Lodge Country Hotel
Moor Lane
Forge Valley
East Ayton
Scarborough, North Yorkshire
01723 864227

Sherborne (West Camel)
The Walnut Tree
West Camel
Nr Sherborne
Somerset BA22 7QW
01935 851292

Shipton-under-Wychwood
The Lamb Inn
Shipton-Under-Wychwood
Oxfordshire OX7 6DQ
01993 830465

Shipton-under-Wychwood
The Shaven Crown Hotel
High Street
Shipton-under-Wychwood
Oxfordshire OX7 6RA
01993 830330

Skipton (Elslack)
The Tempest Arms
Elslack
Nr Skipton
North Yorkshire BD23 3AY
01282 842450

Southport (Formby)
Treetops Country House Restaurant
Southport Old Road
Formby
Nr Southport
Merseyside L37 0AB
01704 879651

Stonor (Henley-on-Thames)
The Stonor Arms
Stonor
Nr Henley-on-Thames
Oxfordshire RG9 6HE
01491 638354

Stow-on-the-Wold
The Kingshead Inn And Restaurant
The Green
Bledington
Nr Kingham
Oxfordshire OX7 6HD
01608 658365

Stow-on-the-Wold
The Royalist
Digbeth Street
Stow-on-the-Wold
Gloucestershire GL54 1BN
01451 830670

Stratford-upon-Avon (Alveston)
Baraset Barn Restaurant
Pimlico Lane
Alveston
Stratford-upon-Avon
Warwickshire CV37 7RF
01789 295510

Stratford-upon-Avon
The Blue Boar Inn
Temple Grafton
Alcester
Warwickshire B49 6NRE
01789 750010

Telford (Norton)
The Hundred House Hotel
Bridgnorth Road
Norton
Nr Shifnal, Telford
Shropshire TF11 9EE
01952 730353

Tewkesbury
The Bell Hotel
Church Street
Tewkesbury
Gloucestershire GL20 5SA
01684 293293

Thame, Nr Oxford
Thatchers Inn
29/30 Lower High Street
Thame
Nr Oxford
Oxfordshire OX9 2AA
01844 212146

Thelbridge
Thelbridge Cross Inn
Thelbridge
Nr Witheridge
Devon EX17 4SQ
01884 860316

Thorpe Market
Green Farm Restaurant And Hotel
North Walsham Road
Thorpe Market
Norfolk NR11 8TH
01263 833602

Torquay (Kingskerswell)
The Barn Owl Inn
Aller Mills
Kingskerswell
Devon TQ12 5AN
01830 872130

Totnes (Staverton)
The Sea Trout Inn
Staverton
Nr Totnes
Devon TQ9 6PA
01803 762274

Troutbeck, nr Windermere
The Mortal Man Hotel
Troutbeck
Nr Windermere
Cumbria LA23 1PL
015394 33193

Tunbridge Wells
Royal Wells Inn
Mount Ephraim
Tunbridge Wells
Kent TN4 8BE
01892 511188

Twyford (Knowl Hill)
The Bird in Hand
Bath Road
Knowl Hill
Twyford
Berkshire RG10 9UP
01628 826622/822781

Upton-upon-Severn, Nr Malvern
White Lion Hotel
High Street
Upton-upon-Severn
Worcestershire WR8 0HJ
01684 592551

Walberswick
The Anchor
Walberswick
Suffolk IP18 6UA
01502 722112

Weobley
Ye Olde Salutation Inn
Market Pitch
Weobley
Herefordshire HR4 8SJ
01544 318443

West Witton (Wensleydale)
The Wensleydale Heifer
West Witton
Wensleydale
North Yorkshire DL8 4LS
01969 622322

Whitewell
The Inn At Whitewell
Forest Of Bowland
Clitheroe
Lancashire BB7 3AT
01200 448222

Winchcombe
Wesley House
The High Street
Winchcombe
Gloucestershire GL54 5LJ
01242 602366

Winchester
The Wyckeham Arms
75 Kingsgate Street
Winchester
Hampshire SO23 9PE
01962 852824

Withypool
The Royal Oak Inn
Exmoor National Park
Withypool
Somerset TA24 7QP
01643 831236

Worthing (Bramber)
The Old Tollgate Restaurant & Hotel
The Street
Bramber
Steyning
West Sussex BN44 3WE
01903 879494

Wroxham
The Barton Angler Country Inn
Irstead Road
Neatishead
Nr Wroxham
Norfolk NR12 8YD
01692 630740

Yattendon
The Royal Oak Hotel
Yattendon
Newbury
Berkshire RG16 0UF
01635 201325

Chepstow
Castle View Hotel
16 Bridge Street
Chepstow
Gwent NP6 5EZ
01291 620349

Dolgellau (Penmaenpool)
George III Hotel
Penmaenpool
Nr Dolgellau
Gwynedd LL40 1YD
01341 422525

Llanarmon DC
The West Arms Hotel
Llanarmon Dc
Nr Llangollen
Clwyd LL20 7LD
01691 600665

Llandeilo (Rhosmaen)
The Plough Inn
Rhosmaen
Llandeilo
Dyfed SA19 6NP
01558 823431

Montgomery
The Dragon Hotel
Montgomery
Powys SY15 6AA
01686 668359

Welshpool (Berriew)
The Lion Hotel And Restaurant
Berriew
Nr Welshpool
Powys SY21 8PQ
01686 640452

Banchory (Royal Deeside)
Potarch Hotel
By Banchory
Royal Deeside
Kincardineshire AB3 4BD
013398 84339

Comrie
Comrie Hotel
Comrie
Perthshire PH6 2DY
01764 670239/330

Drymen
The Winnock Hotel
The Square
Drymen
Stirlingshire G63 0BL
01360 60245

Glenisla
The Glenisla Hotel
Kirkton of Glenisla
By Alyth
Perthshire PH11 8PH
01575 582223

Isle Of Skye (Eilean Iarmain)
Isle Ornsay Hotel
Eilean Iarmain
Isle Of Skye IV43 8QR
01471 833332

Kylesku, Sutherland
Kylesku Hotel
Kylesku
By Lairg
Sutherland IV27 4HW
01971 502231/200

Loch Gilphed
Cairnbann Hotel
By Loch Gilphed
Argyll PA31 8SJ
01546 603668

NORTHERN IRELAND
IRELAND
To Stranraer, Cairnryan
To Liverpool, Douglas
To Holyhead, Douglas
To Holyhead, Liverpool
To Pembroke Dock
To Swansea
Fishguard
Coleraine
Londonderry
LONDONDERRY
LETTERKENNY
DONEGAL
BALLYMENA
ANTRIM
Carrickfergus
CRAIGANTLET
Bangor
NEWTOWN-ARDS
BELFAST (ALDERGROVE)
Belfast
TYRONE
PORTAFERRY
FERMANAGH
Armagh
ARMAGH
DOWN
Newry
MONAGHAN
SLIGO
RIVERSTOWN
MAYO
LEITRIM
CARRICKMACROSS
Dundalk
CAVAN
KNOCK
ROSCOMMON
LOUTH
CONNEMARA
CONG
LONGFORD
Drogheda
WESTMEATH
MEATH
GALWAY
BUSHYPARK
Galway
DUBLIN
MALAHIDE
OFFALY
Dun Laoghaire
Bray
Gort
BIRR
KILDARE
LAOIS
WICKLOW
CLARE
NENAGH
NEWMARKET-ON-FERGUS
SHANNON
Limerick
ADARE
LIMERICK
TIPPERARY
Kilkenny
CARLOW
GOREY
THOMASTOWN
KILKENNY
WEXFORD
Tralee
KERRY
Clonmel
Wexford
WATERFORD
Waterford
ROSSLARE
KILLARNEY
CORK
KENMARE
Cork
SKIBBEREEN
0 20 40 60 80 100 Kilometres
0 10 20 30 40 50 Miles
JOHANSENS RECOMMENDED HOTEL
JOHANSENS RECOMMENDED COUNTRY HOUSE

JOHANSENS RECOMMENDED HOTEL
JOHANSENS RECOMMENDED INN OR RESTAURANT
JOHANSENS RECOMMENDED COUNTRY HOUSE
To Dublin/ Dun Laoghaire
Holyhead
ANGLESEY
CONWY
LLANDUDNO
CAERNARFON
GWYNEDD
BETWS-Y-COED
PORTMEIRION VILLAGE
CRICCIETH
ABERSOCH
HARLECH
BARMOUTH
DOLGELLAU
TYWYN
MACHYNLLETH
ABERYSTWYTH
HOLYWELL
CLYWD
MOLD
CORWEN
BALA
LLANARMON DYFFRYN CEIRIOG
LLANGOLLEN
LAKE VYRNWY
LLANFYLLIN
WELSHPOOL
MONTGOMERY
POWYS
WIGAN
LIVERPOOL
MERSEYSIDE
GREATER MANCHESTER
Manchester
SADDLEWORTH
GLOSSOP
HAYFIELD
ALTRINCHAM
MANCHESTER AIRPORT
WILMSLOW
ALDERLEY EDGE
KNUTSFORD
PRESTBURY
CHESHIRE
SANDIWAY
CHESTER
WILLINGTON
NANTWICH
LEEK
Stoke
ONNELEY
Whitchurch
STAFFORDSHIRE
OSWESTRY
Stafford
SHREWSBURY
TELFORD
WOLVERHAMPTON
SHROPSHIRE
BRIDGNORTH
WEST MIDLANDS
BIRMINGHAM
BELBROUGHTON
CHADDESLEY CORBETT
LUDLOW
BRIMFIELD
CLEOBURY MORTIMER
BROMSGROVE
REDDITCH
LEOMINSTER
HEREFORD & Worcester WORCESTER
ALCESTER
KINGTON
WEOBLEY
LLANGAMMARCH WELLS
MALVERN
UPTON-ON-SEVERN
EVESHAM
HEREFORD
LEDBURY
BROADWAY
HAY-ON-WYE
TEWKESBURY
WINCHCOMBE
BRECON
ROSS-ON-WYE
CHELTENHAM
GLOUCESTER
CRICKHOWELL
MONMOUTH
GLOUCESTERSHIRE
ABERGAVENNY
STONEHOUSE
CIRENCESTER
GWENT
USK
STROUD
MINCHIN HAMPTON
TINTERN
CHEPSTOW
TETBURY
MALMESBURY
NEWPORT
BADMINTON
CASTLE COMBE
CHIPPENHAM
FORD
BOX
To Rosslare
FISHGUARD
ST DAVID'S
DYFED
Carmarthen
Pembroke Dock
TENBY
LLANDEILO
WEST GLAMORGAN
SWANSEA
MID-GLAMORGAN
To Cork
BRIDGEND
CARDIFF
SOUTH GLAMORGAN
CARDIFF
BRISTOL
AVON
BATH
HUNSTRETE
BRADFORD-ON-AVON
CHEDDAR
BECKINGTON
WILTSHIRE
WELLS
WARMINSTER
COMBE MARTIN
LYNTON
LYNMOUTH
MIDDLECOMBE
MINEHEAD
WOOLACOMBE
SIMONSBATH
EXMOOR
EXFORD
KILVE
WITHYPOOL
BARNSTAPLE
INSTOW
DULVERTON
WIVELISCOMBE
SOMERSET
CASTLE CARY
CLOVELLY
SOUTH MOLTON
TAUNTON
MONTACUTE
SHERBORNE
STURMINSTER NEWTON
ISLES OF SCILLY
DEVON
THELBRIDGE
MORCHARD BISHOP
SEAVINGTON ST MARY
Blandford Forum
CHEDINGTON
EVERSHOT
WIMBORNE MINSTER
DORSET
HATHERLEIGH
HONITON
BEAMINSTER
AXMINSTER
BOURNEMOUTH
ASHWATER
OKEHAMPTON
EXETER
SIDMOUTH
BEER
BRIDPORT
DORCHESTER
POOLE
WAREHAM
TINTAGEL
CHAGFORD
LAUNCESTON
LIFTON
MORETON-HAMPSTEAD
DODDISCOMBSLEIGH
NEW POLZEATH
PORT GAVERNE
BOVEY TRACEY
PADSTOW
HAYTOR
ILSINGTON
DARTMOOR
NEWTON ABBOT
CONSTANTINE BAY
TAVISTOCK
ASHBURTON
NEWQUAY
CORNWALL
TORQUAY
STAVERTON
ST KEYNE
PLYMOUTH
TOTNES
PELYNT
LOOE
PLYMOUTH
NORTH HUISH
ST AGNES
ST AUSTELL
TALLAND-BY-LOOE
KINGSBRIDGE
CAMBORNE
ST IVES
PORTLOE
SALCOMBE
Penzance
HELSTON
ST MAWES
FALMOUTH
PORTHLEVEN
HELFORD
To Santander
To Roscoff
To Guernsey
0 20 40 60 80 100 Kilometres
0 10 20 30 40 50 Miles

To Zeebrugge
To Rotterdam
SADDLEWORTH
GREATER MANCHESTER
Manchester
SOUTH YORKSHIRE
DONCASTER
GLOSSOP
HAYFIELD
SHEFFIELD
WILMSLOW
CASTLETON
GRINDLEFORD
ALDERLEY EDGE
PRESTBURY
CALVER
DRONFIELD
BASLOW
ASHFORD-IN-THE-WATER
BAKEWELL
LINCOLN
WOODHALL SPA
MATLOCK
LEEK
DERBYSHIRE
NOTTINGHAMSHIRE
LINCOLNSHIRE
BIGGIN BY HARTINGTON
BELPER
FULBECK
ASHBOURNE
STAFFORDSHIRE
NOTTINGHAM
DERBY
BURNHAM MARKET
THORPE MARKET
FAKENHAM
GREAT SNORING
NORTH WALSHAM
BURTON UPON TRENT
CASTLE DONNINGTON
GRIMSTHORPE
Stafford
STAPLEFORD
KING'S LYNN
WROXHAM
GREENHILL
QUORN
OLD CATTON
NORWICH
LICHFIELD
LEICESTERSHIRE
OAKHAM
STAMFORD
NORFOLK
LEICESTER
RUTLAND WATER
WOLVERHAMPTON
UPPINGHAM
ATHERSTONE
FENNY DRAYTON
GLASTON
PETERBOROUGH
KINGSBURY
HINCKLEY
WEST MIDLANDS
BIRMINGHAM
BECCLES
LUTTERWORTH
GISSING
ELY
THETFORD
HUSBANDS BOSWORTH
BIRMINGHAM
DISS
BELBROUGHTON
Kettering
SOUTHWOLD
CHADDESLEY CORBETT
COVENTRY
RUGBY
NORTHAMPTONSHIRE
HUNTINGDON
FRESSINGFIELD
WALBERSWICK
HOCKLEY HEATH
BROMSGROVE
REDDITCH
WARWICK
BURY ST EDMUNDS
CLAVERDON
ALDEBURGH
STRATFORD-UPON-AVON
Northampton
CAMBRIDGE
CASTLE ASHBY
CAMBRIDGESHIRE
ALCESTER
BADBY
SUFFOLK
Worcester
WARWICKSHIRE
BEDFORD
To Gothenburg/Esbjerg/Hamburg
WOODBRIDGE
UPTON-ON-SEVERN
EVESHAM
CHIPPING CAMPDEN
BEDFORDSHIRE
LONG MELFORD
IPSWICH
MILTON KEYNES
LAVENHAM
BROADWAY
BANBURY
TEWKESBURY
BLOCKLEY
FLITWICK
ADDERBURY
Felixstowe
WINCHCOMBE
MORETON-IN-MARSH
CLAVERING
DEDHAM
Harwich
UPPER SLAUGHTER
KINGHAM
To Hook of Holland
STANSTED
STANSTED
BUCKINGHAMSHIRE
STOW-ON-THE-WOLD
COLCHESTER
CHELTENHAM
LUTON
LUTON
BISHOP'S STORTFORD
GREAT DUNMOW
SHIPTON-UNDER-WYCHWOOD
LOWER SLAUGHTER
BOURTON-ON-THE-WATER
To Zeebrugge
GLOUCESTER
WOODSTOCK
AYLESBURY
WARE
ESSEX
GLOUCESTERSHIRE
HERTFORDSHIRE
EASINGTON
STROUD
BURFORD
OXFORD
TRING
ST ALBANS
CHELMSFORD
BIBURY
THAME
CIRENCESTER
BAMPTON
FAIRFORD
OXFORDSHIRE
MINCHIN HAMPTON
MEYSEY HAMPTON
HADLEY WOOD
DORCHESTER-ON-THAMES
TETBURY
WALLINGFORD
STONOR
EXLADE STREET
MALMESBURY
SWINDON
MARLOW
GREATER LONDON
HURLEY
London
CASTLE COMBE
GORING-ON-THAMES
MAIDENHEAD
STREATLEY-ON-THAMES
BRAY-ON-THAMES
HENLEY
LONDON
Sheerness
FORD
SONNING-ON-THAMES
TWYFORD
RICHMOND-UPON-THAMES
DARTFORD
CHIPPENHAM
YATTENDON
WINDSOR
ETON
HEATHROW
BOX
MARLBOROUGH
NEWBURY
BERKSHIRE
ASCOT
HAMPTON COURT
Ramsgate
To Dunkerque
WEYBRIDGE
CANTERBURY
COBHAM
To Oostende
WILTSHIRE
MAIDSTONE
BASINGSTOKE
SURREY
GUILDFORD
REDHILL
KENT
WARMINSTER
GATWICK
TUNBRIDGE WELLS
ASHFORD
DOVER
ANDOVER
GODALMING
HAMPSHIRE
HASLEMERE
GATWICK
Folkestone
To Calais
Channel Tunnel
SALISBURY
WINCHESTER
HANDCROSS
NUTLEY
To Boulogne
To Boulogne
CUCKFIELD
BUXTED
NEW ROMNEY
SOUTHAMPTON
MIDHURST
PETWORTH
RYE
PULBOROUGH
EAST SUSSEX
FORDINGBRIDGE
UCKFIELD
BATTLE
Southampton
WEST SUSSEX
STORRINGTON
WINCHELSEA
Blandford Forum
LYNDHURST
Portsmouth
AMBERLEY
HERSTMONCEUX
ARUNDEL
WIMBORNE MINSTER
BROCKENHURST
BEAULIEU
CHICHESTER
BRIGHTON
ALFRISTON
WORTHING
Newhaven
NEW MILTON
LYMINGTON
Cowes
BOURNEMOUTH
POOLE
BOURNEMOUTH
WAREHAM
ISLE OF WIGHT
To Dieppe
THE CHANNEL ISLANDS
GUERNSEY
GUERNSEY
SARK
JERSEY
JERSEY
To Guernsey
To Bilbao
To St Malo
To Cherbourg
To Caen
To Le Havre
To Jersey
To Cherbourg

EDINBURGH
GLASGOW
Rothesay
LOTHIAN
IRVINE
TROON
STRATHCLYDE
PEEBLES
BORDERS
KELSO
CORNHILL-ON-TWEED
ABINGTON
MOFFAT
NORTHUMBERLAND
DUMFRIES AND GALLOWAY
Dumfries
Cairnryan
NEWTON STEWART
DALBEATTIE
CORBRIDGE
ANTRIM
To Larne
To Belfast
Stranraer
Larne
PORTPATRICK
GATEHOUSE OF FLEET
AUCHENCAIRN
Carrickfergus
Bangor
Belfast
CUMBRIA
BARNARD CASTLE
SEE INSET ON RIGHT
DOWN
ISLE OF MAN
Kendal
ASKRIGG
Douglas
Heysham
BOLTON-BY-BOWLAND
SKIPTON
WHITEWELL
LANCASHIRE
Fleetwood
Blackpool
HAWORTH
HEBDEN BRIDGE
PRESTON
To Dublin
SOUTHPORT
WIGAN
SADDLEWORTH
GREATER MANCHESTER
Manchester
LIVERPOOL
MERSEYSIDE
GLOSSOP
To Dublin/ Dun Laoghaire
ALTRINCHAM
HAYFIELD
MANCHESTER AIRPORT
WILMSLOW
ALDERLEY EDGE
KNUTSFORD
PRESTBURY
LLANDUDNO
Holyhead
ANGLESEY
CONWY
HOLYWELL
CHESHIRE
SANDIWAY
CLWYD
CHESTER
WILLINGTON
CAERNARFON
MOLD
BETWS-Y-COED
GWYNEDD
NANTWICH
LEEK
PORTMEIRION VILLAGE
CORWEN
Stoke
CRICCIETH
BALA
LLANGOLLEN
Whitchurch
ONNELEY
STAFFORDSHIRE
LLANARMON DYFFRYN CEIRIOG
HARLECH
OSWESTRY
ABERSOCH
LAKE VYRNWY
Stafford
DOLGELLAU
BARMOUTH
LLANFYLLIN
SHREWSBURY
WELSHPOOL
TELFORD
TYWYN
MACHYNLLETH
WOLVERHAMPTON
MONTGOMERY
SHROPSHIRE
BRIDGNORTH
WEST MIDLANDS
ABERYSTWYTH
BELBROUGHTON
POWYS
CLEOBURY MORTIMER
CHADDESLEY CORBETT
LUDLOW
BRIMFIELD
BROMSGROVE
REDDITCH

CORNHILL-ON-TWEED
BELFORD
BAMBURGH
ALNWICK
NORTHUMBERLAND
CORBRIDGE
NEWCASTLE
TYNE AND WEAR
DURHAM
NEWTON AYCLIFFE
BARNARD CASTLE
DARLINGTON
Middlesbrough
CLEVELAND
WHITBY
EGTON
GOATHLAND
CRATHORNE
NORTH YORKSHIRE
ROSEDALE ABBEY
APPLETON-LE-MOORS
KIRKBYMOORSIDE
SCARBOROUGH
WEST WITTON
ASKRIGG
MIDDLEHAM
EAST WITTON
HELMSLEY
PICKERING
HOVINGHAM
MALTON
BOLTON ABBEY
HARROGATE
SKIPTON
YORK
OTLEY
WETHERBY
HUMBERSIDE
HAWORTH
BRADFORD
LEEDS
BEVERLEY
HEBDEN BRIDGE
HALIFAX
Hull
WEST YORKSHIRE
Wakefield
HUDDERSFIELD
SADDLEWORTH
DONCASTER
SOUTH YORKSHIRE
Manchester
GLOSSOP
HAYFIELD
CASTLETON
SHEFFIELD
WILMSLOW
GRINDLEFORD
ALDERLEY EDGE
PRESTBURY
CALVER
DRONFIELD
BASLOW
ASHFORD-IN-THE-WATER
BAKEWELL
LINCOLN
WOODHALL SPA
MATLOCK
LEEK
DERBYSHIRE
NOTTINGHAMSHIRE
LINCOLNSHIRE
BIGGIN BY HARTINGTON
FULBECK
ASHBOURNE
BELPER
STAFFORDSHIRE
NOTTINGHAM
DERBY
BURNHAM MARKET
THORPE MARKET
FAKENHAM
GREAT SNORING
NORTH WALSHAM
BURTON UPON TRENT
CASTLE DONNINGTON
GRIMSTHORPE
Stafford
STAPLEFORD
KING'S LYNN
WROXHAM
GREENHILL
QUORN
LEICESTERSHIRE
NORWICH
OLD CATTON
LICHFIELD
OAKHAM
STAMFORD
RUTLAND WATER
LEICESTER
UPPINGHAM
NORFOLK
WOLVERHAMPTON
ATHERSTONE
FENNY DRAYTON
GLASTON
PETERBOROUGH
KINGSBURY
HINCKLEY
WEST MIDLANDS
BIRMINGHAM
LUTTERWORTH
HUSBANDS BOSWORTH
ELY
THETFORD
GISSING
BECCLES
DISS
Kettering
SOUTHWOLD
BELBROUGHTON
COVENTRY
RUGBY
NORTHAMPTONSHIRE
FRESSINGFIELD
WALBERSWICK
To Stavanger/Bergen
To Gothenburg
To Esbjerg
To Hamburg
To Zeebrugge
To Rotterdam
CARLISLE
BRAMPTON
ALSTON
CUMBRIA
PENRITH
KESWICK-ON-DERWENTWATER
LAKE ULLSWATER
APPLEBY-IN-WESTMORLAND
BUTTERMERE
GRASMERE
AMBLESIDE
TROUTBECK
WINDERMERE
HAWKSHEAD
Kendal
HAWES
NEWBY BRIDGE
WITHERSLACK
CARTMEL
GRANGE-OVER-SANDS
KIRKBY LONSDALE
Heysham
JOHANSENS RECOMMENDED HOTEL
JOHANSENS RECOMMENDED INN OR RESTAURANT
JOHANSENS RECOMMENDED COUNTRY HOUSE
0 20 40 60 80 100 Kilometres
0 10 20 30 40 50 Miles

Scrabster
KYLESKU
Stornoway
ACHILTIBUIE
STRATH BRORA
Ullapool
Tarbert
ISLE OF HARRIS
ISLE OF SKYE
ISLE OF SKYE
TORRIDON
ELGIN
FORRES
INVERNESS
INVERNESS
HIGHLAND
ARDELVE
DRUMNADROCHIT
GRANTOWN-ON-SPEY
ISLE OF SKYE
WHITEBRIDGE
AVIEMORE
Ardvasar
Mallaig
BEASDALE
FORT WILLIAM
TAYSIDE
KILLIECRANKIE
PITLOCHRY
KENTALLEN OF APPIN
ABERFELDY
Lochaline
APPIN
BLAIRGOWRIE
ISLE OF ERISKA
DUNKELD
ISLE OF MULL
OBAN
SCONE
PERTH
KILCHRENAN
COMRIE
CALLANDER
PORT OF MENTETH
KINBUCK
KINROSS
CENTRAL
DRYMEN
FINTRY
LOCHGILPHEAD
LOCH LOMOND
DUNOON
EDINBURGH
GLASGOW
Rothesay
GLASGOW
LOTHIAN
IRVINE
STRATHCLYDE
TROON
ABINGTON
MOFFAT
Coleraine
DUMFRIES AND GALLOWAY
Londonderry

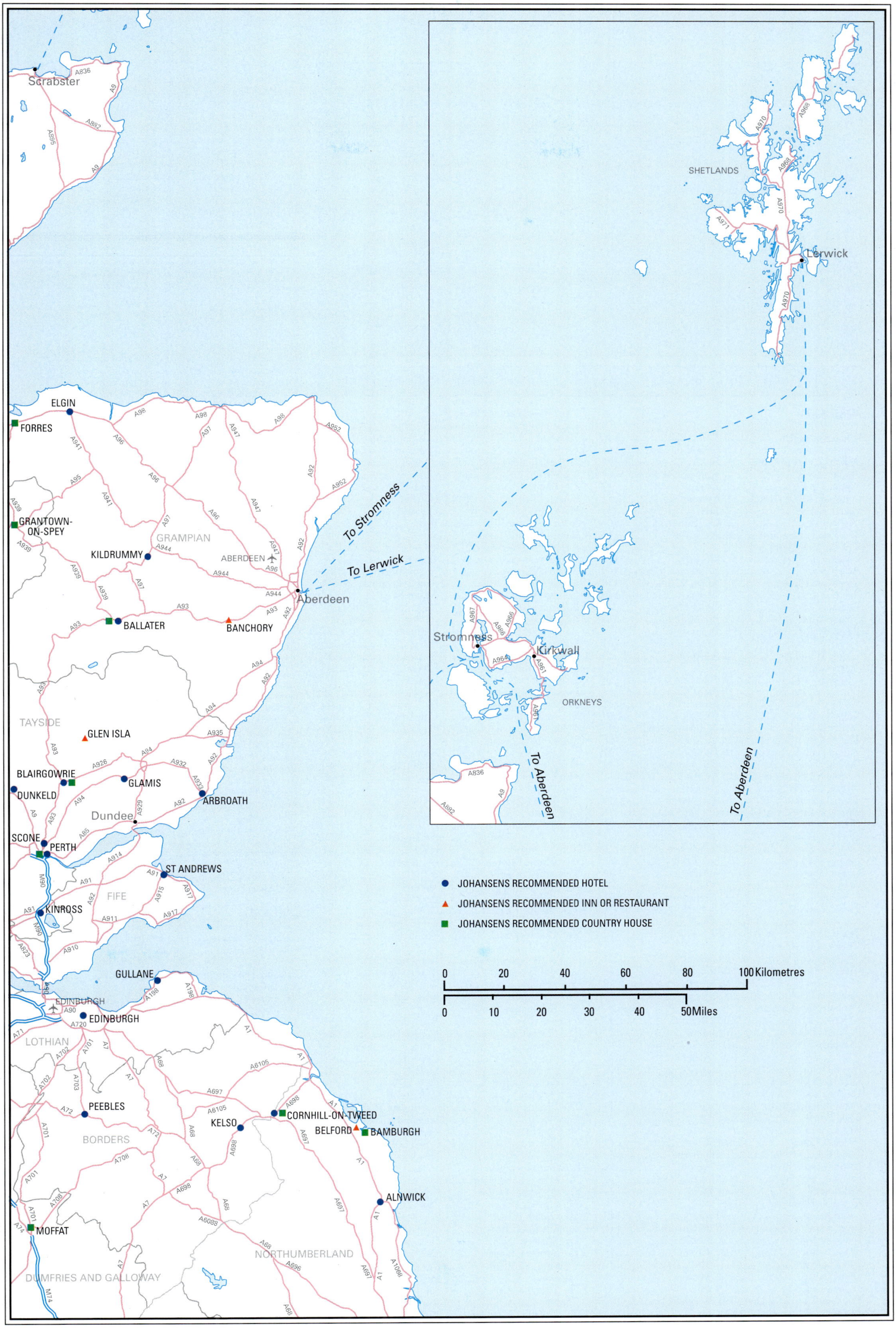
Scrabster
SHETLANDS
Lerwick
ELGIN
FORRES
To Stromness
To Lerwick
GRANTOWN-ON-SPEY
GRAMPIAN
KILDRUMMY
ABERDEEN
Aberdeen
BALLATER
BANCHORY
Stromness
Kirkwall
ORKNEYS
To Aberdeen
To Aberdeen
TAYSIDE
GLEN ISLA
BLAIRGOWRIE
DUNKELD
GLAMIS
ARBROATH
Dundee
SCONE
PERTH
ST ANDREWS
FIFE
KINROSS
JOHANSENS RECOMMENDED HOTEL
JOHANSENS RECOMMENDED INN OR RESTAURANT
JOHANSENS RECOMMENDED COUNTRY HOUSE
0 20 40 60 80 100 Kilometres
0 10 20 30 40 50 Miles
GULLANE
EDINBURGH
EDINBURGH
LOTHIAN
PEEBLES
KELSO
CORNHILL-ON-TWEED
BELFORD
BAMBURGH
BORDERS
ALNWICK
MOFFAT
NORTHUMBERLAND
DUMFRIES AND GALLOWAY

To enable you to use your 1996 Johansens Recommended Country Houses and Small Hotel Guide more effectively, the following four pages of indexes contain a wealth of useful information about the establishments featured in the Guide. As well as listing the hotels alphabetically, by region and by county, the indexes also show at a glance which Country Houses offer certain specialised facilities.

The indexes are listed as follows:

- Alphabetically by region
- By county
- With a swimming pool
- With tennis
- With fishing nearby
- With shooting facilities
- With conference facilities for 30 delegates or more
- Double rooms for £50 or under
- Single rooms for £30 or under
- Index of advertisers

1996 Johansens Recommended Country Houses listed alphabetically by region

1996 Johansens Recommended Country Houses by county

Country Houses with a swimming pool

Country Houses with tennis

Country Houses with fishing nearby

Country Houses with shooting nearby

Country Houses with conference facilities for 30 delegates or more

Country Houses with single rooms for £30 per night or under

Country Houses with double rooms for £50 per night or under

Index of Advertisers

NEW

Recommended Hotels in Europe 1996

A stunning new publication from Johansens.

Discover over 120 of the finest establishments in more than 20 European countries.

From French chateaux to German castles, Italian palaces and Belgian town houses, there is something to please business and leisure travellers alike. There are recommendations in famous European cities such as Paris, Rome and Salzburg, as well as some located in inspirational countryside with superb views.

On sale at all good bookstores or direct from the publisher at £9.95 plus p&p. Call the credit card hotline on 0800 269397 to place your order.

JOHANSENS 1996 RECOMMENDED

GUEST SURVEY REPORT

Name and location of hotel: ______________________ Date of visit: ____________

Name and address of guest: ______________________

______________________ Postcode: ____________

Please tick one box in each category below:	Excellent	Good	Disappointing	Poor
Bedrooms				
Public Rooms				
Restaurant/Cuisine				
Service				
Welcome/Friendliness				
Value For Money				

PLEASE return your Guest Survey Report form!

Occasionally we may allow other reputable organisations to write with offers which may be of interest.

If you prefer not to here from them, tick this box ☐

To: Johansens, FREEPOST (CB264), 175-179 St John Street, London EC1B 1JQ

Your own Johansens 'inspection' gives reliability to our guides and assists in the selection of Award Nominations

GUEST SURVEY REPORT

Name and location of hotel: ______________________ Date of visit: ____________

Name and address of guest: ______________________

______________________ Postcode: ____________

Please tick one box in each category below:	Excellent	Good	Disappointing	Poor
Bedrooms				
Public Rooms				
Restaurant/Cuisine				
Service				
Welcome/Friendliness				
Value For Money				

PLEASE return your Guest Survey Report form!

Occasionally we may allow other reputable organisations to write with offers which may be of interest.

If you prefer not to here from them, tick this box ☐

To: Johansens, FREEPOST (CB264), 175-179 St John Street, London EC1B 1JQ

Your own Johansens 'inspection' gives reliability to our guides and assists in the selection of Award Nominations

GUEST SURVEY REPORT

Name and location of hotel: ______________________ Date of visit: ____________

Name and address of guest: ______________________

______________________ Postcode: ____________

Please tick one box in each category below:	Excellent	Good	Disappointing	Poor
Bedrooms				
Public Rooms				
Restaurant/Cuisine				
Service				
Welcome/Friendliness				
Value For Money				

PLEASE return your Guest Survey Report form!

Occasionally we may allow other reputable organisations to write with offers which may be of interest.

If you prefer not to here from them, tick this box ☐

To: Johansens, FREEPOST (CB264), 175-179 St John Street, London EC1B 1JQ

Your own Johansens 'inspection' gives reliability to our guides and assists in the selection of Award Nominations

Order Coupon

To order Johansens guides, simply indicate which publications you require by putting the quantity(ies) in the boxes provided. Choose you preferred method of payment and return this coupon (NO STAMP REQUIRED). You may also place your order using FREEPHONE 0800 269397 or by fax on 0171 490 2538.

❑ I enclose a cheque for £______________ payable to Biblios PDS Ltd (Johansens book distributor).
❑ I enclose my order on company letterheading, please invoice me. (UK companies only)
❑ Please debit my credit/charge card account (please tick)
❑ MASTERCARD ❑ VISA ❑ DINERS ❑ AMEX

Card Number ______________________________

Signature ______________________ Expiry Date ____________

Name (Mr/Mrs/Miss) ______________________________

Address ______________________________

____

______________________ Postcode ____________

(We aim to despatch your order with 10 days, but please allow 28 days for delivery)

Occasionally we may allow reputable organisations to write to you with offers which may interest you. If you prefer not to hear from them, tick this box ❑

CALL THE JOHANSENS CREDIT CARD ORDER SERVICE FREE ☎ **0800 269397**

	PRICE	QTY	TOTAL
save £10 WHEN YOU BUY A SET OF ALL THREE 1996 UK JOHANSENS GUIDES	£35.80		
Boxed presentation set of three 1996 UK Johansens guides with slip case	£39.00		
Johansens Recommended Hotels in Great Britain & Ireland 1996	£21.90		
Johansens Recommended Inns with Restaurants in Great Britain 1996	£11.95		
Johansens Recommended Country Houses and Small Hotels in Great Britain & Ireland 1996	£11.95		
Johansens Recommended Hotels in Europe 1996	£11.95		

ALL PRICES INCLUDE HANDLING AND UK POSTAGE ONLY **38J**

Outside the UK add £3 for each single guide ordered, or £5 for a set or boxed set to cover additional postage. ***PRICES VALID UNTIL 31/12/96***

Post free to:
JOHANSENS, FREEPOST (CB264), HORSHAM, WEST SUSSEX RH13 8ZA

Order Coupon

To order Johansens guides, simply indicate which publications you require by putting the quantity(ies) in the boxes provided. Choose you preferred method of payment and return this coupon (NO STAMP REQUIRED). You may also place your order using FREEPHONE 0800 269397 or by fax on 0171 490 2538.

❑ I enclose a cheque for £______________ payable to Biblios PDS Ltd (Johansens book distributor).
❑ I enclose my order on company letterheading, please invoice me. (UK companies only)
❑ Please debit my credit/charge card account (please tick)
❑ MASTERCARD ❑ VISA ❑ DINERS ❑ AMEX

Card Number ______________________________

Signature ______________________ Expiry Date ____________

Name (Mr/Mrs/Miss) ______________________________

Address ______________________________

____

______________________ Postcode ____________

(We aim to despatch your order with 10 days, but please allow 28 days for delivery)

Occasionally we may allow reputable organisations to write to you with offers which may interest you. If you prefer not to hear from them, tick this box ❑

CALL THE JOHANSENS CREDIT CARD ORDER SERVICE FREE ☎ **0800 269397**

	PRICE	QTY	TOTAL
save £10 WHEN YOU BUY A SET OF ALL THREE 1996 UK JOHANSENS GUIDES	£35.80		
Boxed presentation set of three 1996 UK Johansens guides with slip case	£39.00		
Johansens Recommended Hotels in Great Britain & Ireland 1996	£21.90		
Johansens Recommended Inns with Restaurants in Great Britain 1996	£11.95		
Johansens Recommended Country Houses and Small Hotels in Great Britain & Ireland 1996	£11.95		
Johansens Recommended Hotels in Europe 1996	£11.95		

ALL PRICES INCLUDE HANDLING AND UK POSTAGE ONLY **38J**

Outside the UK add £3 for each single guide ordered, or £5 for a set or boxed set to cover additional postage. ***PRICES VALID UNTIL 31/12/96***

Post free to:
JOHANSENS, FREEPOST (CB264), HORSHAM, WEST SUSSEX RH13 8ZA

Order Coupon

To order Johansens guides, simply indicate which publications you require by putting the quantity(ies) in the boxes provided. Choose you preferred method of payment and return this coupon (NO STAMP REQUIRED). You may also place your order using FREEPHONE 0800 269397 or by fax on 0171 490 2538.

❑ I enclose a cheque for £______________ payable to Biblios PDS Ltd (Johansens book distributor).
❑ I enclose my order on company letterheading, please invoice me. (UK companies only)
❑ Please debit my credit/charge card account (please tick)
❑ MASTERCARD ❑ VISA ❑ DINERS ❑ AMEX

Card Number ______________________________

Signature ______________________ Expiry Date ____________

Name (Mr/Mrs/Miss) ______________________________

Address ______________________________

____

______________________ Postcode ____________

(We aim to despatch your order with 10 days, but please allow 28 days for delivery)

Occasionally we may allow reputable organisations to write to you with offers which may interest you. If you prefer not to hear from them, tick this box ❑

CALL THE JOHANSENS CREDIT CARD ORDER SERVICE FREE ☎ **0800 269397**

	PRICE	QTY	TOTAL
save £10 WHEN YOU BUY A SET OF ALL THREE 1996 UK JOHANSENS GUIDES	£35.80		
Boxed presentation set of three 1996 UK Johansens guides with slip case	£39.00		
Johansens Recommended Hotels in Great Britain & Ireland 1996	£21.90		
Johansens Recommended Inns with Restaurants in Great Britain 1996	£11.95		
Johansens Recommended Country Houses and Small Hotels in Great Britain & Ireland 1996	£11.95		
Johansens Recommended Hotels in Europe 1996	£11.95		

ALL PRICES INCLUDE HANDLING AND UK POSTAGE ONLY **38J**

Outside the UK add £3 for each single guide ordered, or £5 for a set or boxed set to cover additional postage. ***PRICES VALID UNTIL 31/12/96***

Post free to:
JOHANSENS, FREEPOST (CB264), HORSHAM, WEST SUSSEX RH13 8ZA

GUEST SURVEY REPORT

Name and location of hotel: ______________________ Date of visit: __________

Name and address of guest: ______________________

______________________ Postcode: __________

Please tick one box in each category below:	Excellent	Good	Disappointing	Poor
Bedrooms				
Public Rooms				
Restaurant/Cuisine				
Service				
Welcome/Friendliness				
Value For Money				

PLEASE return your Guest Survey Report form!

Occasionally we may allow other reputable organisations to write with offers which may be of interest.

If you prefer not to here from them, tick this box ☐

To: Johansens, FREEPOST (CB264), 175-179 St John Street, London EC1B 1JQ

Your own Johansens 'inspection' gives reliability to our guides and assists in the selection of Award Nominations

GUEST SURVEY REPORT

Name and location of hotel: ______________________ Date of visit: __________

Name and address of guest: ______________________

______________________ Postcode: __________

Please tick one box in each category below:	Excellent	Good	Disappointing	Poor
Bedrooms				
Public Rooms				
Restaurant/Cuisine				
Service				
Welcome/Friendliness				
Value For Money				

PLEASE return your Guest Survey Report form!

Occasionally we may allow other reputable organisations to write with offers which may be of interest.

If you prefer not to here from them, tick this box ☐

To: Johansens, FREEPOST (CB264), 175-179 St John Street, London EC1B 1JQ

Your own Johansens 'inspection' gives reliability to our guides and assists in the selection of Award Nominations

GUEST SURVEY REPORT

Name and location of hotel: ______________________ Date of visit: __________

Name and address of guest: ______________________

______________________ Postcode: __________

Please tick one box in each category below:	Excellent	Good	Disappointing	Poor
Bedrooms				
Public Rooms				
Restaurant/Cuisine				
Service				
Welcome/Friendliness				
Value For Money				

PLEASE return your Guest Survey Report form!

Occasionally we may allow other reputable organisations to write with offers which may be of interest.

If you prefer not to here from them, tick this box ☐

To: Johansens, FREEPOST (CB264), 175-179 St John Street, London EC1B 1JQ

Your own Johansens 'inspection' gives reliability to our guides and assists in the selection of Award Nominations

Order Coupon

To order Johansens guides, simply indicate which publications you require by putting the quantity(ies) in the boxes provided. Choose you preferred method of payment and return this coupon (NO STAMP REQUIRED). You may also place your order using FREEPHONE 0800 269397 or by fax on 0171 490 2538.

❑ I enclose a cheque for £______________ payable to Biblios PDS Ltd (Johansens book distributor).
❑ I enclose my order on company letterheading, please invoice me. (UK companies only)
❑ Please debit my credit/charge card account (please tick)
❑ MASTERCARD ❑ VISA ❑ DINERS ❑ AMEX

Card Number ______________________________

Signature ______________________ Expiry Date __________

Name (Mr/Mrs/Miss) ______________________________

Address ______________________________

____

______________________ Postcode __________

(We aim to despatch your order with 10 days, but please allow 28 days for delivery)

Occasionally we may allow reputable organisations to write to you with offers which may interest you. If you prefer not to hear from them, tick this box ❑

CALL THE JOHANSENS CREDIT CARD ORDER SERVICE FREE ☎ **0800 269397**

	PRICE	QTY	TOTAL
save £10 WHEN YOU BUY A SET OF ALL THREE 1996 UK JOHANSENS GUIDES	£35.80		
Boxed presentation set of three 1996 UK Johansens guides with slip case	£39.00		
Johansens Recommended Hotels in Great Britain & Ireland 1996	£21.90		
Johansens Recommended Inns with Restaurants in Great Britain 1996	£11.95		
Johansens Recommended Country Houses and Small Hotels in Great Britain & Ireland 1996	£11.95		
Johansens Recommended Hotels in Europe 1996	£11.95		

ALL PRICES INCLUDE HANDLING AND UK POSTAGE ONLY **38J**

Outside the UK add £3 for each single guide ordered, or £5 for a set or boxed set to cover additional postage. ***PRICES VALID UNTIL 31/12/96***

Post free to:
JOHANSENS, FREEPOST (CB264), HORSHAM, WEST SUSSEX RH13 8ZA

Order Coupon

To order Johansens guides, simply indicate which publications you require by putting the quantity(ies) in the boxes provided. Choose you preferred method of payment and return this coupon (NO STAMP REQUIRED). You may also place your order using FREEPHONE 0800 269397 or by fax on 0171 490 2538.

❑ I enclose a cheque for £______________ payable to Biblios PDS Ltd (Johansens book distributor).
❑ I enclose my order on company letterheading, please invoice me. (UK companies only)
❑ Please debit my credit/charge card account (please tick)
❑ MASTERCARD ❑ VISA ❑ DINERS ❑ AMEX

Card Number ______________________________

Signature ______________________ Expiry Date __________

Name (Mr/Mrs/Miss) ______________________________

Address ______________________________

____

______________________ Postcode __________

(We aim to despatch your order with 10 days, but please allow 28 days for delivery)

Occasionally we may allow reputable organisations to write to you with offers which may interest you. If you prefer not to hear from them, tick this box ❑

CALL THE JOHANSENS CREDIT CARD ORDER SERVICE FREE ☎ **0800 269397**

	PRICE	QTY	TOTAL
save £10 WHEN YOU BUY A SET OF ALL THREE 1996 UK JOHANSENS GUIDES	£35.80		
Boxed presentation set of three 1996 UK Johansens guides with slip case	£39.00		
Johansens Recommended Hotels in Great Britain & Ireland 1996	£21.90		
Johansens Recommended Inns with Restaurants in Great Britain 1996	£11.95		
Johansens Recommended Country Houses and Small Hotels in Great Britain & Ireland 1996	£11.95		
Johansens Recommended Hotels in Europe 1996	£11.95		

ALL PRICES INCLUDE HANDLING AND UK POSTAGE ONLY **38J**

Outside the UK add £3 for each single guide ordered, or £5 for a set or boxed set to cover additional postage. ***PRICES VALID UNTIL 31/12/96***

Post free to:
JOHANSENS, FREEPOST (CB264), HORSHAM, WEST SUSSEX RH13 8ZA

Order Coupon

To order Johansens guides, simply indicate which publications you require by putting the quantity(ies) in the boxes provided. Choose you preferred method of payment and return this coupon (NO STAMP REQUIRED). You may also place your order using FREEPHONE 0800 269397 or by fax on 0171 490 2538.

❑ I enclose a cheque for £______________ payable to Biblios PDS Ltd (Johansens book distributor).
❑ I enclose my order on company letterheading, please invoice me. (UK companies only)
❑ Please debit my credit/charge card account (please tick)
❑ MASTERCARD ❑ VISA ❑ DINERS ❑ AMEX

Card Number ______________________________

Signature ______________________ Expiry Date __________

Name (Mr/Mrs/Miss) ______________________________

Address ______________________________

____

______________________ Postcode __________

(We aim to despatch your order with 10 days, but please allow 28 days for delivery)

Occasionally we may allow reputable organisations to write to you with offers which may interest you. If you prefer not to hear from them, tick this box ❑

CALL THE JOHANSENS CREDIT CARD ORDER SERVICE FREE ☎ **0800 269397**

	PRICE	QTY	TOTAL
save £10 WHEN YOU BUY A SET OF ALL THREE 1996 UK JOHANSENS GUIDES	£35.80		
Boxed presentation set of three 1996 UK Johansens guides with slip case	£39.00		
Johansens Recommended Hotels in Great Britain & Ireland 1996	£21.90		
Johansens Recommended Inns with Restaurants in Great Britain 1996	£11.95		
Johansens Recommended Country Houses and Small Hotels in Great Britain & Ireland 1996	£11.95		
Johansens Recommended Hotels in Europe 1996	£11.95		

ALL PRICES INCLUDE HANDLING AND UK POSTAGE ONLY **38J**

Outside the UK add £3 for each single guide ordered, or £5 for a set or boxed set to cover additional postage. ***PRICES VALID UNTIL 31/12/96***

Post free to:
JOHANSENS, FREEPOST (CB264), HORSHAM, WEST SUSSEX RH13 8ZA

GUEST SURVEY REPORT

Name and location of hotel: ______________________ Date of visit: __________

Name and address of guest: ______________________

______________________ Postcode: __________

Please tick one box in each category below:	Excellent	Good	Disappointing	Poor
Bedrooms				
Public Rooms				
Restaurant/Cuisine				
Service				
Welcome/Friendliness				
Value For Money				

PLEASE return your Guest Survey Report form!

Occasionally we may allow other reputable organisations to write with offers which may be of interest.

If you prefer not to here from them, tick this box ☐

To: Johansens, FREEPOST (CB264), 175-179 St John Street, London EC1B 1JQ

Your own Johansens 'inspection' gives reliability to our guides and assists in the selection of Award Nominations

GUEST SURVEY REPORT

Name and location of hotel: ______________________ Date of visit: __________

Name and address of guest: ______________________

______________________ Postcode: __________

Please tick one box in each category below:	Excellent	Good	Disappointing	Poor
Bedrooms				
Public Rooms				
Restaurant/Cuisine				
Service				
Welcome/Friendliness				
Value For Money				

PLEASE return your Guest Survey Report form!

Occasionally we may allow other reputable organisations to write with offers which may be of interest.

If you prefer not to here from them, tick this box ☐

To: Johansens, FREEPOST (CB264), 175-179 St John Street, London EC1B 1JQ

Your own Johansens 'inspection' gives reliability to our guides and assists in the selection of Award Nominations

GUEST SURVEY REPORT

Name and location of hotel: ______________________ Date of visit: __________

Name and address of guest: ______________________

______________________ Postcode: __________

Please tick one box in each category below:	Excellent	Good	Disappointing	Poor
Bedrooms				
Public Rooms				
Restaurant/Cuisine				
Service				
Welcome/Friendliness				
Value For Money				

PLEASE return your Guest Survey Report form!

Occasionally we may allow other reputable organisations to write with offers which may be of interest.

If you prefer not to here from them, tick this box ☐

To: Johansens, FREEPOST (CB264), 175-179 St John Street, London EC1B 1JQ

Your own Johansens 'inspection' gives reliability to our guides and assists in the selection of Award Nominations

Order Coupon

To order Johansens guides, simply indicate which publications you require by putting the quantity(ies) in the boxes provided. Choose you preferred method of payment and return this coupon (NO STAMP REQUIRED). You may also place your order using FREEPHONE 0800 269397 or by fax on 0171 490 2538.

❑ I enclose a cheque for £____________ payable to Biblios PDS Ltd (Johansens book distributor).

❑ I enclose my order on company letterheading, please invoice me. (UK companies only)

❑ Please debit my credit/charge card account (please tick)

❑ MASTERCARD ❑ VISA ❑ DINERS ❑ AMEX

Card Number ______________________________

Signature ______________________ Expiry Date __________

Name (Mr/Mrs/Miss) ______________________________

Address ______________________________

____

______________________ Postcode __________

(We aim to despatch your order with 10 days, but please allow 28 days for delivery)

Occasionally we may allow reputable organisations to write to you with offers which may interest you. If you prefer not to hear from them, tick this box ❑

CALL THE JOHANSENS CREDIT CARD ORDER SERVICE FREE ☎ **0800 269397**

save £10	PRICE	QTY	TOTAL
WHEN YOU BUY A SET OF ALL THREE 1996 UK JOHANSENS GUIDES	£35.80		
Boxed presentation set of three 1996 UK Johansens guides with slip case	£39.00		
Johansens Recommended Hotels in Great Britain & Ireland 1996	£21.90		
Johansens Recommended Inns with Restaurants in Great Britain 1996	£11.95		
Johansens Recommended Country Houses and Small Hotels in Great Britain & Ireland 1996	£11.95		
Johansens Recommended Hotels in Europe 1996	£11.95		

ALL PRICES INCLUDE HANDLING AND UK POSTAGE ONLY **38J**

Outside the UK add £3 for each single guide ordered, or £5 for a set or boxed set to cover additional postage. ***PRICES VALID UNTIL 31/12/96***

Post free to:
JOHANSENS, FREEPOST (CB264), HORSHAM, WEST SUSSEX RH13 8ZA

Order Coupon

To order Johansens guides, simply indicate which publications you require by putting the quantity(ies) in the boxes provided. Choose you preferred method of payment and return this coupon (NO STAMP REQUIRED). You may also place your order using FREEPHONE 0800 269397 or by fax on 0171 490 2538.

❑ I enclose a cheque for £____________ payable to Biblios PDS Ltd (Johansens book distributor).

❑ I enclose my order on company letterheading, please invoice me. (UK companies only)

❑ Please debit my credit/charge card account (please tick)

❑ MASTERCARD ❑ VISA ❑ DINERS ❑ AMEX

Card Number ______________________________

Signature ______________________ Expiry Date __________

Name (Mr/Mrs/Miss) ______________________________

Address ______________________________

____

______________________ Postcode __________

(We aim to despatch your order with 10 days, but please allow 28 days for delivery)

Occasionally we may allow reputable organisations to write to you with offers which may interest you. If you prefer not to hear from them, tick this box ❑

CALL THE JOHANSENS CREDIT CARD ORDER SERVICE FREE ☎ **0800 269397**

save £10	PRICE	QTY	TOTAL
WHEN YOU BUY A SET OF ALL THREE 1996 UK JOHANSENS GUIDES	£35.80		
Boxed presentation set of three 1996 UK Johansens guides with slip case	£39.00		
Johansens Recommended Hotels in Great Britain & Ireland 1996	£21.90		
Johansens Recommended Inns with Restaurants in Great Britain 1996	£11.95		
Johansens Recommended Country Houses and Small Hotels in Great Britain & Ireland 1996	£11.95		
Johansens Recommended Hotels in Europe 1996	£11.95		

ALL PRICES INCLUDE HANDLING AND UK POSTAGE ONLY **38J**

Outside the UK add £3 for each single guide ordered, or £5 for a set or boxed set to cover additional postage. ***PRICES VALID UNTIL 31/12/96***

Post free to:
JOHANSENS, FREEPOST (CB264), HORSHAM, WEST SUSSEX RH13 8ZA

Order Coupon

To order Johansens guides, simply indicate which publications you require by putting the quantity(ies) in the boxes provided. Choose you preferred method of payment and return this coupon (NO STAMP REQUIRED). You may also place your order using FREEPHONE 0800 269397 or by fax on 0171 490 2538.

❑ I enclose a cheque for £____________ payable to Biblios PDS Ltd (Johansens book distributor).

❑ I enclose my order on company letterheading, please invoice me. (UK companies only)

❑ Please debit my credit/charge card account (please tick)

❑ MASTERCARD ❑ VISA ❑ DINERS ❑ AMEX

Card Number ______________________________

Signature ______________________ Expiry Date __________

Name (Mr/Mrs/Miss) ______________________________

Address ______________________________

____

______________________ Postcode __________

(We aim to despatch your order with 10 days, but please allow 28 days for delivery)

Occasionally we may allow reputable organisations to write to you with offers which may interest you. If you prefer not to hear from them, tick this box ❑

CALL THE JOHANSENS CREDIT CARD ORDER SERVICE FREE ☎ **0800 269397**

save £10	PRICE	QTY	TOTAL
WHEN YOU BUY A SET OF ALL THREE 1996 UK JOHANSENS GUIDES	£35.80		
Boxed presentation set of three 1996 UK Johansens guides with slip case	£39.00		
Johansens Recommended Hotels in Great Britain & Ireland 1996	£21.90		
Johansens Recommended Inns with Restaurants in Great Britain 1996	£11.95		
Johansens Recommended Country Houses and Small Hotels in Great Britain & Ireland 1996	£11.95		
Johansens Recommended Hotels in Europe 1996	£11.95		

ALL PRICES INCLUDE HANDLING AND UK POSTAGE ONLY **38J**

Outside the UK add £3 for each single guide ordered, or £5 for a set or boxed set to cover additional postage. ***PRICES VALID UNTIL 31/12/96***

Post free to:
JOHANSENS, FREEPOST (CB264), HORSHAM, WEST SUSSEX RH13 8ZA

North American Order Coupon

To order Johansens guides in North America, simply indicate which guide(s) you wish by entering the quantity in the boxes provided. Select your preferred method of payment and forward whole Order Coupon by mail to Johansens at the address given at the bottom of this coupon.

PLEASE PRINT

Your Name

Street Address

Town/City

State/Province Zip/Post Code

☐ I enclose a check for US $ payable to JOHANSENS.

☐ Please debit my credit/charge card account the amount of US $ in favor of JOHANSENS.

☐ MasterCard ☐ Diners ☐ Amex ☐ Visa ☐ Discover ☐ Carte Blanche

Card No

Expiry date

Signature Date

Mail to: JOHANSENS, 30 Edison Drive, Wayne, New Jersey 07470

SAVE $5

		Qty	US$ Total
When you buy all three 1996 UK Johansens guides	US$49.75 + $8.25 s&h		
Boxed presentation set of three 1996 UK Johansens guides	US$58.75 + $8.75 s&h		
Johansens Recommended Hotels in Great Britain & Ireland 1996	US$24.95 + $6.00 s&h		
Johansens Recommended Inns with Restaurants in Great Britain 1996	US$14.95 + $4.75 s&h		
Johansens Recommended Country Houses in Great Britain & Ireland 1996	US$14.95 + $4.75 s&h		
Johansens Recommended Hotels in Europe 1996	US$14.95 + $4.75 s&h		

All items shipped UPS Ground Service. Canadian customers or for experdited delivery details telephone 1-800 213 9628 (24 Hours). New Jersey customers, please add appropriate sales tax. Please allow 21 days for delivery.

BILLING ADDRESS OF CREDIT/CHARGE CARD, IF DIFFERENT FROM ABOVE

Street Address

Town/City

State/Province Zip/Post Code

North American Order Coupon

To order Johansens guides in North America, simply indicate which guide(s) you wish by entering the quantity in the boxes provided. Select your preferred method of payment and forward whole Order Coupon by mail to Johansens at the address given at the bottom of this coupon.

PLEASE PRINT

Your Name

Street Address

Town/City

State/Province Zip/Post Code

☐ I enclose a check for US $ payable to JOHANSENS.

☐ Please debit my credit/charge card account the amount of US $ in favor of JOHANSENS.

☐ MasterCard ☐ Diners ☐ Amex ☐ Visa ☐ Discover ☐ Carte Blanche

Card No

Expiry date

Signature Date

Mail to: JOHANSENS, 30 Edison Drive, Wayne, New Jersey 07470

SAVE $5

		Qty	US$ Total
When you buy all three 1996 UK Johansens guides	US$49.75 + $8.25 s&h		
Boxed presentation set of three 1996 UK Johansens guides	US$58.75 + $8.75 s&h		
Johansens Recommended Hotels in Great Britain & Ireland 1996	US$24.95 + $6.00 s&h		
Johansens Recommended Inns with Restaurants in Great Britain 1996	US$14.95 + $4.75 s&h		
Johansens Recommended Country Houses in Great Britain & Ireland 1996	US$14.95 + $4.75 s&h		
Johansens Recommended Hotels in Europe 1996	US$14.95 + $4.75 s&h		

All items shipped UPS Ground Service. Canadian customers or for experdited delivery details telephone 1-800 213 9628 (24 Hours). New Jersey customers, please add appropriate sales tax. Please allow 21 days for delivery.

BILLING ADDRESS OF CREDIT/CHARGE CARD, IF DIFFERENT FROM ABOVE

Street Address

Town/City

State/Province Zip/Post Code

North American Order Coupon

To order Johansens guides in North America, simply indicate which guide(s) you wish by entering the quantity in the boxes provided. Select your preferred method of payment and forward whole Order Coupon by mail to Johansens at the address given at the bottom of this coupon.

PLEASE PRINT

Your Name

Street Address

Town/City

State/Province Zip/Post Code

☐ I enclose a check for US $ payable to JOHANSENS.

☐ Please debit my credit/charge card account the amount of US $ in favor of JOHANSENS.

☐ MasterCard ☐ Diners ☐ Amex ☐ Visa ☐ Discover ☐ Carte Blanche

Card No

Expiry date

Signature Date

Mail to: JOHANSENS, 30 Edison Drive, Wayne, New Jersey 07470

SAVE $5

		Qty	US$ Total
When you buy all three 1996 UK Johansens guides	US$49.75 + $8.25 s&h		
Boxed presentation set of three 1996 UK Johansens guides	US$58.75 + $8.75 s&h		
Johansens Recommended Hotels in Great Britain & Ireland 1996	US$24.95 + $6.00 s&h		
Johansens Recommended Inns with Restaurants in Great Britain 1996	US$14.95 + $4.75 s&h		
Johansens Recommended Country Houses in Great Britain & Ireland 1996	US$14.95 + $4.75 s&h		
Johansens Recommended Hotels in Europe 1996	US$14.95 + $4.75 s&h		

All items shipped UPS Ground Service. Canadian customers or for experdited delivery details telephone 1-800 213 9628 (24 Hours). New Jersey customers, please add appropriate sales tax. Please allow 21 days for delivery.

BILLING ADDRESS OF CREDIT/CHARGE CARD, IF DIFFERENT FROM ABOVE

Street Address

Town/City

State/Province Zip/Post Code

MAIL TO:

JOHANSENS
30 EDISON DRIVE
WAYNE
NEW JERSEY 07470

MAIL TO:

JOHANSENS
30 EDISON DRIVE
WAYNE
NEW JERSEY 07470

MAIL TO:

JOHANSENS
30 EDISON DRIVE
WAYNE
NEW JERSEY 07470